An
introduction
to
PERSONAL ADJUSTMENT

*If a man does not keep pace
with his companions, per-
haps it is because he hears
a different drummer. Let
him step to the music
which he hears, however
measured or far away.*

HENRY DAVID THOREAU

An

introduction

to

1958

BOSTON

ALLYN AND BACON, INC.

EDWARD C. GLANZ

Professor and Chairman
Psychology and Guidance Division
Boston University Junior College

ERNEST B. WALSTON

Professor and Chairman
Guidance Department
College of General Education
Boston University

PERSONAL ADJUSTMENT

A new approach to guidance and counseling

Copyright, 1958 by ALLYN AND BACON, INC.,
470 Atlantic Avenue, Boston. All rights reserved. No part of this book may
be reproduced in any form, by mimeograph or any other means, without permission in writing from the publisher. Printed in the United States of America.

Library of Congress Catalog Card Number: 58-10153

Library of Congress Catalog Card Number: 58-10252

T_he origins_ of this book involve the efforts of many individuals in addition to the authors. The material is an outgrowth of a decade of experience in two colleges of Boston University: the College of General Education and the Junior College. Significant contributions to the material were made by those listed below.

CONTRIBUTORS

Vernon A. Anthony   *Registrar and Assistant Professor, Psychology and Guidance Division, Boston University Junior College*

Howard O. Armstrong   *Director of Student Activities, Wright Junior College, Chicago, Illinois*

Vincent F. Calia   *Assistant Professor, Psychology and Guidance Division, Boston University Junior College*

Robert W. Hayes   *Instructor, Psychology and Guidance Division, Boston University Junior College*

James F. Penney   *Assistant Professor, Psychology and Guidance Division, Boston University Junior College*

George C. Rogers, Jr.   *Instructor, Psychology and Guidance Division, Boston University Junior College*

Ivy A. Winterton   *Instructor, Psychology and Guidance Division, Boston University Junior College*

Vernon A. Anthony completed the original draft of Chapters 14, 15, and 16; Vincent F. Calia, Chapters 8 and 11; Howard O. Armstrong, Chapter 6; Robert W. Hayes, Chapters 3 and 5; James F. Penney, Chapter 7; George C. Rogers, Jr., Chapters 10 and 12; and Ivy A. Winterton, Chapter 9.

An *Introduction to Personal Adjustment* is designed to provide a meaningful understanding of personal adjustment and personality in college. The chapters of the book offer an opportunity for each student to become involved in a process of self-analysis, self-evaluation, and self-understanding. Critical thinking becomes the application of such learnings.

Each individual, through interaction with the varied experiences of life, develops characteristic patterns of behavior designed to meet and solve the many problems of living. Psy-

FOREWORD

chologists know such characteristic patterns of behavior as personality. A significant aspect of understanding personality is the degree to which the individual is able to view and evaluate his or her own characteristic patterns of behavior. Thus individuals not only act in a particular fashion but are able, through hindsight and foresight, to perceive and to judge their own actions. To the degree that an individual is able to assess his or her behavior realistically, the person is said to possess self-understanding. The process of an individual systematically viewing the operation and effectiveness of personality is self-analysis. This book deals primarily with the concepts of individual personality, self-analysis, and self-understanding. The fundamental thesis of the book can therefore be stated as:

> To the degree that each person, through self-analysis, can begin to know and to appreciate successfully his or her own personality and the degree of self-understanding present in that personality, the following achievements are possible:
>
> 1. critical thinking
> 2. educational growth
> 3. effective consideration of the future
>
> Guidance and counseling foster the achievement of these objectives. The ultimate goal is the independent functioning of each student in these areas.

The approach to critical thinking through the study of psychology is divided into four major sections.

Part I begins with the immediate problem of the college student, adjustment to college. Part II provides a theoretical foundation in the principles of psychology related to the understanding of an individual. The concepts of psychology considered are behavioral causes, learning processes, and personality development and functioning. Part III allows the student to begin the process of self-analysis. The areas important in an individual's functioning in personal, academic, and work worlds are examined. An opportunity to integrate these factors into a self-analysis essay closes Part III. Part IV provides for the application of the knowledge gained through self-analysis; occupational and educational planning serve as a testing ground for new, reordered, or reinforced self-understandings. Various appendices are offered to aid in the understanding of the text material.

Individual counseling, group discussions, and other guidance procedures are desirable with the use of this book. The growth of self-analysis and self-understanding is not possible through a usual textbook approach. Counseling and counselors are the "change agents" through which the psychological content of the book can be utilized by students. The text supplies necessary psychological data and information; counseling and guidance become processes or tools for growth.

An Introduction to Personal Adjustment is constructed as a textbook and as a student handbook for a basic and integrative personal experience within a total educational process. When this book is used as a foundation for a total guidance and counseling program within a school or college, every student can be involved. When individual classes use this book as a text for an introductory psychology or adjustment course, the size of the class or classes will determine the number of students involved. Whether an entire student body of an institution or a small class of students is involved, the process is similar; each individual studies the psychology of personal adjustment in college, and each student moves from self-study to involvement in future planning.

The conception of guidance and counseling in this book is significantly different from traditional programs. The usual plan of orientation, group activities, individual counseling, occupational planning, and other facets of a guidance and counseling program have been unified and are presented within a student-centered source book. The topics cover many areas traditionally included in "General Psychology" or in such courses as "Personal and Social Psychology," "Psychology of Adjustment," or others. Guidance and counseling through psychology, therefore, can become an integral part of the curriculum. Administrators will find that the traditional "Orientation Course," "Mental Hygiene," "Group Guidance," "Individual Counseling," "Occupational Analysis," and other topics are adequately covered here.

The developmental history of this book as an orientation and guidance text has shown the value of spacing the work over an entire year. A topic or chapter per week is the normal pace for the first semester. The second semester, with a major research paper, is conducted at a slower speed. Lectures, classes, small group meetings, and individual counseling sessions are the major learning procedures utilized in this approach.

A first course in psychology based on this text will normally be a one semester course. Supplementary readings can be drawn from the bibliographies or from other sources.

Individual counseling will increase the effective use of this book. The teacher-counselor's relationship to each student is vital to the success of the program and the growth of the student. Individual differences among students will be great. Some students will need much assistance from their teacher-counselor; other students will need only brief but careful supervision. Flexibility is the key word for any person planning to use this book within a guidance program or in a beginning course in psychology. No guidance or counseling program can be foisted upon the students of a particular institution. Variations in emphasis of psychological test use, group activities, and in virtually every step and unit will be needed.

The book *An Introduction to Personal Adjustment* can be used with the book entitled *Basic Study Skills* (Wilcox, Allyn and Bacon, Inc., 1958). This book stresses critical analysis of self with regard to reading, writing, vocabulary building, library techniques, and study habits. The two books are designed as companion volumes. The use of these two approaches to learning in an academic situation will provide a useful foundation for students interested in obtaining a meaningful education.

This book has been written for student readers. The ideas that each student will encounter in these pages may occasionally be confusing or puzzling. This experience should be common to all students at one time or another. The ultimate effectiveness of the words in this book, the efforts of a counselor or teacher, and the educational process of learning depend upon the willingness, energy, and effort expended by the student. The facts, principles, interpretations of experiences, and psychological learnings, all of which can be derived from these pages, must be related to the person actively engaged in the learning process. The value of the material must be measured by its use and incorporation into the individual learner's view and understanding of himself.

The nature of the material is such that students will usually become deeply involved in a study of psychological concepts. The attitudes and actions of the student are closely related to his understanding that the psychological experience to which the book is dedicated is that *emotional as well as intellectual understanding is necessary for each student.*

Acknowledgments

Many professional psychologists and specialists in the fields of counseling and guidance have aided in innumerable ways to make this book possible. Francis McElaney aided in editing selected portions of the appendices. George Getchell provided much of the art work and the diagrams. Delores Getchell typed the manuscript, completed the lettering, and served as proofreader, indexer, and counselor to the authors. Secretarial assistance was also provided by Joan Marsh. Appreciation is gratefully extended to all.

Pictures were supplied by the Boston University Photo Service; School and College Relations, Boston University; Stephen Grohe, Hingham Photo Service; The Psychological Corporation; Alston Studios, and Burbank Photo Service. The photograph on the title page was kindly supplied by the Iowa State Teachers College, Cedar Falls, Iowa. Many publishers and authors have graciously extended permission to quote their materials. All quotations and, whenever possible, ideas have been identified within the text with proper reference to sources.

Last of all, but certainly not least, acknowledgment is needed and extended to the editors of Allyn and Bacon, Inc.; they are a sincere, hardworking, but demanding group!

EDWARD C. GLANZ
ERNEST B. WALSTON

TABLE OF CONTENTS

xi

9 VOCATIONAL INTEREST

10 CONCEPT OF APTITUDES

11 INTELLIGENCE AND SCHOLASTIC APTITUDE

12 THE OTHER FACTORS

13 PROCESS OF SELF-ANALYSIS

PART FOUR: *Occupational and educational planning — 215*

14 IMPORTANCE OF PLANNING

15 OCCUPATIONAL AND EDUCATIONAL INFORMATION

16 OCCUPATONAL AND EDUCATIONAL RESEARCH PAPER

APPENDICES

College is an opportunity for growth and enjoyment

Part I

ORIENTATION
TO COLLEGE

*An old adage demands that you "Start where you are!"
The problem is often "Where am I?" Part I is concerned
with the problems of students who have just entered
college. Chapters are offered in three areas of major
concern: psychology, critical thinking, and college; motivation and values in college; and learning in college.*

*An overview of the total field of psychology is pre-
sented in Chapter 1. Along with a historical perspective, a survey of the present-day dimensions of psychol-*

ogy is offered. An analysis of several basic concepts in psychology and critical thinking concludes this introductory chapter. The second chapter is an examination of the relationships of motivation and values to success in college. The fields of philosophy and education as well as psychology demand that a student be as vitally concerned with these areas as in traditional subject-matter learnings. Practical learning techniques are presented in Chapter 3.

T*he intricacies* of human behavior have long been of interest
to man, but, for centuries, the causes, effects, and implications of man's behavior were only dimly understood. Psychology is a relative newcomer to the intellectual and academic world, since modern-day psychology dates from the
late nineteenth century. The study of man in a detailed and
methodical fashion is thus less than one hundred years old.
Earlier approaches to psychology were most often the specu-
lative ventures of philosophers into the nature of man. These

Chapter 1

PSYCHOLOGY,
COLLEGE, AND LIFE

early reflections aided in establishing a foundation for modern-day psychology but were unable satisfactorily to explain
man, man's behavior, and how man had become what he was.

Psychology, as a discipline or approach to knowledge, is
the systematic and organized study of man and the behavior
of man. Experimental approaches to sensations, reaction
times, and other relatively simple aspects of behavior led to
the establishment of laboratories of psychology in American
and European universities in the last quarter of the nineteenth century. Within these laboratories man and man's behavior were subjected to experiment and analysis.

Introspection, or reports from the human subject concerning reactions, feelings, impressions, or thoughts, as well as
other responses, was an early method of the first laboratory
experimenters in psychology. Other experiments were conducted in the area of individual differences in responses to
varying stimulations. Light, heat, pain, pressure, and other
stimuli were used to provoke man into behaving. This behavior was observed, recorded and analyzed. Conclusions
were reached, hypotheses determined, and further experiments

3

conducted in order to obtain significant facts about man and his actions.

These investigations into man's behavior soon led to questions that were almost unanswerable through experimentation with humans, so animals of all types were utilized as substitutes. More data were collected, and hypotheses developed from this type of experimenting in order to uncover psychological facts and to build theories concerning man and his behavior.

Soon other pioneers joined in the study of man. Man's introspective reports were held to be unimportant; man's actions were viewed as supreme and were seen as the only area for legitimate concern to the psychologist. "Introspectionism," "behaviorism," "functionalism," "Gestalt," and many other novel approaches to man and his actions began to appear, and "schools" of psychology were developed. Charges and countercharges, emotionalism, and confusion were almost the order of the day. Each group claimed to know the route to more perfect knowledge.

The "schools" period of psychology extended well into the twentieth century. From the perspective obtained just since that time, however, it appears that the new discipline of psychology passed through its "storm-and-stress" period in relatively rapid fashion. A more mature, systematic study of man in the field of psychology has led to specialization and to more carefully defined differences of approach at the present time. The "schools" of psychology have served to highlight the many-sided nature of psychology. The contributions of men in all of these areas have provided foundations for the present state of psychology. "Schools" have not entirely disappeared. New theories and approaches to various aspects of psychology still attract adherents and followers. As new knowledge is uncovered, it is explored, utilized, and applied in all areas of psychology.

Prior to examining the present status of the field of psychology it is important to trace one other basic source of present-day psychology. At approximately the same time that the early psychological laboratories were being founded, a young medical doctor in Vienna, Sigmund Freud, was exploring the peculiarities and abnormal behavior of individual patients. Freud was a practicing physician and was concerned with individuals rather than experiments and the laboratory. He treated various types of problems that appeared to have little or no physical basis. His work and relationships with his patients stimulated him into writing and speculating about man. Freud's contributions in theory and design in the field of psychology stemmed directly from his clinical practice. His genius for creative thought developed a parallel design for the new field of psychology.

The names of men such as Freud, Wilhelm Wundt, John Watson, William James, John Dewey, and others are woven throughout the early (and even recent) history of psychology. The story of these men and their work (52),* (19), (138), (135) is the story of the origins of psychology.

* Numbers in parentheses refer to Bibliography starting on page 329.

DIMENSIONS OF MODERN PSYCHOLOGY

Present-day psychology can be divided conveniently into three major areas, *experimental* or *scientific psychology, applied psychology,* and *clinical psychology.*

Experimental or scientific psychology

The early tradition of laboratory study and experiment in psychology has continued into the present day. The laboratory psychologists of today are concerned with hypothesis, theory, fact, and knowledge. All psychological data concerning needs, drives, stresses, and all other aspects of man's behavior are subjected to rigorous testing and examination in order to further the entire field of psychology. This laboratory, experimental, or scientific approach to the study of man and his behavior is at the center of virtually all psychological knowledge. Early experiments on man in simple acts and responses, animal experiments, and later complex psychological experimentation led to exhaustive testing on the nervous system, drives (thirst and hunger), learning (mazes, conditioning, and insight), and other factors. Such experimentation began to offer theories and plausible explanations for both animal and human behavior. These early psychological scientists built hypotheses and theories and then retested them on animals and, when possible, applied them to man.

Modern experimental and scientific psychology is as broad as the total field of psychology. Every aspect of human behavior is now the legitimate subject matter of the laboratory experimenter: high-altitude tolerance, food deprivation, frustration, aggression, intelligence factors, children's developmental habit patterns, authoritarian personality development, motivation, and hosts of other problems now are involved in the testing, measuring, observing, and evaluation processes. Earlier experimentation in learning, drives, and other areas also continued. The many aspects of applied psychology and clinical psychology are thoroughly dependent upon the creative contributions of this dimension of modern psychology.

Applied psychology

The showroom of modern psychology is applied psychology. Early in the twentieth century psychology was the province of the almost solitary practitioner or experimenter; awareness and use of psychology have grown exceptionally since that time. World War I, with the psychological testing of the ability levels of millions of men in the Armed Forces, marked the first large-scale impact of applied psychology. The need to classify and utilize the talents of men from all walks of life allowed the psychologist to come out of the laboratory and into the practical world to solve and help to solve various problems of everyday life. Everyone in our society today is involved in the application of psychological knowledge in countless ways that are both important and casual. The classroom, the family, business, hospitals, and many other phases of our community, personal, and industrial life have been affected by psychology.

Recent textbooks on the subject of applied psychology (23) (63) list many of the significant aspects of psychology in everyday life. Such chapters are in the following list:

BURTT (23) *Applied Psychology,* 2nd edition (chapter topics):

1. Intelligence
2. Individual Differences
3. Learning in School
4. Personal Efficiency
5. Vocational Guidance
6. Mental Disorders
7. Psychotherapy
8. Psychology and Testimony
9. Crime Detection
10. Crime Prevention
11. Employment
12. Industrial Efficiency
13. Fatigue, Monotony, and Accidents
14. Morale
15. Advertising
16. Attention and Memory (Advertising)

HEPNER (63) *Psychology Applied to Life and Work,* 3rd edition (major sections and chapter topics):

I. *Introduction*
II. *Understanding the Individual's Behavior through the Adjustment Concept*
   Persons and Problems, Adjustment Activities Positive, Negative, Functional Ailments, Treating the Maladjusted, Counseling, Counseling Interviews.
III. *Personal Problems*
   Personality Development, Mental Work and Study, Choosing a Vocation, Job Advancement, Dating, Courtship and Marriage, Children's Adjustment.
IV. *Industrial Psychology*
   Hiring Employees, Testing, Merit Ratings, Job Evaluation, Working Conditions, Group Dynamics, Supervising Employees, Communication and Morale, Communication Media and Methods, Employee Relations, Organized Labor, Leadership Trends.
V. *The Consumer*
   Markets, Advertising, Salesmanship.
VI. *Research*
   Psychological Research Reports.

Clinical psychology

The individual human being and his behavior have always been a prime concern of the field of psychology and of psychologists. C. M. Louttit in Watson's *Readings in Clinical Psychology* (135:3) defines clinical psychology as follows: "It is in dealing with . . . individual problems that one of the most important services of psychology is to be found, and it is this individual work which constitutes, in a general way, the field of clinical psychology." Louttit immediately states why even this definition is unsatisfactory because of its general nature and the many detailed problems that are obscured by so broad a treatment of the field. Sigmund Freud's early work in the clinical field has influenced all of psychology and particularly the personal understanding and help offered to individuals so typical of clinical psychology. Freud's treatment of mentally disturbed patients and other early attempts by European and American pioneers to aid children in their adjustments were among the earliest milestones in the clinical-psychology field.

Alfred Binet, a French pioneer in the field, offered the first widely acceptable intelligence test in the early 1900's. This device was a forerunner of the many tests now currently available to clinicians dealing with intelligence, aptitudes, interests, achievement, and personality.

Diagnosis through psychological testing and other devices concomitant with treatment through counseling and other individual procedures have always loomed large in the work of any clinical psychologist. The clinical psychologist thus attempts to apply the principles of psychology to the individual.

PSYCHOLOGY AND ADJUSTMENT

In individual adjustment psychology is both applied and used clinically. Through a study of psychology, its applications, and its use in a semiclinical or clinical setting, students can be aided in obtaining a more satisfactory adjustment to the environment of college, the growth process of education, and life in general. In order to enter into a study of psychology and its applications in critical thinking and personal adjustment, various basic concepts concerning psychology and adjustment need to be examined.

Growth of personality

Two basic principles in psychology are that (a) all behavior is caused and that (b) each individual behaves in a unique fashion. Psychologists technically refer to these unique patterns of a person's behavior as personality. Personality is thus the individual's "way of life," and this way of life is caused.

Personality is largely the result of the interacting forces of heredity and environment. Structural aspects of personality (physical appearance, physical skills, and traits) stem from heredity; functional aspects of personality (methods of problem solving and adjusting) are learned from the individual's interaction with environment. At birth personality begins to form. (Prenatal life appears to affect personality in a structural sense only.) The passage of time and the interaction of heredity and environment allow each person to develop a unique personality and a particular way of life. The individual at the same time, of course, is also undergoing life experiences. Personality is thus formed out of life experiences and in turn is an approach to life and its problems.

Learning and differentiation. Learning and differentiation are the processes involved in the building of personality. Learning is a process of *acquiring* a particular aspect or pattern of behavior or of *changing* behavior. Differentiation, as an aspect of learning, is the selection or "picking out" of life and its experiences a meaningful portion of that life and experience. To demonstrate how differentiation may be viewed as a part of the process called learning, some rather familiar examples of the learning process may be examined. The newborn baby probably does not at first make a distinction between his "self" and his environment. His fist, doubling and moving in front of his face, he does not recognize at first as a part of his "self," any more than he knows that the colorful toy swinging over his crib is a part of his environment. Slowly he differentiates the sights, sounds, and touch of things around him as not a part of himself. He feels hunger and soon learns that his cry is effective in bringing someone who will satisfy his need. Before long he perceives that his mother's face appearing before him also brings the promise of the fulfillment of his needs. He differentiates between his mother and any other moving figure that might appear over the edge of the crib.

In time he differentiates the sound he makes to summon his mother; he learns that "mama," or an approximation of that sound, will secure for him the person who will most likely minister to his needs. Later he differentiates between milk and water and between the sounds of the names "milk" and "water." This differentiation is learning, and it is a process that continues through life.

To explain differentiation in another way, it could be said that the detail of a particular learning process is differentiated out of the general ground of life experience when the individual feels a need to perceive the detail, or when he is taught to be aware of the detail. The first crayon drawings of the kindergarten child may not differentiate between men and women. When he learns to distinguish men and women as such, he does it by sorting out detail. His teacher may bring this detail into focus by showing the young artist how to pile curls on the head of the female figure or to draw an approximation of the difference in clothes between the sexes.

Throughout life differentiation and learning are the processes used to build personality. The individual's interaction with environment is a constant process with early experiences determining the patterns of future response and behavior. The early years of life are therefore most significant in that these years are formative of basic personality structure.

Self-concept. A controlling factor in personality is the self-concept that the individual builds and learns for himself. Various authors,

Snygg and Combs (116), Murphy (98), and Jersild (68), as well as others, have stressed this recent concept in psychology. These authors see the "self-concept" of the individual as a *core* of personality. The "self as seen by the self" is a disarming definition of self by Snygg and Combs. Actually, this concept of self as seen by the self is basic to an understanding of personality.

Self-pictures begin to be learned at an early age. This gradually emerging pattern of self-beliefs, attitudes, and values is deepened and broadened as life progresses. As a concept of self develops, its control function increases and matures. The self-concept encompasses all areas of life. The individual builds a concept of self out of almost unlimited self-pictures or personal reactions to experience. The individual sees himself as a person with abilities, skills, capacities, and limitations, and on a present operating level as he would like to be and as others see him. Intelligence or nonintelligence, handsomeness or ugliness, aggression or submission, and forwardness or retiringness are only a few of the hundreds of dimensions of personality, and each person sees himself in a particular, unique fashion in all of these dimensions. As a core element of personality the self-concept is much more than a view of self in various "traits" or habit patterns. The self-concept is the *total* psychological view that the individual has of himself as a being or organism in an environment; this environment is the world and its elements as seen by him and is unique and self-perceived. Reality for each person is also self-conceived and perceived.

The total or fully developed, controlling self-concept of a person can seldom, if ever, be fully known by an individual himself or by others. Aspects or elements of this basic view of self may be seen as the individual meets and adjusts to life and as the self-concept determines patterns of adjustment. Portions of the self-concept (or perhaps self-pictures) can be isolated, viewed, and partially understood as psychological tools and procedures are utilized.

Personality in action. Adjustment is the process of meeting life's problems, and is personality and the self-concept aspect of personality in action. Self-pictures, or elements of the self-concept, may not match reality as others see the individual in action. The physical weakling may see himself as the star athlete; the homely girl may see herself as a beauty-contest winner. Maladjustment results when the self-concept or self-picture is widely out of accord with reality or the individual is unable to meet or cope with the problems and demands of life upon the self.

Each individual needs to function in many varied aspects of life. Through learning and differentiation, self-concept and personality are constantly developing and functioning. The child at birth must eat, sleep, eliminate waste materials, and begin to live in a human society. The methods and procedures of life and problem-solving actions, even in these early days, set the patterns that are to follow. The child, as he grows and meets the world, must respond and exist. The neighborhood, school, work, and marriage are illustrations of the everyday activities that present problems of life that must be faced by the individual. The self-concept as the core of personality directs the personality or patterns of adjustment.

Self-pictures, adjustment patterns, intelligence, abilities, talents, and interests are all important elements within self-concept and personality that allow the individual to succeed or to fail in life. Psychologists and particularly clinical psychologists are interested and skilled in investigating and studying these various aspects of personality in action. The tools and techniques used by them are available, in partial form or perhaps with lesser skill, to the beginning student of psychology. The individual can partially view and study personality or the self in action. This text is designed to aid students in viewing selected elements of their own personalities in action.

Personality and college

The individual functions in a social world, which at first is narrow and restricted. As time passes this social environment extends outward beyond the home and family into school, friends, and job. The college student is closing one chapter of life and opening another. College marks the close of childhood and early adolescence and lays the foundation for a life career. Students enter college as adolescents and hopefully graduate as adults. The college years, therefore, provide the environment within which this last major developmental task of growth must be accomplished.

College students are fortunate in being mature enough to understand various principles of psychology, personality, and adjustment and yet young enough still to profit in their own lives from the application of their learning. Certain aspects of personality are significant and vital for all college students. The process of understanding and utilizing the principles of personality can be particularly rewarding, and an over-all view of them can help to orient the prospective reader and aid in a "stocktaking" or viewing of one's self as these principles function in college.

College and adjustment. The college student is living in an unusual and somewhat false environment that demands certain behavior characteristics that are not always called for in other surroundings. This uncommon situation is often recognized by referring to college as "an ivory tower" or as a place inhabited by "eternal adolescents." Actually, college life is a smaller "slice" of life, with emphasis upon selected portions of personality, and demands particular adjustment patterns. The following areas of personality and an individual's functioning in a college environment are particularly important for college students.

1. *Motivation.* "Why did I come to college?" This question sometimes haunts the new college student as he faces the bewildering first few days of a new existence. What can psychology offer to the student of human behavior who wishes not only to answer this question for himself now but in the future. "Why do I do (or want) what I do?" Certainly, this question is significant and vital for the new student of psychology.

2. *Learning.* "Why do I learn?" "How do I learn?" College demands that each student be proficient in subjects of varying complexity and significance. What can psychology offer in the area of efficient and effective learning? What permits a person to acquire knowledge that previously was unknown? How is knowledge retained and utilized in examinations and in life? The college student is a learner. Perhaps to be a learner about learning is also important.

3. *Social maturity.* What is maturity? How may a person know whether he or she is a mature, consistent, integrated person or personality? Life makes many demands upon the individual; how can each personality meet the conflicting problem-solving dilemmas of everyday existence? College students frequently become leaders in their communities and in their relations with others. A stable, integrated, socially mature personality is important for all students.

4. *Interest.* "What do I like to do?" "I used to like that but I don't like it any more!" These statements are common in college. What is the significance of interest? Does it determine aptitude, or is it related to intelligence? What is vocational interest? Interest can serve as the stimulus to a creative life of broad satisfaction or a narrow sterile life of frustration and boredom; certainly, this merits study.

5. *Aptitude.* "What can I do best?" This is a question asked by not only college students but students of all levels. College students, concerned with planning their futures, are particularly needful of answers to this question. How do musicians, painters, engineers, teachers, salesmen, and so many other wage-earners differ in talent or aptitude? Again, the student who is beginning college needs to seek answers.

6. *Intelligence.* Sometimes called ability, talent, scholastic aptitude, or simply brains, intelligence is a significant factor in college life. Arguments as to whether intelligence is a structural (inherited) factor, an aspect of personality (learned) or a combination of these forces is a problem of psychology. Intelligence, in any case, is an aspect of personality without an adequate amount of which a college student soon will become a "former" college student.

There are many questions surrounding intelligence. How much is needed in college? How much is needed in a job? Is intelligence related to adjustment or happiness? Obviously, these are questions to which there is no easy or quick answer. The student beginning psychology, however, needs to be concerned with the answer and its applications.

7. *Vocational planning.* An eternally demanding question for all persons not working is, "What job shall I take?" Even for those who have tentatively chosen their life's work the nagging anxiety that they have improperly selected their vocational goal is a fearful worry at times. What factors should be considered in selecting an occupation? How can data be obtained? How can one know whether he can succeed or not? Psychology, clinical psychology, and guidance are special approaches to this problem. What are the answers to these questions?

Understanding personality. The student of psychology needs to know and appreciate that merely reading about principles of psychology may have no effect upon one's own self-concept or behavior. Psychological knowledge is a powerful tool, but as with any tool it may be unused or misused or misunderstood.

A primary requisite to the understanding of personality in college, and in life, is a thorough acquaintance with the contributions made by the many creative thinkers, writers, and specialists in the field of psychology who have given us such variety and depth of knowledge of human beings and human behavior. The facts, principles, forces, and ramifications of human behavior must then be the raw material out of which each individual builds a more thorough understanding of his own self, personality, and life. Such data, however, as raw material, must be used, applied and tested. Thinking, learning, experiencing, planning, revising, and evaluating, and again, thinking, learning, experiencing, planning, revising, and evaluating—such is the process of utilizing the knowledge gained in the field of psychology. Such a process of application or experience can seldom if ever be solitary, introspective, and self-taught. Classroom experience, directed projects, shared group discussions, individual conferences and interviews are the elements of an environment in which these processes of application must take place.

CRITICAL THINKING

Problem solving and adjustment processes of life involve experience of a primary type or level. To select from this primary level or type of experiencing those elements, principles, and learnings that will aid in future problem solving and adjustment processes of living demands thinking of a higher level of abstraction than direct first-hand experiencing. Critical thinking is the process of drawing meaningful conclusions, generalizations, or applications out of present experience for future use.

Critical thinking requires that present experience be organized, ordered, and interpreted so that it will effectively influence future experiences. Psychology has taught that man is not solely a rational being. Man is influ-enced by his hopes, fears, dreams, and unrealistic or realistic perception of himself in fact—by a multitude of factors other than reason or intellect. True critical thinking involves more than rational thought; critical thinking in psychology demands that all elements within man and his behavior be accorded a proper place in the developing of conclusions or generalizations for the future.

Reason or intellect can function in a helpful fashion when man allows his reason to include all elements of behavior important for critical think-ing. Various elements of personality have been listed as important for students in college. As an individual is able to understand and experience learnings in personal adjustment in college and life, various conclusions, generalizations, and new applications of learning for future behavior may be possible.

Psychology, particularly the applied and semiclinical study of self, per-sonality, adjustment, and self-evaluation, is a demanding taskmaster. There are no easy, simple keys to an understanding of psychology or to magical changes in personality. The mysteries of old have been revealed as puzzles rather than insoluble predicaments; solutions are slow, frustrating, and many times tortuous because of their very nature. Knowledge, facts, forces, and ramifications concerning human behavior are necessary for a reason-able understanding of the personal adjustment processes of the student in college. The material in the succeeding chapters has been selected to apply most appropriately to the college student. The supporting learning proc-esses, directed experiences, and procedures necessary for utilizing these psychological principles have also been provided. The student needs first to know and understand the material, then to apply it and experience it. Knowledge of human behavior and guided experience in its application, theoretical and practical learnings, provide the data for the development of meaningful conclusions, generalizations and applications—critical thinking.

The organization of the approach in this book to psychology and critical thinking stresses four parts. Part I is concerned with a broad over-all view of college and life. Emphasis is given to motivation, values, and learning in college. Part II is a presentation of some of the most basic material in the entire field of psychology concerning human beings and human behavior. The causes of human behavior, learning, personality, and social maturity are the major topics of Part II. Part III will involve the student in a study of psychological knowledge significant for self-understanding and self-analysis. Individual differences, interests, aptitudes, and intelligence are the major concerns of this unit. Part IV is concerned with the application of the previous sections and examines the process and problem of educational and vocational planning.

The process or procedures important to the effective application of the principles present in the four parts of the book are presented in various chapters and in the appendices. Chapter 13, "The Process of Self-Analysis," and Chapter 16, "The Educational and Occupational Research Paper," are designed to be learning and experiencing processes for students. Each of these chapters deals with a significant application of the understanding of the principles of adjustment, self-concept and personality. Each of these two chapters is an integral portion of the two application sections of the book. The "autobiography," "self-analysis essay," outline and worksheets, the "psychological test glossary," "psychological test profiles," "case studies for group discussion," examples of self-analysis essays, and efficient and effective study-habit routines are included in the appendices. The student and the teacher-counselor must enter into a joint, shared investigation into psychology, personality, and adjustment.

SUPPLEMENTARY SOURCES

Boring, E. G., *A History of Experimental Psychology* (2nd ed.). New York: Appleton-Century-Crofts, Inc., 1950.

Boring, E. G., H. S. Langfeld, and H. P. Weld, *Foundations of Psychology*. New York: John Wiley & Son, Inc., 1948.

Fry, C., and E. G. Rostow, *Mental Health in College*. New York: Commonwealth Fund, 1942.

Hepner, H. W., *Psychology Applied to Life and Work* (3rd ed.). Englewood Cliffs, N. J.: Prentice-Hall, Inc., 1957.

Klein, D. B., *Mental Hygiene* (rev. ed.). New York: Henry Holt & Company, Inc., 1956.

Morgan, Clifford T., *Introduction to Psychology*. New York: McGraw-Hill Book Company, Inc., 1956.

Patty, W. L., and Louise S. Johnson, *Personality and Adjustment*. New York: McGraw-Hill Book Company, Inc., 1953.

Ruch, F. L., *Psychology and Life* (4th ed.). Chicago: Scott, Foresman and Company, 1953.

Schneiders, Alexander A., *Personal Adjustment and Mental Health*. New York: Rinehart & Company, Inc., 1955.

Watson, R. I., *Readings in the Clinical Method in Psychology*. New York: Harper & Brothers, 1949.

Woodworth, R. S., *Contemporary Schools of Psychology* (rev. ed.). New York: The Ronald Press Company, 1948.

A *question* that each individual needs to ask himself very soon after college has begun is, "Why did I come to college?" It is a question that needs to be answered on various levels. It is a question to which various replies are offered every day, but it is not a question that is thoroughly understood or thoroughly answered on any day.

The ready answer that almost anyone may give to this question is "I came to college in order to obtain an education." Is this, however, an answer or is it a cliché? Is it an

Chapter 2

MOTIVATION AND VALUES IN COLLEGE

easy way to parry, to meet a difficult situation with an easy answer? "To obtain an education" is an answer that is practical and useful when one is discussing such a problem with friends, families, or others. It is also an answer that is reasonably acceptable to one's self. It is an answer, though, that is sometimes not a particularly adequate or meaningful answer. Many times, it may be a rationalization—a good reason rather than the real reason. The answer to the question "Why did I come to college" can help to illuminate the problem of understanding motives, emotions and values.

The United States Armed Forces recognized the importance of motives, emotions, and values. They produced and showed to many millions of servicemen a series of films, entitled "Why We Fight." These films demonstrated many of the basic issues involved in World War II. These motion pictures served to answer the question for some servicemen, but certainly not for all. Some servicemen perhaps felt as the college student does when someone asks, "Why did you come to college?", and he says, "To obtain an education." The soldier may have answered to a similar question, "Why

15

are you fighting?"—"I'm fighting because we are at war." This answer, similar to the college student's answer, is a "good" reason, but is not necessarily a *real* reason. The United States Armed Forces recognized the importance for each individual of the problem of awareness of why he fought.

Philosophers, political analysts, and psychologists have said that one of the most basic differences between the American army personnel and any other army personnel has been the awareness of the individuals in the American service system of the concept of why they fought. The question of motivation and values became highlighted again when the Korean War broke out in 1950. At this time when American troops were sent to a far-off land, many people in the United States raised the question, "Why?" There were no motion pictures to assist the particular individuals fighting in the battles, or the parents of the servicemen who were killed overseas in Korea. In spite of this problem of confusion in motivation, other servicemen felt very clear in their response to what they felt to be a basic call to the defense of freedom and democracy throughout the world. This comparison of college students and soldiers fighting in a war can only serve to highlight the importance of motives, emotions, and values when individual behavior is analyzed.

MOTIVATION

To return to the problem of the college student who is asked the question "Why did you come to college," perhaps an answer may be found in the commonplace experiences of all students. If such an answer can be extracted from the everyday experience of students, motivation may then be understood as a meaningful concept in psychology as well as an active force that can be operative within a person and, particularly, within a student's life.

Several years ago at Boston University, where this book was developed and has been used, freshmen students were asked to complete a questionnaire dealing with the reasons for college attendance. The list of reasons given by these students is here reproduced. These reasons are first listed without comment, without any question of their validity.

1. To learn more about myself.
2. To develop life goals.
3. To develop intellectual abilities.
4. To prepare for a vocation.
5. To improve learning power.
6. To acquire preprofessional training.

7. To improve my social standing.
8. To meet new people.
9. To have a good time.
10. To acquire a better understanding of people.
11. To increase my knowledge of problems of our age.
12. To develop an appreciation of culture.
13. To live up to family tradition.
14. To do the right thing.

These answers, that in many ways vary from the very serious attempts of students to analyze their own reasons for college attendance to the rather trite, common, acceptable phrases that people feel that others expect of them, exemplify some of the feelings of students looking at their own problems of college attendance.

In order to examine motivation from a different view, a series of questions that are asked and expressed in a personal fashion may help each student to look more clearly into his or her own motivational pattern. These questions are as follows:

1. Who decided that you should go to college?
2. When was the decision made to go to college?
3. Have you ever made a personal commitment to yourself that a college education is one of the primary goals of your life?
4. Who is paying for your college education?
5. If you are working, how much do you contribute toward the expense of your own education?
6. Can you read effectively?
7. Do you like to read?
8. Who chose your educational program in high school?
9. Who decided what program you should take in college?
10. Would you be willing to attend college for two or four years and receive no academic degree, simply being satisfied with the education?
11. Would you be willing to accept your degree today, dated and signed by the president of the college, forgetting any further attendance or further striving for an education?
12. Is education something that is desirable and good—but for others rather than for yourself?
13. What forces are keeping you in college today, tomorrow, and the day after that? Why don't you drop out of college?

These questions are designed to raise issues in the minds of students with regard to the underlying reasons for college attendance. These questions raise problems with regard to motives operative in each student's college attendance. The answers may be simple or complex; the answers, however, when viewed in light of a theoretical discussion of motivation, may help each student to understand his own motives and motivational patterns more effectively.

Basic drives

Man is motivated by various basic drives, both organic and social. Organic drives, such as hunger, thirst, and sex, are physiologically based. Social drives or needs, such as security, self-esteem, affection, acceptance, and independence, are learned and arise out of a person's interaction with the environment.

Organic drives are not immediately discernible in the causation of behavior in most college students. Social drives, however, are clearly visible in almost all forms of student behavior. Psychological security, self-esteem, affection, acceptance, and independence are all involved in the normal college activities of students.

Social drives are significant in the decision to attend college, the selection of a college, and behavior at college. Typical of the operation of social drives in college behavior is the determining effect of needs for acceptance and independence. The group behavior of college students is notorious in our society. The swallowing of goldfish, raccoon coats, and other fads of the 1920's and '30's belong to the group codes of an earlier college generation. Each college generation develops its own peculiar fads or fashions. Such developments seem to begin with students who need to establish a reputation for their independence, and shortly thereafter hordes of students copy such behavior in order to gain acceptance in the eyes of other students. The social drives of independence and acceptance also operate in normal or usual behavior as well. Many of the everyday group and individual actions of students are caused by needs for acceptance or independence or both.

The drive or need for self-esteem is basic in a continuing sense in all of college as in life. The desire for a college education, the ever-present need to study, effective self-discipline, the selection of courses, and the area of specialization—in fact all of college—are often dominated by a drive for self-esteem. Many students may consciously deny that an active striving for self-esteem is present in their personalities, for even to obtain the immediate respect of others it is, at times, desirable to deny the need for such respect. It is often more acceptable for a person to express his own need for self-esteem through an emphasis on long-range security.

Affection is often encountered in normal heterosexual relations, comradeship, and in faculty-student relationships. The bond between fraternity brothers and sorority sisters and the total tie between the college and the student is an affective relationship.

Social drives and needs thus are intertwined in all student behavior in college. Each student needs carefully to analyze and evaluate the forces and effects of a social nature that can influence daily and long-range behavior. A knowledge of these causative forces of behavior can aid each student in beginning the process of self-analysis and self-appraisal.

Emotions and college

College has long been known as a place where emotionalism is commonplace. Sometimes in life after college (at alumni gatherings) a person will attribute emotions to college that actually were not present, but actual college attendance holds many emotional experiences important for the present student.

Fear, anticipation, confusion, frustration, elation, and dejection are only a few of the deeply felt emotions present in the everyday life of college. Many situations can evoke an emotional response or an emotional anticipation:

1. Arriving at college
2. The first day of college
3. The confusion of registration
4. The first class
5. The first examination
6. The course final examination
7. The first college dance
8. Failure
9. The Dean's List
10. The football game
11. Becoming "pinned" (fraternity)
12. The "Prom"
13. Dismissal
14. Going home
15. Graduation

Each of these occurrences or events can bring on a host of emotional or psychological feelings within a person. The *desire* to experience such emotions or the *fear* of experiencing these emotions can serve as a basic motivating force in each student's college life. Even when emotions do not serve as basic motivating factors they influence and affect behavior.

From a multitude of possible emotions as basic or influencing factors in behavior, two illustrations are presented. Fear of failure often can drive students to almost impossible hours of study. The imagination can picture a homecoming to friends, family, or a community after dismissal from college. Failure, actually, the *fear* of failure, thus can explain certain students' behavior. Satisfaction, although more basic in determining all of life's behavior than even fear, is most often an afterfeeling following the completion of an act or part of the anticipation of an act, rather than an emotion accompanying an act. A good grade on an examination, the successful tryout for the team, the big dance, and graduation—all of these activities may perhaps be a result of certain social drives such as prestige or self-esteem, or even independence, but the emotion of satisfaction looms large in each.

All behavior can be analyzed in terms of its emotional counterpart. All action, except the simplest forms of behavior, evokes an emotional feeling either before, during or after its occurrence. Human beings respond to emotions, and all students are emotionally involved in college.

Defining and recognizing values

Values have been said to be the primary beliefs and internal feelings of an individual. Such values are difficult to bring out into the open because of the diversity of situations that appear to call for different and varying systems. Just as motivation can sometimes be more clearly seen and understood in light of the commonplace everyday problems of life, so value structures can be many times more apparent through an analysis of average day-to-day problems.

1. What do you want most from life: money—prestige—power—success—happiness?
2. In planning for a vocation what are the most important factors in a future job: security—prestige—salary—promotion potential—satisfying work—surroundings—coworkers?
3. What kind of success do you most desire: business success—personal power and prestige—a secure and happy family—community prestige?
4. Whose respect do you most desire: family—coworkers—the boss—the community—other people—the church?
5. In a crisis who or what do you think of first: position—prestige—family—job—future—the boss—integrity—character?

These questions are difficult to answer. Each question can have many answers. Answers may vary according to an interpretation of the question. The responses to such questions can, however, quickly reveal value structure and primary personal beliefs. A rank order of values, or a hierarchy of personal beliefs is a desirable attribute of all students. "First things first," but what or which is first for each person? When a crisis occurs, first values become apparent. Crisis or conflict, problem or confusion; each can only reveal, not determine, present value structure.

College life as a freshman contains a series of crises and problems. Value structures and motivations are often sorely tried and sometimes altered. Students may find, for various reasons, that the conflict or crisis is too severe, and they leave. Psychology, guidance, and counseling are concerned with freshman success and failure. As students are able to uncover, study, and structure motives and values, college can be encountered as a challenge rather than as a trial.

THEORY AND PRACTICE

Just as motives, drives, emotions, and values have been studied and analyzed, perhaps it is desirable to scrutinize college and education as a goal or objective for students. Why should students strive for a college education; to what end should motives be directed; what can lead to emotional satisfaction; what can be valued?

College and education hold for all students many complex rewards. To attempt to say that a common outcome for all students is desirable is to violate all of the commonly accepted principles of education. Yet, for all students there needs to be something to strive for and to seek. "Why *should* one go to college?" An analysis of the reasons commonly listed for college attendance and an attempt at a general conclusion can perhaps help students in building an adequate and effective, though not identical, value and motivational system or pattern.

Financial gain

Financial gain is one of the most popular reasons for going to college. In the view of some people all those who attend college can assure themselves of a larger income for the rest of their lives. As an investment, of course, education is in a sense an attempt to obtain a financial reward. This, therefore, is certainly a useful and realistic reason for attending college. Complete insistence on this, however, as a dominating force, would be undesirable. Human-relations experts, psychologists, and philosophers have told us that although human beings must work to live, they cannot live to work. If college can only prepare one for work and fails in enabling one to live a fuller and more satisfying life, then college is a failure in every way in spite of the amount of money that has been earned by any individual.

The quick roads to wealth are not to be found in educational institutions. An apprenticeship with an embezzler, a crooked gambler, or a dishonest businessman would perhaps prove to be more fruitful and rewarding. A college education will certainly be of some financial help, but such assistance will depend upon the state of national or international affairs. In the event of depression, war, pestilence, or famine, college graduates will certainly suffer along with other citizens. Each individual's health, his ability to get along with others in the field of work, his personal attributes, and many other factors will affect the financial reward that can be derived from college training and education. Financial reward can legitimately enter into thinking about the value of a college education; if it dominates planning, however, it must be faced that this is shortsightedness. There are other and more superior values in college education that will be of more worth and more value in terms of either prosperity or depression. There are values that can be obtained from college that support failing spirits, even when all other circumstances are such that despair would seem to be appropriate.

Social success

Social success is another commonly accepted reason for attending college. It is probable that this is the reason for college attendance more often among young women than young men, although it is by no means absent from masculine thinking. About social matters there can be much discussion. The social value of college attendance will be affected by the mores and customs of a particular community in which the individual resides as well as the type of work in which the person is engaged. The social values attached by some people to attendance in college will not be obtained if a person does not fulfill personally and professionally the promise indicated by college attendance. In the last analysis the social reward from college and education will not come automatically with the possession of a degree. The implementation of social success will depend upon the individual and the circumstances of the environment in which he may work and live.

There are real social values in college. These are to be found in the daily contacts with other students who are engaged in a common intellectual

SCHOOL AND COLLEGE RELATIONS

Faculty members influence education in many ways

process. In addition, there are experiences and contacts resulting from participation in extracurricular and student activities such as athletic, music, dramatic, fraternity, and club life as well as a host of others that may enliven the scene at every school or college. An experience with some of these activities may serve to expand or change one's patterns of personal traits.

Even if there are real and legitimate social values to be derived from college attendance it cannot safely be maintained that this should be the primary reason for going to college. Students with no better purpose than this might be able to find schools that have objectives that would provide the satisfaction of these desires. It stands to reason that these students, in the long run, will fail to attain that same degree of happiness and success that other students can attain by attending a college that inculcates and stresses constructive learning and total education rather than the narrow concept of social growth.

Other reasons

There are always those who go to college because others wish them to do so, the "others" usually being parents. In such cases the judgment or values of the parents have been substituted for those of the student. Perhaps the parents may be right, although they themselves may have been influenced by one or a combination of the reasons that have already been discussed. Parents are also sometimes right in feeling that once the unwilling scholar has been "shanghaied" into college, he will like school and proceed to settle down and succeed. There are tragic cases, however, in which this particular doctrine has not proved successful. Usually, a year or less is enough to convince parents in such cases that there is no hope in trying further, and the impatient young man or woman is released from the intellectual shackles of college and abandoned to the perhaps kindlier worlds of business or matrimony.

There are others who go to college because "work" is a distasteful word. There may be colleges that aspire to harbor such leisure-loving individuals, but reputable institutions are likely to prove beds of nettles and thorns. A few months, or a year at most, and college has given most of these persons all that they can use of college and education.

Other persons enter college because their friends have entered. This group can be defined as a subspecies of the larger group who enter for social reasons. Sometimes such students catch the true spirit of a college and of education and stay on to do worth-while work. More often they are cut off in the bud by the blight of examinations and grades.

There are also young people who attend some colleges to lay the basis for a professional career in athletics. Some of these gentlemen are unfortunate cases academically, and do not last very long. Others are scholars as well as athletes and are a credit to themselves and to the institutions they represent. This, of necessity, is a small group, and as long as its members are good scholars they certainly have a legitimate reason for attending college.

There are still other persons who go to college because they have found life a riddle and hope that a better answer will come out of their study period. They are likely to be in the older age groups. Some of these individuals make the best students, whereas others become more confused and discouraged and vanish early from the scene.

There are many other unique and peculiar reasons for college attendance. Each freshman class brings new reasons. Fortunately, there is still another view as to why a student may go to college: *to obtain an education*—with all of the total implications of the word "education."

College and education

To conclude a discussion of motivation, emotions, values, and education, it is necessary to attempt to answer accurately and positively the original question posed, "Why come to college?" A positive and accurate statement for each person must result from the total effect of all of the years of life experience preceding college entrance, yet to answer the question, "Why come to college?" one must answer in the future tense, "to obtain an education."

A student concerned with education knows that the purpose of education is to share in the observation and criticism of the ideas of great thinkers throughout the world; education sharpens the powers of thinking and communication and stresses critical analysis, problem solving, and citizenship.

Who is better able to understand the blows of fate if not the man or woman who has a knowledge of history and economics that enables the understanding if not always the anticipation of the causes and results of fate? College students may be able to understand if not to predict business depressions or wars. Who can best plan the choice of a marriage partner and the management of family living, if not the man or woman who has had a chance to study psychology, biology, philosophy, and all of the other important subjects relating to the problems of man's relationship to man? Solving the complex relationships that exist in business, social, and family life may be accomplished more effectively by the person who has the chance to study the findings of experts in such matters than by one who must face such problems with only a knowledge gained in the painful school of experience.

Who would deny that all people are concerned with the mysteries of human life, its origin, its development, and ultimate goal? Who would argue that the study of philosophy and science will not yield specific answers and ideals that will enable a man to work out a method of adjusting himself to these omnipresent dilemmas? It is unlikely that any person would maintain that an appreciation of order and symmetry and an understanding of the structure that makes for beauty in architecture, sculpture, painting, music, and literature are not assets to one who wishes to make the most of living. College is the place where one can gain insight into such matters.

All of these subjects are the foundation of education; the broad domain of intellectual and emotional life is open for exploration by the young person who comes with the purpose of learning. If a person has come for other purposes, all of this domain may be overhung with a mist that cannot be pierced. There is hope for the student when he can become aware of the great vistas that will be opened by further study and thought after college and throughout life.

SUMMARY

Organic drives are seldom involved in everyday behavior (normal satisfactions are easily obtained in most cases), but social drives—such as security, self-esteem, acceptance, affection, and independence—emotional needs, and developed values are all intertwined in each student's daily life in college.

Students, when they are able to see more clearly the reasons why they act as they do, are able to begin the process of self-analysis; individual differences become apparent in each person's behavior, and other facets of personality can be meaningfully examined.

Many students attend college for marginal or particularly peculiar reasons. Other students are unclear in their reasons for attending college, and simply state that they are seeking a "college education." Thoughtful students do seek a "college education" but with all of the full meanings of the term "education"; they are usually more aware of the various values of college and their own motivations in seeking an education.

SUPPLEMENTARY SOURCES

Bennett, Margaret E., *College and Life* (4th ed.). New York: McGraw-Hill Book Company, Inc., 1952.

Heyns, Roger W., *The Psychology of Personal Adjustment*. New York: The Dryden Press, Inc., 1958.

Jersild, Arthur T., *In Search of Self*. New York: Bureau of Publications, Teachers College, Columbia University, 1955.

Kelley, Janet A., *Guidance and Curriculum*. Englewood Cliffs, N. J.: Prentice-Hall, Inc., 1955.

Landis, Paul H., *So This Is College*. New York: McGraw-Hill Book Company, Inc., 1954.

Murphy, Gardner, *Personality, A Bio-Social Approach to Origins and Structure*. New York: Harper & Brothers, 1947.

Siedman, Jerome, ed., *The Adolescent*. New York: The Dryden Press, Inc., 1953.

Snygg, Donald, and Arthur W. Combs, *Individual Behavior*. New York: Harper & Brothers, 1949.

Stephens, Nancy P., and Robert Hoppock, "College Courses and Careers," *Psychology and Guidance Journal*, 34 (1956), pp. 502-503.

————, "Junior College Courses and Careers," *Vocational Guidance Quarterly*, 3 (1954), pp. 21-23.

Many *students* have found high school a rewarding and profitable experience, and learning was an exciting and interesting process. Other students found high school an experience and process simply to be endured. College can offer for students the promise of a meaningful education or perhaps a "sentence" to be served because of the "judgment" of parents or society. Effective and efficient learning procedures or methods can determine whether college is to be a highly valued experience or a "necessary evil" to be endured.

Chapter 3

LEARNING IN COLLEGE

Students learn each day of their lives. Education is the process of disciplined, ordered, and meaningful learning rather than chance, disorganized, or incidental learning. An understanding of learning and learning procedures can aid college students in obtaining the maximum value from education.

Attendance at school is required by law until the age of sixteen for students in most states of the United States. In addition, social pressures have dictated that adolescents finish high school prior to beginning a career. Cultural forces within American society place great stress upon education. Many jobs are unavailable to nonhigh-school graduates. Many students accede to these social pressures and forces, but simply attend high school and make no attempt to learn or profit from it.

Many high-school students do not study; most students enrolled in high school, however, do graduate. The serious student, who has attempted to seek knowledge and understanding, is joined in the graduation procession by the student who appears to be graduating because of his "endurance" or "staying power."

Serious and nonserious students seek and obtain admission to college since students of ability may possess all degrees of seriousness and devotion to study. Most colleges, however, will not grant diplomas earned only through "attendance." The American view of college life is often a conglomeration of football games, pregame rallies, fraternities, junior proms, and dormitory bull sessions. Seldom is college portrayed as an opportunity for an education through study, effort, and learning. Serious students will seek a balanced approach to all of the requirements of college; the "attending" students may be lured into a false sense of academic security because of the rush and rash of activity in college.

The tragedy of student failure in college is sometimes due to inefficient and ineffective study and learning procedures rather than a lack of ability. Many students must accept the consequences of failure that are a direct result of habits and approaches to learning acquired in high school.

This chapter is a discussion of the major methods that can be utilized by students interested in serious study and learning in college. College, learning, and education can become meaningful as an understanding of learning procedure is obtained.

Learning and methods of learning are two related but significantly different conceptual areas of study. Learning as a psychological and biological process of changing behavior, adopting new means of problem solving, or acquiring knowledge is a function and property of all human beings. Learning as a psychological and biological process is presented in a later chapter. Practical methods of learning are subjects of interest to applied psychologists and particularly to students or "learners" and are presented in this chapter.

Learning can be defined as the process that allows a person (organism), through experience, to act in a particular fashion in response to the stimuli arising within the organism or the environment surrounding the organism (after Murphy's [98] approach). More simply, learning is the process of changing one's behavior, adopting new methods of problem solving, or acquiring knowledge, attitudes, or values.

Many factors have been isolated and accepted as conditions important in promoting successful learning. Two important factors to be considered in this chapter are self-involvement and an absence of "threat" (psychological danger) to the self. Self-involvement implies a strong self-interest or "investment" by the person in the process of learning. The absence of "investment" or self-involvement can usually produce only incidental or casual learning. "Threat" to the individual can inhibit or diminish learning. Emotional upset or the need for defensive behavior by the individual can preclude or prevent learning.

Self-involvement and the absence of "threat" to the self or self-picture of the individual are important since they are related to the concept that persons learn to enhance or defend the self. (116) Students who have been put "on the spot" can probably recall the "threat" inherent in such a learning situation in school. The lack of interest or self-investment, for example, in abstract mathematics courses or perhaps other "nonvalued" courses will aid students in recalling situations or courses where self-involvement was low or lacking. These factors are most significant to students in college since they stress the relationship of learning and motivation.

Selected examples of traditional and student-centered learning methods will now be offered with particular reference to self-involvement and psychological threat.

TRADITIONAL OR FORMAL LEARNING

Much has been written defending and criticizing the traditional methods of learning. All of the arguments for and against traditional learning are not to be repeated in this section. The student is advised to consult a standard textbook on the psychology of learning for a more complete description of this aspect. This section attempts to introduce briefly those methods that have been used for generations by students in college. Some of the major aspects of each method of traditional learning will be described. The major emphasis of the chapter will be on student-centered learning. The decision to stress the newer methods is based on the hope that a balance can be struck between the two learning methods. To be sure, it is desirable to keep the old when it is useful, but also desirable to be certain not to disregard the new simply because it is new and unique.

Lecture

When the word "lecture" is mentioned, one immediately thinks of notebooks opening and students feverishly taking volumes of notes, trying in vain to keep up with an instructor who is expelling gems of wisdom like a machine gun. The approved procedure is to go home, sort out these notes, memorize them, return at some future date, and parrot back these pearls of wisdom to the instructor. Is this learning? Will a change in behavior result from this type of learning experience? It may and it may not. When a lecture is analyzed, what can it do and what can it not do?

A good lecture can transpose the written words of a textbook assignment into a spoken story, emphasizing points that may remain unclear in the text and demonstrating the relationships between the reading assignments and course objectives.

A lecture is more flexible than a book. Books, such as this one, are meant for many different audiences, and will be used in many different ways. A good lecture can unite the loose ends and result in learning; it can show the relationships between the concepts introduced in a text selection.

A lecture can also introduce new material. A good lecturer can, through an interesting presentation, change a dull, dry text assignment into a stimulating problem for the student. Since motivation is largely a result of an external incentive in a lecture situation, and self-involvement may be low, a good lecturer can stimulate and initiate motivation within his students. Sometimes, the enthusiasm and interest in a lecture can serve as immediate stimuli for a student to launch into an interesting problem.

It may be said, then, that the lecture is a method of teaching. Whether learning takes place or not is dependent upon whether the student is sufficiently motivated to become self-involved in the material, and whether he sees the satisfaction of some need in the presentation. The lecturer can present ideas to students, introduce areas of study, and even show the relationships of course content. The lecture is, however, an inefficient approach to learning for most students unless motivation and involvement are high, or the lecture (or lecturer) outstanding. The lecture is best utilized as a supplemental learning procedure.

Class meeting

The second type of traditional educational experience to be considered is the usual type of classroom meeting. Here, in a group of twenty-five to thirty-five or more students, the instructor and the class discuss, further investigate, or expand the lecture and text materials. The usual methods are, first, the lecturette (the little lecture), in which the possibilities for learning are much the same as in the lecture, and secondly, using the question-and-answer or Socratic method, the instructor tries to expand and clarify the lecture and text material. Here, more than in a lecture, the student, rather than being a passive listener, has a greater opportunity to become involved in the discussion and learning process. The skill of the teacher and the subject of the class or course many times can make the classroom meeting a satisfying and efficient learning experience for the student. Students are aware that some classes are continually interesting whereas others are dull. It should be remembered that the fact that whether or not class or section meetings are stimulating is a result of student and instructor involvement. Lethargic or passive classroom behavior on the part of all participants can only lead to minimal learning.

Textbook

The achievement of much of college learning is derived from a textbook approach. Without a degree of familiarity with the subject and a general background of information the student would be at a loss in the best of lectures or class meetings. The use of text material is certainly necessary in every college learning situation. In many college situations the use of textbooks often assumes motivation on the part of students. Even the best of college textbooks, however, seldom read like a best-selling novel; therefore, very often, if the student is to learn from a textbook, his motivation must result from outside incentive factors. Ego or self-involvement is possible; by no means, however, is it a necessary accompaniment of textbook study. Students many times will only study textbooks because of a fear of the consequence (threat) if they do not. Defense of self is therefore often operative. Intrinsic interest and desire to learn when present, however, can provide a powerful stimulus to learning from textbooks.

STUDENT-CENTERED LEARNING

It has been pointed out that the lecture can be used as a content or information source as well as a device for stimulating thought and investigation of the topic under discussion. Classroom work and textbook study complete the usual view of college learning. Group discussions and individual or personal counseling are two major approaches to student-centered learning, and each of these more unusual methods of student learning needs to be carefully investigated and reviewed.

Group discussion

A small group discussion allows a student an opportunity to become (self-) involved in the content of the discussion with little threat or danger to the self. Through this type of student involvement, learning may more effectively take place. The group, as it is being considered in this approach to learning, is an organized discussion group. Its purpose is to explore problems, consider implications and, when possible, arrive at a decision or a conclusion in a problem-solving situation. It is organized with a leader (faculty member or student) and recorder. This section of the book on the group, as a learning device, explains how the group process fits into the learning situation and explains how a group functions.

Much of the material in this book, as well as material in other books, courses, and classes will be discussed in small groups. Why is this small-group method utilized? As the student enters into his first small-group situation, there will seem to be many disadvantages to this type of learning. Certainly, from the view of the instructor and student, it is occasionally very frustrating. It means allowing a group to appear to wander aimlessly at times, with small opportunity to reach a solution to the problem. Sometimes the group situation allows disorder to reign when the co-operation of everyone is not involved in this learning experience, and certainly allows, at times, considerable noise and confusion. In spite of these disadvantages, why, then, is it used?

There are at least two theories as to what education actually is. One of these theories states that education is training for future life situations. A second theory states that education in itself is an experience in living. Each approach has many implications. If the student can reflect upon his own method of living, he will note that most persons in our society are committed to a democratic method of arriving at decisions—that is, the majority rules, but the minority must be heard. One needs to look no further to observe this than local town meetings, city-council meetings, or state legislatures. Here, people who have been duly elected by voting members of a political unit discuss and argue problems that come before them, hear both the majority and the minority, and then decide what action shall be taken.

The members of the two schools of thought on education (one of which advocates training, and the other, experience) agree that, if democratic education is to be realistic from either view, it must move toward a degree of democratic participation by all members. It then becomes necessary for all students to be able to work in a group for at least two reasons. First, since democratic action is taken through the use of groups, it is necessary for the student to learn to utilize the group as a democratic procedure. Secondly, the student needs to be actively (self-) involved in the learning situation; and group discussion provides for such self-involvement.

There is an old adage that says "one learns by doing." There is much truth in this. Anyone who has read a do-it-yourself book on carpentry knows that, although the theory of sawing a board or nailing a nail is fully understood, it is only after a few fingernails have been blackened, a few straight lines resembling ellipses have been drawn, and a few boards have been sawed just an inch too short, that he realizes that one learns by doing. For this reason, then, small-group work needs to be an integral part of the college curriculum. For, in a small group, each and every student is an active participant. Whether he actually participates verbally in the discussion, or whether he sits and observes the give-and-take between members, the student, functioning in a small group, frequently becomes emotionally involved in the activity around him. The student in this situation, then, is the doer (learner) rather than the passive listener or observer.

"All the world's a stage, and all the men and women merely players." Shakespeare's well known concept perhaps points out more graphically than in any other way the fact that in our lives many different roles are played in many different situations. Reflection for a moment upon the playing of roles or acting in a particular fashion in a life situation can aid in the clarification of group and individual behavior. In the daily life of a person he perhaps plays the following roles: in the morning upon arising and upon greeting his parents he is a son or daughter; he leaves his home and boards some type of transportation for school and becomes a commuter; upon arriving at school or college he becomes a student; in the evening he perhaps has a date and becomes "the boy friend" or "girl friend." Here in the period of one day, a person takes on at least five or six different roles in which he acts very differently each time. In the small-group situation, it is seen that there are certain roles that are played within the group. Someone must be the leader of the group; someone must act as recorder or secretary of the group to transcribe the findings and progress; and, thirdly, the remainder of the members of the group are playing the roles of participants. These are not necessarily static roles; all members in a group interact with each other, and all group roles are shared and interchanged. An examination of these special group roles will aid in the understanding of learning through group action.

The leader. Throughout history there have been many varieties of leaders. Dictators or kings have exercised complete power in an *authoritarian* situation. Some countries have had weak or vacillating leadership that allowed all members of a society to do largely as they wished. This is usually called a *laissez-faire* type of leadership. *Democratic* leadership involves respect for, and an understanding of, the wishes, desires, and needs of those who follow.

In a group situation, then, using the terms *laissez-faire, democratic,* and *authoritarian,* how should the leader of the group act? If he is performing as he would at the laissez-faire end of this continuum, he might do absolutely nothing. He would allow the group to function completely without his assistance. It might wander anywhere and discuss anything that happened to concern it; whether it came to any conclusions would not concern the leader in the least. Secondly, the leader might tell the group exactly what to do. He might not only lead the discussion, but drag or push it toward a foregone conclusion in an authoritarian manner. Thirdly, the leader might be a person who is responsible for the methodology by which his group acts but allows it to reach its own decisions. This last-mentioned type of leadership is discussed by Dean Ernest Melby of New York University's School of Education when he talks of the concept of leadership as the process of releasing the creative talents of others (91), which perhaps is another way of saying that in a democratic group situation the most important task of the leader is to develop leadership in others.

Returning to a concept of learning, as discussed earlier in this chapter, one sees that learning is part of the adjustment process—one learns for the purpose of satisfying needs. (116) Social needs are fully as important as are organic needs in a modern society. Taking these two things into con-

sideration—the adjustment process and the social needs of modern man—
it logically follows that if the group is to be used as a situation for effective
learning it must provide opportunities for such needs to be met and such
processes to take place. Lewin (79) found in his experiments with club
groups that only in the democratic group with democratic leadership was
there the necessary social status for all individuals and the necessary co-
operation for the group to work toward a goal satisfactory to all. Research
has also shown that some of the characteristics of an authoritarian or autocratic group were individual antagonism and frustration resulting in aggressive behavior toward the leader, whereas in the laissez-faire or anarchistic
situation there was an aimlessness that hindered the group from moving
toward a conclusion of any problem. Learning appears to flourish most frequently, therefore, in a democratic group with democratic leadership.

If it has been shown through research that learning can take place most
effectively through leadership of a democratic nature, we then must ask how
a democratic leader functions. A more recent theory of democratic leadership is that it is a developed and acquired attribute; leaders can be trained
to lead a certain group in doing certain tasks. Leadership is not restricted
to any particular class or any particular person. An example that helps to
strengthen this theory is the fact that we all know friends or acquaintances
who are leaders in one field and yet followers in another area: the very successful businessman who is a leader when he is in his factory but when he
arrives home at night assumes the role of a very meek follower with a domi-
neering wife; or the laborer, perhaps a bricklayer or a mason, who is a follower in his trade, taking orders from the foreman, and yet when he attends
a labor-union meeting is a leader and is a controlling influence over the
other members of his group. At some times in our lives all of us will lead;
at other times all of us will follow.

If students were asked, "What does a democratic leader do?", it might be
imagined that the first response would be: "That's very easy, he leads; he
utilizes democratic procedures in aiding a group to the solution of a given
problem." This answer is true, but would the person who asked this question now have any more idea as to what he would actually do if he were
confronted with a leadership situation? The responsibility for leading the
group toward the solution of a problem involves the leader in at least four
basic functions.

First, he is responsible for regulating the discussion of the group. That
is, he is responsible for keeping the group from wandering too far afield
from the problem under consideration. For example, if the topic under discussion by the group is automobile traffic in downtown Boston, and, during
the discussion, the group begins to discuss the fact that the runways at
Logan International Airport in Boston are too short for some airliners to
land, it is one of the functions of the leader of the group to bring the dis-

cussion back to the main point so that it will continue toward its stated objective.

Secondly, the leader is responsible for focusing the discussion. As has been said before, each member of the group may have a different opinion and a different idea as to the possible solution of a problem. As part of the task of focusing a discussion, the leader must be certain that the points being made by each member of the group are well understood by all others. This function, at times, calls for considerable interpretative skills on the part of the leader. Here again the leader must be sensitive to the feelings and the ideas of the person for whom he is interpreting. His interpretations must be objective and they must be complete if he is to remain a proficient leader.

A third responsibility of the leader is that of guiding discussions. A group is a group only as long as each of its members is able to express his opinion and is able to comment upon the opinions of others. If the discussion is dominated by any individual to the exclusion of other individuals the group is no longer functioning in the most advantageous way.

Fourthly, and perhaps most difficult for the leader, is the problem of interpretation of the content during the discussion. If there are ten members on a certain committee and each member has given his opinion as to what the problem actually is, it then becomes a function of the leader to interpret what each person has said. The leader needs to highlight the topics of agreement, when it seems possible to do so, and to recognize and accept those about which considerable disagreement exists.

In summary, the functions of a leader revolve around the idea that, in a democratic discussion, the leader's task is to bring out the "best" that is present in the members of the group. He accomplishes this through regulating the discussions, focusing the discussion upon the goal, guiding the discussion so that all members have a chance to voice their opinions, and interpreting the opinions of others so that a final conclusion can be reached.

Group recorder. The recorder serves three functions. First, in the usual discussion group the recorder is responsible for putting on paper the conclusions of the group and the intermediate notes necessary to reach a conclusion. This does not mean a verbatim recording of the statements of each participant but rather a sorting of the material and a process of summarizing ideas into meaningful conclusions. The second function of the recorder is to help the leader in the summarization of discussion material. This is an important check against the leader in the problem of understanding what others have said. The recorder's third function is to be a group member. In fact, in a small group every person is a member first and holds any other responsibility secondly.

Group members. A group becomes a group and remains a group as long as it is united in discussion or as it moves toward the solution of a given problem; it must have a goal; and to be successful, it must move toward that goal. The roles of leader and recorder are important, but ultimately the success or failure of any group depends upon its members. They have definite functions and responsibilities.

First of all, the members of a group must maintain an attitude that will help lead the group toward a solution of the problem. This attitude must be one of co-operation with the other members of the group as long as the group itself is moving along the road to solution.

Secondly, the group members are responsible for electing or selecting a leader and a recorder who will meet their needs. The group members are responsible for knowing the necessary attributes of a good leader and for picking the person in their group who can best fill this role.

Thirdly, the group must be continually sensitive to the activities of both the leader and the recorder to see that they are fulfilling the responsibilities of their different roles. If the group finds, or individual members of the group find, that the leader is not fulfilling the role that has been assigned to him, it is the responsibility of the group members to take leadership away from this member and assign it to some other person who will perform the necessary functions.

Fourthly, it is the responsibility of each member of a discussion group to contribute as much as possible to the discussion. Just as it is a responsibility of the leader to bring out the best of the participants, it is the responsibility of the members to give their best to the group.

Fifthly, it is necessary for each member of the group to respect the other members of the group. This means that no one person should try to dominate the discussion and that the members must keep in mind that the one goal of the group is to move toward a solution of its given problem.

Sixthly, just as it is a responsibility of the leader to keep the discussion from wandering too far afield, it is a responsibility of the participants not to allow a discussion to become disorganized. Certainly, it is necessary for all aspects of a problem to be considered if a final solution is possible, but when a member feels that the discussion has wandered so far from the topic that decisions reached can have little bearing on the final solution of the problem, it is the function of the member of the group to bring this to the attention of the leader or to mention it himself.

Finally, just as the leader must be sensitive to the feelings of each member of the group, so must the members of the group be sensitive to the feelings of each other member. Each person must be continually aware that in any problem under consideration there will be disagreement and that many times this disagreement goes deeper than pure, intellectual argumentation. The disagreements that most people have are at least partly emotionally based. Members of the group must be continually sensitive to the personalities and feelings of the other members and although they may feel sure that they are right, they must understand that other members of the group may feel as secure in their own views.

Group discussion has been presented as a procedure in which student (or self) involvement can be high, and threats to the individual (self) can be minimal. These two conditions can serve to heighten learning and thinking. Students will need to practice and improve their group-learning skills, or the benefits of such an approach will be lost in the confusion of argument, digression, and frustration.

Personal counseling

Personal counseling of the student by a trained counselor is desirable and useful to help students in the process of self-understanding. Personal counseling offers (as did small-group discussion) a unique student-centered learning experience. The psychological principles discussed in this book are offered to students in a fashion designed to induce a high degree of self-involvement in the learning process. Personal counseling offers an atmosphere in which self-involvement is high and threat to self is low. Students, in counseling, are progressing in individual learning.

As was stated earlier in this chapter, learning normally involves a change in behavior. The student, in a nonthreatening, individual counseling session, may review his past behavior and plan for the future. The high level of self-involvement in a student-and-counselor learning situation allows students to perceive changes in behavior that can lead to a more satisfactory and realistic adjustment to a college program.

Counseling usually begins with personal problems or questions. The student is soon, however, involved in questions arising out of the text of the psychology course, other texts, other courses, and soon the entire educational process. Counseling can become, therefore, a part of the total educational experience of each student.

Counseling has long been a process of one person's aiding another to solve problems or to change behavior patterns. Such changes in behavior or solutions to problems that can arise from counseling must be attributed to learning—learning that takes place during counseling.

Theorists and writers in the area of counseling have been puzzled for many years concerning the actual processes that take place in successful experiences of counseling. Significant insights, self-understandings, even changed life plans, may result from counseling. The best explanations of how counseling can effect such changes in behavior emphasize that meaningful and efficient learning occur as the individual is able, in a nonthreatening environment, to reorder his own feelings, attitudes, values, emotions, and motives in life. Counseling of a personal nature, then, fulfills all of the requirements for successful student-centered learning. Counseling carries to a normal, expected conclusion the principles of effective learning. The student becomes the center of the learning process.

Functions. Counseling in conjunction with learning and the educational process has at least three functions. The student, first of all, may need help in understanding more fully his course or academic work and study. Such a personal relationship between the teacher or counselor and the student is as old as the teaching process. In a personal conference the student's motivation is usually high, the self is not threatened, and the individual is as completely involved as is theoretically possible. Learning in such a situation has its best chance of success.

Secondly, the student is able, through counseling, to solve more efficiently his educational or personal problems or both. Through a review of past behavior and a contemplation of future behavior, the student can better perceive the relationships of his personality and abilities to the goals that he has set forth for himself. Failure in an academic situation usually means more than "more work, more time, and more effort." It usually means that some further insight into the relationships between behavior and the academic situation is necessary. Through counseling, the achievement of such insights is often possible.

Thirdly, the student is in college to receive training and education toward goals and objectives that he has set for himself. The more effectively this can be done, the more the student can obtain from his college experience. Here, also, counseling is an effective tool in the student's attainment of his goals. Through greater insight and a clearer self-picture, the student is better able to obtain that which college can offer him. Complete and realistic introspection is not possible because the individual, rather than being realistic, will tend to defend himself. It then remains for counseling to bridge the gap between the world of reality and the student's own self-concept or self-picture. When this is done, but only to the degree that it is done, will any actual change in behavior and progress toward goals result.

Counseling relationship. Students many times have difficulty in understanding, preserving and contributing to the relationship that should exist between a counselor and a student. Students may expect that counselors will dispense "advice" or "tell students what to do." Other students may perceive the counselor as a "censor," "a disagreeable pessimist," or "an unrealistic optimist." Actually, the counselor never attempts to assume these stated roles. A counselor is a partner in the learning process that takes place in counseling. The counselor serves as an interested, accepting, and understanding individual with whom students may talk, discuss, or explore the past, present, or future.

Counselors, many times, can serve as vital sources of information. Test scores, vocational information, educational resources, and even interpretations of school policy are examples of information that counselors may offer to students. This "information-giving role" must not be distorted into a "decision-making role." Students should always try to be responsible for their own decisions.

Students will find that a counselor can aid them in looking at all sides of a problem, in viewing possible alternative patterns of action, or in evaluating completed or proposed patterns of behavior. The counselor, ideally, has no personal bias or mental attitude of prejudgment to foist upon students. Counselors are interested in aiding each person to achieve his own personal goals or objectives. Unrealistic optimism or disagreeable pessimism is an attitude gained from the student's actual contact with the world of reality (perhaps as temporarily represented by the counselor) rather than something injected into the relationship by the counselor. Counseling as learning is both an experience in living and preparation for future living.

SUMMARY

A basic objective of democratically oriented education is to provide well informed, balanced, and competent democratic citizens. This becomes the objective of the college learning situation. One of the related objectives of college must therefore be to create the most efficient learning situations possible, so that the student is able to attain the basic objective academically and personally in accord with his level of scholastic aptitude or capacity.

It has been the aim of this chapter to review the different types of learning situations that usually exist in a college program, and to introduce and discuss other types that are unique or unusual. The question of whether there is any best method of creating a learning situation arises. The answer to this query, of course, is that there is not. Students and teachers respond, because of individual differences, to many different types of learning situations.

There does seem to be some indication that if self-involvement and the enhancement and protection of the self-picture (or concept) are to be considered important for student motivation, some of the student-centered types of learning situations may at times provide the best opportunity for learning to take place. This certainly does not mean that the teacher-centered practices of lecture, class meetings, and text assignments are not useful, but it does mean that the emphasis of the college program should be balanced so that students may be active partners in the learning process and not mere "sponges" for knowledge.

The student and the teacher share an equally responsible role in creating meaningful learning situations. Teachers, counselors, and all educators are interested in providing an environment and an atmosphere within which students may discover facts, relate ideas, and develop concepts. The application of learnings becomes the pragmatic test of an education. The student must enter into the process of learning and education. It becomes the student's responsibility to create an atmosphere of co-operation and of willingness to take advantage of opportunities that the instructor creates. The best student-centered learning situation can be useless if the student does not allow himself to become involved in the learning situation. College can create the opportunities, but the student must take advantage of them.

Group work and counseling are two illustrations of student-centered learning procedures. These techniques require equal involvement and responsibility on the part of both the teacher-counselor and the student.

SUPPLEMENTARY SOURCES

Benne, D., and N. Muntyan, *Human Relations in Curriculum Change*. New York: The Dryden Press, Inc., 1951.

Bennett, M. E., *College and Life* (4th ed.). New York: McGraw-Hill Book Company, Inc., 1952.

————, *Guidance in Groups*. New York: McGraw-Hill Book Company, Inc., 1955.

Bugelski, B. R., *The Psychology of Learning*. New York: Henry Holt & Company, Inc., 1956.

Brayfield, Arthur H., ed., *Readings in Modern Methods of Counseling*. New York: Appleton-Century-Crofts, Inc., 1950.

Callis, Robert, Paul C. Polmantier, and Edward Roeber, "Five Years of Research in Counseling," *Journal of Counseling Psychology*, 4 (1957), pp. 119-123.

Cartwright, D., and A. F. Zander, *Group Dynamics: Research and Theory*. New York: Row, Peterson & Company, 1953.

Haiman, Franklyn S., *Group Leadership in Democratic Action*. Boston: Houghton Mifflin Company, 1951.

Hoppock, Robert, *Occupational Information*. New York: McGraw-Hill Book Company, Inc., 1957.

Sherif, Muzafer, and Carolyn W. Sherif, *Groups in Harmony and Tension.* New York: Harper & Brothers, 1953.

Shoben, E. J., Jr., "Psychotherapy as a Problem in Learning," *Psychological Bulletin,* 46 (1949), pp. 366-392.

Thelen, H., *Dynamics of Groups at Work.* Chicago: The University of Chicago Press, 1954.

Application of psychological knowledge is vital to all

FOUNDATIONS OF
SELF-ANALYSIS AND
SELF-APPRAISAL

Psychology is the systematic and organized study of man and man's behavior. The principles of psychology that underlie man's behavior are presented in Part II.

Chapter 4 is an analysis of age-old theories of why man behaves as he does, and a survey of man's current understandings of the causes of behavior. Chapter 5 is a study of the major theories of how man changes his behavior or acquires new beliefs, attitudes, or values. Learning theories are presented as a process that, when

*combined with the basic causes of behavior, can pro-
duce particular personality patterns. Chapter 6 is the
third step in the analysis of the process whereby each
person becomes a unique, particular individual. Personality is seen as the characteristic way in which a person
approaches and solves the problems of life. Chapter 7
deals with an analysis of personality in action and the
development of physiological, social, and psychological
maturity.*

Man has long sought to isolate, define, and measure the many factors that appear to cause behavior. He accepts the concept that behavior is caused, but finds that his behavior is the most complex of all among the living organisms. An explanation of the concept of causation seems to be the pot of gold at the end of the rainbow. Early philosophical writings attributed man's behavior to the effects of the elements, such as blood or bile, within the body. Philosophers have continued to wrestle with these problems with only par-

Chapter 4

CAUSES OF
HUMAN BEHAVIOR

tial success until almost the present day. In the comparatively recent past psychologists, at first considered renegade philosophers, began to study the problem. Success was not immediate, but progress was made. Psychologists have now formulated meaningful hypotheses and theories of behavior. Exact and precise answers, particularly in individual cases, are still not available, but reasonable and partially proved hypotheses and theories now exist. The speculation of the past was largely an exercise of logic and reason with little concern for any practical application or testing of the theories developed. The rule of reason, intellect, and rational processes prevented the development of an experimentally-oriented science of psychology. The reality of life and the validity of experience finally provided a testing ground for the theories, ideas, and concepts of psychologists. As thought processes were validated, knowledge and understanding in the field of psychology progressed. This chapter will examine some of the early psychological theories of behavior as well as the more currently accepted theories that attempt to explain, at least partially, the behavior of man.

45

EARLY THEORIES OF BEHAVIOR

Man has always been concerned with the "why" of his behavior. Man attributed the varying reactions and adjustments of himself and his brothers to good or evil spirits, witches, the planets and the moon, mesmerism—the list is endless. In more recent times, psychologists and scholars have offered theories that seem better to satisfy the modern mind.

Sigmund Freud

Sigmund Freud, an Austrian physician who lived from 1856 to 1939, is generally acknowledged to be the outstanding pioneer of modern psychology. A practicing physician, a clinical observer of human behavior, and, most of all, a brilliant creative thinker, he presented the first widely known and partially accepted theory of human behavior.

Freud's theories, except as pioneering and illuminating contributions to human behavior, are beyond the province, scope, and design of this book. His early theories are today entirely accepted by some people, in modified form by many, and not at all by others. To trace the development of his ideas into modern-day practice is a task beyond the college freshman. Various authors (3), (70) have attempted to outline Freud's ideas, and interested readers may wish to refer to these sources. Freud's theories in oversimplified and perhaps (for some) distorted fashion will be briefly viewed as examples of early strivings to understand man and the behavior of man. Selected principles of Freudian theory will also be examined in order to see their historical significance in terms of today's beliefs. This brief summary is based on *An Outline of Psychoanalysis,* by Sigmund Freud. (52)

Sigmund Freud saw man as a psychological organism composed of three major forces that directed behavior. Freud labeled these forces the *ego,* the *superego,* and the *id*. Freud believed that man began with an id, which represented vague animalistic or unconscious urges or strivings within the personality. Experience and interaction with environment soon allowed the individual to differentiate an ego and superego from the id. Freud believed the ego to be the reality or worldly-contact portion of the id and postulated that the ego served as a directing, mediating, and controlling force in human behavior. The superego, developed in turn from the ego, became the conscience or inhibiting factor in behavior. The ego and superego thus controlled behavior. Freud imagined the id to be the remaining unconscious larger reservoir of urges and strivings that seldom saw the daylight of contact with reality.

Freud's view of man seemed to solve many problems of explaining the actions of man. Behavior could be attributed to an ego, superego, or id. The naïve student may rightly ask, "Where were these things or forces located?" and "Where did they come from?" Freud always wrote of these factors as almost "physical" forces or "mind areas." The naïve student would have uncovered a basic problem. Where do the id, ego, and super-ego come from, reside, and how do they influence behavior? These were problems never clearly resolved. It is sufficient to say that a meaningful explanation of man had been presented though certainly not proved.

Freud postulated two basic instincts that served as the forces existing behind the id, ego, and superego. He called these forces "Eros" and the "destructive instinct" (Thanatos). (52:20) These two forces were seen as the basic causes of all of man's behavior. "Eros" was defined as an instinct for life or self-preservation. The destructive instinct represented the urge to destroy, even one's self, through death.

Freud wrote of various modifications of these basic instincts. Through "sublimation," "displacement," or other mechanisms, man's behavior could be understood. The two basic "instincts" served as the driving mo-tivating forces in man.

Freud practiced, spoke, and wrote as a prophet in a new land. His con-tributions in psychology are legion. The importance of early childhood in personality formation, the human being as a dynamic learning mechanism, and the problem-solving or adjustive nature of man are but a few of the literally hundreds of ideas emanating from his creative mind.

The many contributions of Freud influence all of the current beliefs about man and the causes of man's behavior. Freud's early theories have undergone many revisions. His concepts of ego, superego, and id have been modified. The "self," the "self-concept," and "personality patterns" are related in modern-day psychology. Freud's definition of instincts in their pure form is not accepted today. Drives, needs, motives, emotions, and the adjustment process are utilized instead. His pioneering, however, has made possible current-day knowledge. Modern psychologists may worship or curse Freud and his ideas, but none can ignore his contributions. He stands alone as a prophet, philosopher, and psychologist in modern-day psychological theory.

Theory of instincts

Early in the twentieth century American psychologists also began to at-tempt to explain man's behavior in terms of "instinctual" behavior. Ob-servation of the behavior of human beings led to a conclusion that many actions were common to all persons. Through observation of man, theor-ists speculated that there were unlearned forces inherent within men that led to certain types of behavior. These unlearned forces were called instincts. An instinct was defined as a complex behavior pattern, present at birth or at an appropriate time, unlearned, and found in all persons. Instinct was a "natural" impulse or guide to action. Early psychologists believed that man's behavior could be explained if all of man's "instincts" were discovered and catalogued. Man was presumed to have, according to various lists of differing lengths, a pugnacious instinct (to fight), a self-preservation instinct, a gregarious instinct (to seek others' company), a maternal instinct (for women only), a power instinct, a love instinct, and many others.

The instinct theory as presented most comprehensively by McDougall (86) gained considerable acceptance. Many references as to why man acts as he does can even now be found, using the instinct theory as an explanation. In fact and in proof, however, the instinct theory did not fare well. Various "instincts" were found to be present in some but not all individuals. Other "instincts" were found to be present at times but not at other times within the same individual. The exceptions became so numerous that the entire theory had to be discarded by most psychologists. At the same time, many investigators began analyzing "instincts" and found that, through theories of instinct, behavior was being *labeled* or *described* but not explained. A new and different cause was needed in order to explain man's behavior.

Animal instincts are talked of when we do not understand why animals behave as they do. Animal instincts simply describe and do not explain behavior; much is still unknown of "instinctual" animal behavior. Further research and investigation may or may not place animal instincts in the same obsolete category to which human instincts have been relegated.

ADJUSTMENT AND BEHAVIOR

Man's behavior, through analysis and experimentation, appeared to be directed toward the satisfaction of various needs. Psychologists reasoned that, if the needs and drives (basic motivating forces) of man could be investigated and then the process used to satisfy these needs also investigated, man's behavior could be understood.

Early investigators, well represented by the thorough presentations of Woodworth (138), found that various stimulations would produce particular reactions in individuals. It was found early that if the lack of water (a thirst need) was used as a stimulus then all manner of attempts would be used by thirsty individuals to satisfy such a need. Many stimuli were discovered that would produce identical or nearly identical responses; other stimuli would produce varied responses. Then it was found that not only were the stimuli (basic needs or superficial provokers to action) important in order to determine human response or action, but that the individual stimulated and reacting was also involved in the process.

It was a significant advance in the understanding of man's behavior when research and investigation determined that not only were simple causes needed to understand man's behavior but that man himself was involved. This process of "stimulus" (to man) and "response" (man acting) had to go through the organism called man. A formula expressing this was written as S—O—R or $S + O = O + R$. In this shorthand "S" stood for stimulus, "O" for organism or man, and "R" for response or action. Man's behavior and the *causes* for man's acting as he did were slowly beginning to be understood. If enough could be learned about "S" (stimulus), "O" (man), and "R" (response) behavior could be understood.

"Stimulus-response" theory and investigation began to reward the psychologists and investigators. Early successes were numerous, but problems occurred. Complex behavior still could not be understood. Further refinement and more careful analysis of man and his behavior were necessary.

Even after advances in understanding had been made through an analysis of the stimuli acting upon man and man's responses, a more thorough explanation of the process involved was desirable. It was clear that there were many needs and drives (stimuli) acting upon man, but he was constantly being thwarted or frustrated in his desire to achieve the satisfaction of such needs or drives. Psychologists finally were able to integrate these many factors in the theory of the "adjustment process."

The adjustment process is as follows (adapted from Shaffer's [113] presentation of the concepts involved, and Dashiell's original diagram [40]).

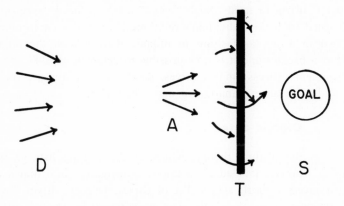

"D" represents drives, needs, or stimuli acting upon man. Man wanted water, food, air, or other basic needs. "T" stands for the thwarting, blocking or frustrations that man encountered in obtaining his desired goal or satisfactions, "S." "A" represents the means by which man solved his problems (mechanisms of adjustment).

An example will serve to illustrate and further to explain the adjustment process. A man is thirsty, "D," his chemical balance and tissue moisture level is beginning to be upset. The man begins to seek means of obtaining satisfaction, "S." The drive leads to activity. If water is at hand (a glass by his chair), he can easily solve his problem (achieving satisfaction). If water is not nearby "T" (frustration or thwarting) occurs. He must go to the kitchen or the well to solve the problem; "A" (adjustment mechanism) represents the means he selects.

All problems of life may be seen in terms of the adjustment process. Man has needs, drives, objectives, or goals, and life is full of blocks, frustrations, or thwartings. Man, in order to solve his problems, fulfill his needs, and achieve his satisfactions, must solve his problems, *adjust,* or die.

The adjustment process, basic as it is to all of psychology and life, will need to be re-examined in light of further areas of study. In order to understand the causes of man's behavior, man's process of adjustment to life needs to be understood; a return to the basic causes of man's behavior is in order.

Psychologists discovered through research and investigation that all of man's behavior could not be understood by external instincts or simple stimuli. The adjustment process as an explanation of the process of behavior finally was offered as basic to behavior causation. At the same time, progress was made in the study of drives or needs. Man's organic or physiological needs were studied and clarified. At the same time, social forces operating on man led to a conception that man, as a social animal, had "social" drives or needs. Such "social" drives or needs were presumed to be learned from the individual's relationships with his environment, but functioned in a similar fashion to organic drives. With the adjustment process as a background it is now possible to delineate the "D" portion of the adjustment process: man's drives, needs, and desires are motivating forces leading to an explanation of man's behavior.

Organic drives

Contrary to the instinct theory, which produced long lists of complex patterns of behavior labeled as instincts, investigation into man's organic needs produced a short, simple list of drives. Organic drives have been defined in many ways. A simple view is expressed by saying: *an organic drive is a physiologically based impetus to action or behavior.* Rather than attempting to explain in one concept all that was involved in a particular pattern of behavior, a theory of drives was an attempt to describe the simple urges and needs of life. Many lists of organic drives have been postulated (110), (99), (95), based upon much experimentation. In spite of various lists there exists much basic agreement about organic drives that was not present when instincts were catalogued.

Three fundamental types of human organic drives have been organized and defined. These types are: (a) needs, (b) discharges, and (c) avoidances. *Needs* are composed of such factors as thirst, hunger, oxygen (breathing) and certain sensory gratifications. *Discharges* are concerned with sex (secretions), lactation, carbon dioxide (breathing), and elimination functions. *Avoidances* involve pain, extreme heat or cold, and certain harmful or irritating substances (such as acids, or alkalies). All of these organic drives lead to action. As such, drives are *not* at all similar to instincts, with which investigators attempted to explain *all* of a complex behavioral pattern. Organic drives lead to an increase in the activity level of man. The use of need-satisfiers or balance-restorers such as water, milk, beer, champagne, or various foods is not determined by organic drives but by learning. A baby with hunger needs in Western societies will be given cow's milk or human milk. Children in other societies or in subcultural units of Western society may use goat's milk or other substances. The particular objects or means used to obtain satisfaction of human organic needs (drives) are determined by availability and culturally influenced learning. Such complex behavior, although stemming from or resulting from organic drives, is determined and greatly influenced by learning, the process of the individual's adjusting and solving problems in a particular society or culture.

Social drives

Progress was made in listing, exploring, and verifying various organic drives. Man's complex behavior patterns, however, were still confusing. Man, a member of society, developed needs that seemed to have no organic or physical base. Social drives or needs, arising out of man's interaction with other men, offered a counterpart to man's organic drives. Social tensions and lacks operate in the same fashion as do physical drives. Need is generally a more comprehensive term, but for purposes of comparative understanding, drive and need will be used as though virtually interchangeable. Perhaps if man were a solitary rather than a social animal, such social drives or needs would not be present. Various experiments have been attempted to test such a hypothesis but clear-cut evidence is not available.

Experimentation and research in the development of social drives and needs have thus far been most fruitful, and Gesell, Jersild, and Cole (56), (66), (33) have reported on much of it. The original research and clinical observations of Gesell and his associates at Yale University have also contributed much concerning the developmental patterns of human behavior in children, and Jersild and Cole have reported on research dealing with children's patterns of social behavior. Such experimentation and study of human behavior have helped to provide a broad understanding of the development of social drives and needs. The present analysis of social drives and needs can proceed without a detailed study of original work underlying the theories. Students who wish to investigate these writings may refer to the indicated sources and the reported research.

Social drives or needs are not as easily classified or catalogued as were organic drives. Social drives are more complex because of their roots in man's relationships to man. Most authors agree on security, self-esteem, affection, acceptance, and independence as being basic social drives. Terms or words such as status, mastery, and others are also used but their concepts are included in the classification offered here.

Security. Man strives for the satisfaction of both physical and psychological security. Food, clothing, and shelter are needed for basic physical security. Psychological security is more complex and involves the individual's inner feeling of safety or certainty in a world of conflict, confusion, or doubt. Security is perhaps the most basic of all social needs or drives; it includes the achievement of success in areas such as self-esteem, affection, acceptance, and independence and is also a pervasive need for man as a social being.

Self-esteem. Man needs to feel a sense of worth and balanced importance in life. A person strives to obtain a meaningful existence in his own eyes and in the eyes of others. Man lives and works among people. The respect and regard of others is important, but one must also possess respect and regard for one's self. Man strives to gain self-esteem; such strivings are learned in a social world.

Affection. Man lives among men. Love serves as a bond between men. Romantic love is only a more precise aspect of affection between men as coinhabitants of a common world. Complete self-sufficiency appears to be an imaginary concept. Man may achieve various levels of self-sufficiency, but affection toward and from other human beings underlies and surrounds true self-sufficiency. Self-sufficiency therefore contains an ability to give and accept affection. Loneliness of fact or spirit is a symptom and result of affection that is missing.

Acceptance. Man as a member of a human society is dependent upon other men. An interrelated, specialized society forces economic dependence. Psychological interdependence and man's need for affection produce a concomitant need for acceptance by other men. Man depends upon the regard and respect of others. When such regard and respect are present from others through the many trials of life, self-acceptance and self-regard tend to result.

Independence. Independence is of a different order from other social drives or needs. In spite of all of man's interrelationships and dependence upon other men, there is need for self-identification as a separate being. When identity has been lost, independence has also vanished. Independence is thus the achievement of security, self-esteem, affection, and acceptance. A person is unique and sovereign while still a member of society.

The presentation of a classification of man's social needs, which serve also as social drives, clearly shows the many overlappings and joint functionings involved in social needs. It is difficult for man to achieve success in one area without at least partial concurrent success in other areas. Failure in one area also usually involves at least partial failure in other areas.

A child at an early age learns to seek the approval and love of his mother, father, family, and others. Approval leads to security, acceptance, affection, and, ultimately, self-esteem. When a child acts in a fashion that parents do not approve, these objects of a child's social drives (such as recognition and love) are withheld, and frustration results. Such approval or disapproval can even begin to operate on the first day of a child's life. Food, love, and parental care are withheld or offered according to parental attitude toward a child's behavior. The child continues to behave in patterns designed to achieve satisfaction of such social needs. Social needs therefore operate, not only in the early days, but also throughout life in the causation of behavior.

A brief summary of social drives or needs can only reveal their complexity and significance. Social drives are more involved and more varied than are organic drives. Organic drives are constantly modified by social drives. All men must eat, but while fulfilling hunger needs, because of social needs, man must eat certain things, eat in certain fashions, and eat at certain times—the ramifications are endless. Organic needs arise from physical functioning, but must exist and be satisfied in social contexts and environments.

Organic and social drives have begun to answer the question of why man behaves as he does. The operation of these drives is infinitely more complex than the illustrations presented. Each day of man's life organic and social drives operate as stimuli to action. Behavior patterns, through learning, are developed. Man, as the perceiving and responding organism, is influenced in his behavior by these drives. Man, however, has yet another basic, causative force operating in his behavior patterns. Emotions serve to cause behavior and to modify behavior by serving as independent drives and by acting upon organic and social drives. Emotions further complicate the study of the causation of behavior. A study of emotions is therefore the third concept to be examined in order to unify the understanding of the causation and modification of behavior through organic and social drives.

EMOTIONS

Organic and social drives can arouse activity and can, at the same time, be viewed as emotional states or feelings within man. When drives or needs are mild there is little emotion or feeling involved. When drives or needs are intense the emotional state or feelings of the individual are intense. A mild thirst need may lead to *concern* for a glass of water. A thirst resulting from abandonment in a desert can involve a state of *fear*—fear of death. Such concern or fear is an emotional state or feeling within the individual.

Emotion is the individual psychological feeling or consciousness that normally accompanies, precedes, or follows an experience. The emotion is not a part of the outside world experienced by a person but is *of* and *within* the person and distinct from the outside world. Emotions are therefore closely related to behavior and in turn related to organic and social drives. Emotions need to be examined and seen independently and in relationship to the organic and social drives underlying behavior.

Emotion has been the subject of much controversy. Instincts and their existence led to debate; emotion and its functioning has led to even more prolonged and heated controversy. Writers state their own favorite definitions; a degree of agreement exists but controversy still remains.

The common area of agreement concerning emotion and its definition appears to be in the statement that emotion is a "stirred-up" state of consciousness or feeling that is within the psychological being of a person but related to and aroused by the experiences and the life of the organism. Emotion is a consciousness or feeling state.

Basic emotions within the life of man have been offered by many writers and research specialists. Some years ago it was firmly believed that fear, rage, and love were the three most basic emotions. These beliefs have been questioned by more careful examination of infants' behavior, and it appears that *general* excitement or distress is the earliest emotional response. Fear, rage, love, specific distress excitement, and delight (113) appear only after several months of life have elapsed.

Emotion as a psychological consciousness also involves the body of the individual experiencing the emotion. An emotional or feeling state is therefore an expression of the total organism; psychological perception and bodily functioning are both involved.

Most persons are familiar with the contributions of the body in emotion but do not relate these physical reactions to the psychological feeling state called emotion. The viscera (the heart, lungs, stomach), endocrine glands, and other organs, the central and autonomic nervous systems, in fact the total physical functioning of the body, are involved in emotion. Intense fear is not merely a perception of a psychological state within the organism, it is also a total response of the physical being. Less intense emotions also involve the body. The nature of emotion is the total response of the organism.

Everyday slang, or so-called "body language," illustrates the physical side of emotion: "That hit me in the pit of my stomach," "It takes guts to endure that," "I have no heart for it." All of these expressions refer to emotional perceptions but are expressed in slang in terms of the body applied to the emotion. Theories about man's original physical need for flight whenever fear was present, or the physical base of rage or love, have all been postulated as reasons why man's physical being is so closely tied to emotion. Certainly, the immediate response of blood pressure, pulse, glandular secretions, metabolism, and other gross or lesser bodily activities in emotion verifies that emotion is a total response of the organism.

Feelings are relatively mild or low-level expressions of emotions and therefore arise out of emotions. Moods are closely related to feelings and emotions and appear to be feelings or emotional states that persist after or before activity or behavior associated with feeling or emotion.

The person or self (the individual's perception of himself) experiences an internal state of consciousness or sensory pleasantness or unpleasantness. Such experience or perception is feeling or mood. Feelings and moods can be not only pleasant or unpleasant, but can exist as an experience of excitement or insensitivity, tension or relaxation, or security or insecurity. Feelings and moods are as infinitely variable as the ability of the language needed to express such concepts.

Emotions, feelings, and moods are a consistent and constant part of man's life. Activity, the anticipation of activity, or the remembrance of activity all involve the psychological expression of emotional feeling or mood.

Emotions are basic to life. Individuals will strive to attain certain emotional states just as they will seek to obtain food or water. Emotions can function independently as drives to stimulate activity. A person can perceive danger (real or unreal), and his fear will lead to action or behavior; anger (justified or irrational) can operate in a similar fashion; and love as a pervasive activity cause is well known. An individual's need, or felt need, of an emotional character can thus substitute in the adjustment process for drives or needs.

Emotions can also function as deterrents to action, "speed-up" agents, or simply change agents in activity aroused by drives. A thirsty man, fearing poisoned water, will not drink. An angered individual may release pent-up aggression by overwork and seek prestige, status or power. Love is well known as a factor that, at times, alone can explain behavior.

Emotion in a more general sense is a broad pervasive factor in not only activity drives but in the entire adjustment process. Man seeks satisfaction or an emotional feeling of well-being in all behavior. Satisfaction may be of a short-term or life-term nature. Satisfaction is an emotional state of being. Satisfaction is a feeling tone based on strong emotion. Emotions, therefore, in a very fundamental sense, are at the roots of all behavior.

One may legitimately ask, concerning unusual behavior, what type of satisfaction is derived from inflicting or experiencing pain or hurt. Some individuals seem to seek only pain or hurt in their actions. Through an involved psychological process (sadism or masochism) even pain can sometimes be satisfying. Other examples could also be given to demonstrate these somewhat involved concepts, but in all human behavior an emotional feeling of satisfaction appears to be basic.

Emotions thus add a third element in the search for foundations of behavior. They are basic to all life and adjustment. Emotions can serve as drives in and of themselves, they can modify or change social or organic drives, and in an all-inclusive sense serve as perhaps the most basic root of behavior in all of man's activities.

MOTIVATION

Basic social and organic drives develop in an individual; varying forces and influences affect their development. Physiology, emotional needs, societal forces, as well as family and cultural pressures, exert their effects. Each individual therefore develops separate and distinct motivational patterns in life. Each person has a unique physiology, a unique pattern of social and emotional needs, a unique family constellation and patterning, and a unique cultural and societal history.

Such extreme differences in individual patterns of motivation at first uncover one reason why each person and each personality is unique. Secondly, such diversity leads to the question of how motivation can be understood if each person is different. The first of these implications needs to be explored whereas the second is partially answered by recent theoretical writings in psychology.

Since learning and motivation make each person unique there are implications of this process that need to be carefully examined. Motivation serves as a force arising out of the past and influencing the future. Philosophers and writers have said, "as the twig is bent the tree will grow," or, "out of today grows tomorrow." Humans more than any other species are able to learn from experience, and through such learnings influence and determine their own futures. Motivation is one of the significant forces determining the future for each individual.

Important personal knowledge of motivation for each person can arise out of study and knowledge of past learnings and present forces operative in personality. The objective of this book is to assist students in the task of self-knowledge and self-understanding in order to allow them to influence their own futures. The task at hand is to analyze the process of how organic and social drives and emotions are modified through learning into motives, values, and motivational patterns that in turn become the causes of behavior.

Motivation and learning

Organic drives or needs, social drives or needs, and emotions have been presented as original stimuli to activity and behavior. The study of the factors and forces underlying behavior is the analysis of *motivation*. Motivation is the study of drives and needs, emotions, and *learning*. Simple arousal of activity cannot explain behavior. The modification, the changing, and the molding of these basic forces into behavior take place through their interaction with learning processes.

Organic and social drives serve as impetuses to activity and behavior. Connecting such basic factors as drives to the complex actions that each person accomplishes every day is a confusing issue. Learning serves as the process unifying such drives and actions. As mentioned before in this chapter, babies can adjust to human, cow's, or goat's milk to satisfy hunger and thirst, and other examples could be given to show how learning acts upon drives. From the moment of birth (and perhaps even in the womb) a child learns. An organic need for food leads to the general activity of restless crying and thrashing. When satisfied with various types of food that are offered the child also learns to prefer certain foods. Hunger conditions later will lead to activity and restlessness again. A schedule of feeding may soon be utilized with the newborn baby. Hunger will occur every two, three, or four hours, but he will learn to control his hunger and to prefer certain foods. Variations are of course involved, but within one day a baby is modifying basic organic and social drives.

Learning continues each day of the new child's life; it ceases when the adult dies. The effects of learning are almost unbelievable. Within one family (brothers, sisters, or twins) unique patterns of personality and life are formed; these differences also exist between families, communities, nations, societies, and cultures. Learning is again the responsible factor for most differences; it is the process leading to differentiation.

Differences between individuals or cultures depend upon how learning changes drives into *motives*. Motives are defined as forces or factors inciting a person to action. Drives, organic or social, needs, or emotions can arouse random activity. When learning occurs a person begins to strive toward a particular method or object as a means of satisfying the original stimulus. Thus, one may possess a "hamburger-eating motive" or a "snake-eating motive." The original stimulus (drive) interacts with environmental forces and available need-satisfiers; individuals develop motives.

Drives are modified through learning into motives. When motives are combined, motivation or motivational patterns result. A man does not purchase a Cadillac automobile, a split-level home, or marry a Jennifer Johnson because of a single particular motive.

Human behavior is complex; motives are less complex. The less complex cannot explain the complex except as the process of how motives become motivational patterns is understood. Man must eat; organic drives explain this function. In order to eat man must work; social drives cause this action to continue. Man must work at a particular occupation. Competition and satisfaction lead to increased security, power, money, and status-derived social drives. The successful man in order to travel to work, to provide transportation for his family, to be safe, to demonstrate his success, and to indicate his status, power, influence, affluence and diverse other things, purchases a Cadillac automobile. None can state that a single drive or motive impels a person to purchase a Cadillac. Other automobiles will serve many needs as well, but in the American culture a Cadillac also serves to tell the world of influence, power, and wealth. As advertising copy has stated, "You're never a stranger when you drive a Cadillac." Presumably, the social drive of "belongingness" can be fulfilled and satisfied with a Cadillac. Of course, a Cadillac only serves to show the diverse causes underlying a single act of man. Man's behavior is complex; when many motives are combined into motivational patterns motivation also becomes complex.

Unifying principle

Snygg and Combs (116) offer a unifying principle in the area of motivation:

The basic human need [is]: the preservation and enhancement of the . . . self.

Human behavior becomes understandable and partially predictable when seen in conjunction with such a principle. This need to defend and enhance the self restates and clarifies the concept of organic and social drives, emotions, motives, learning, and motivation. All behavior of individuals becomes meaningful when seen as related to self, and the basic drives operative within the self. Complex learnings can be built upon such simple beginnings. Prestige, status, educational, personal, and even complex psychological needs can be understood when viewed in the light of the principle offered by Snygg and Combs. Self-preservation and enhancement also always involve emotional satisfaction.

The individualized view of one's self (one's self-picture) is therefore basic in motivation. One acts because one perceives in a particular fashion that which is important. Apples are perhaps liked or disliked not only because of their intrinsic merit but because of the self's view of how the self should view an apple. A Cadillac is the best car, Texas is the best state, Jennifer is the prettiest girl—these statements are judgments of the "self in action." The self is the "grown up 'O' " of the formula S—O—R offered earlier in a discussion of stimulus and response. The organism is involved and influences both stimuli and responses.

Snygg and Combs entitled their book "Individual Behavior." The subtitle of their book is "A New Frame of Reference for Psychology." The approach that has been used in the present discussion on motivation, motives, and drives, as well as the approach in the entire book, also attempts to view the individual self as the center of the learning process. The "self" as a unique self-picture, or self-concept that has been developed and patterned through interaction with heredity, environment, and experience is the subject matter for each student. Each person thus becomes the sum as well as the integration of self-directional forces present and operative in personality and life-adjustment processes.

VALUES

Values are those inner beliefs and feelings that are primary and foremost within the personality of each person. Each individual experiences life in a particular fashion. As motives are derived from drives interacting with the learning and adjustment processes, so values are learned from the experiences of life. Values as learned beliefs and internal feelings are also motives. Values become motives not through external injection or force, but through the result of drives, needs, and learning—an individual developmental process. Values become basic motives, operative in a more fundamental fashion than drives or social needs. Values are overlearned, imbedded feelings of the self. They function as both motives and emotional drives.

Values, as primary beliefs, are not inherited or obtained through a miraculous process of revelation. Psychologists have shown values to be acquired or learned. Values, in order to be learned or acquired, must arise out of life experiences of the individual. Life experiences, as such, therefore, are the forces concomitant with the individual's concept of himself that mold values.

Each individual's value structure at any given moment is the total given product of past experiences. Meaningful, satisfying experiences with people and with an environment can form values. Family, church, community, friends, relatives, and school are the cloth from which values are cut. *Meaningful* and *satisfying* are key words in such learning experiences. Common experiences do not produce common value systems. The individual or self can vary as can the environment; learning depends upon multiple interaction. Examples of such processes are commonplace. Two individuals may undergo the same schoolroom, church, or community experience, but observers are sometimes startled to note the diverse reactions of each of them. The variable that must also be taken into consideration is the individual as he or she is currently undergoing the experience. The self thus influences and is influenced by every meaningful, satisfying experience. The self becomes the unique portion of each life experience. When the self interacts with the environment in a meaningful, satisfying (or uniquely dissatisfying) fashion, values can result.

Gardner Murphy states that attitudes are verbal expressions of values. (98:285) Values are present on the feeling or emotional level of life whereas attitudes are dispositions to action, verbal or physical. Attitude is thus a variable phase of value rather than an exclusive concept unto itself. Deeply held feelings and beliefs can be traced by analysis of action. Attitude links values and action. The learning process allows the analytical reversal of this procedure. As a child learns he develops attitudes, which, when thoroughly accepted and kept as satisfying to the self, become values.

Classification of values

A person may develop virtually an unlimited number of values. As life continues and experiences are added to experiences, values are formed. There is overlapping, and integration, as well as parallel structure in such values. Classification with such confusion can aid in simplifying the problem. A classification of values may be of aid as long as mutually exclusive compartments are not established. Murphy (98) credits Spranger (118), a German writer, as one of the early proponents of a classification of types of value structures. Allport, Vernon, and Lindzey's *Study of Values* (4) also classifies and attempts to measure value patterns. These early and late attempts to classify values are of use to the student studying value structure. The value classification offered is adapted from Murphy, Spranger, and the Allport, Vernon, and Lindzey test manual.

Theoretical. A theoretical value structure involves a concept of life that stresses the "nature of things." As such, the predominating interest of the person concerned with theoretical values is the concept of truth. This value classification stresses the order of life and the systematizing of knowledge about life.

Economic. An economic value structure stresses the relationship of gain and loss within life, particularly with regard to economics or the world of work. The usefulness and particularly the practicality of objects, procedures, and processes are prevailing attitudes within such a value structure.

Esthetic. An esthetic value structure stresses the concern for the sensory or feeling side of life. The satisfaction that one may derive from a particular experience and relationship, or between life and the objects of satisfaction in life, is something of concern within this area of value structure. Esthetics may also be seen in the meaningfulness of form and harmony and the emotional effect of life's experiences.

Social. A social value structure stresses concern for the personal interaction among individuals rather than the abstract or theoretical relationships of man. This value involves the *affective* (affection) relationships of one man to another man.

Political. Political or power values stress the role of power within a man's existence. Individuals sometimes become means to a particular political or power end. The desire for, and question of, personal power, influence, prestige, and status are involved in this structure.

Religious. A religious value structure is not concerned with what might be termed the temporal or localized concern for life. Religious values stress the unity and totality of life and that which lies beyond life as human beings know it. This is a concern for the cosmic or transcendental aspects of man's existence.

SUMMARY

Man's behavior and also the causes of his behavior are complex. Theories concerning these causes have been presented. Early classifications of instincts have been rejected, and instead drives, needs, emotions, motives, and values through interaction with the learning processes have been offered as the best sources for an understanding of the causes of behavior.

Students may wonder how a knowledge of the concepts treated in this chapter can be of aid in self-understanding. The process of self-analysis depends upon what is analyzed. If phrenology or astrology were offered as causes of behavior then these would have to be analyzed in order to establish their effect upon individuals. Drives, needs, emotions, motives, and values, and their incorporation into a personality, will need to be analyzed in Part III of the book.

Prior to becoming involved in the process of self-analysis students will need to examine learning and personality. The area concerned with the causes of behavior is only one of the four major concepts of psychological knowledge that precede self-analysis. Learning as the modifier of the basic causal factors is the next concept to be studied. Personality, the outcome of the interaction of causal factors and learning, is the third concept. Psychological maturity is the fourth concept.

SUPPLEMENTARY SOURCES

Bernard, Harold W., *Toward Better Personal Adjustment* (2nd ed.). New York: McGraw-Hill Book Company, Inc., 1957.

Cole, Luella, *Psychology of Adolescence* (4th ed.). New York: Rinehart & Company, Inc., 1954.

Fry, C., and E. G. Rostow, *Mental Health in College*. New York: Commonwealth Fund, 1952.

Gesell, Arnold, Frances L. Ilg, et al., *Child Development*. New York: Harper & Brothers, 1949.

Jersild, Arthur T., *Child Psychology* (4th ed.). Englewood Cliffs, N. J.: Prentice-Hall, Inc., 1955.

Morgan, Clifford T., *Introduction to Psychology*. New York: McGraw-Hill Book Company, Inc., 1956.

Munn, Norman L., *Psychology* (3rd ed.). Boston: Houghton Mifflin Company, 1956.

Prothro, E. Terry, and P. T. Teska, *Psychology: A Biosocial Study of Behavior*. Boston: Ginn and Company, 1950.

Rogers, Carl R., and R. Diamond, *Psychotherapy and Personality Change*. Chicago: The University of Chicago Press, 1954.

Shaffer, Lawrence F., and E. J. Shoben, *The Psychology of Adjustment* (rev. ed.). Boston: Houghton Mifflin Company, 1956.

Snygg, Donald, and Arthur W. Combs, *Individual Behavior*. New York: Harper & Brothers, 1949.

Problems of learning have always plagued the college student. Some things seem to be learned easily, and yet others seemingly never can be mastered. Why is it that some things are learned so easily? Why is it that seemingly no effort is expended, for instance, in committing the major-league baseball standings to memory, not once, but every day? However, the learning of twenty-five French verbs seems to be an insurmountable task for the same student. Students attend college to learn. Some of them receive excellent grades and

Chapter 5

THEORIES OF LEARNING

graduate with honors. Others with equal intelligence receive failing grades and are not allowed to finish their college education. The question then becomes: What is learning; how does it take place; and, perhaps more important, why does it take place?

This chapter is a discussion of some of the psychological explanations of the process of learning in the human being. With the advent of experimental psychology, at approximately the turn of the twentieth century, psychologists began to study scientifically the phenomenon known as learning. Since that time, and continuing into the present, psychologists have been studying learning. As in many other problems of science, however, the process of how one learns and why the process of learning takes place has never been precisely stated as a single, distinct conceptual theory. It becomes the objective of this chapter not to attempt to explain learning, but to present some of the theories and concepts of learning that are partially understood and currently under investigation.

Learning, like many other phenomena on this earth, is

much easier to observe than it is to explain. It is a relatively easy task to observe and describe many seemingly different types of learning in the psychological laboratory, but to say exactly how or why this learning takes place is a more difficult problem. It is far easier to understand and utilize practical applications of learning than it is to understand learning theories and apply them directly in various learning situations. The student is cautioned not to adopt any one of these theories as the final answer to the problem of learning; it is suggested, however, that the final answer lies not wholly in one theory, but partly in all theories. Individuals differ, and so do the ways in which they learn. Portions of all theories of learning are applicable to each learning situation.

ORIENTATION TO LEARNING THEORY

Like any other term that is to be used over and over again, learning must be defined. The definition (from Murphy, 98) of learning offered earlier needs reviewing. Learning allows a person, through experience, to act in a particular fashion in response to the stimuli arising within or outside the organism. More simply, learning is the process of changing one's behavior, adopting new methods of problem solving, or acquiring knowledge, attitudes, or values.

A person learns to ride a bicycle, to drive a car, new facts, and new relationships. Through experience, new responses are possible. In the act of learning the concept of change is contained. When a change takes place in the behavior of, or the knowledge possessed by, an individual something has been learned. This change may not be as readily observable as the process of learning to ride a bicycle or to drive a car, but it is there. One of the most unobservable types of learning is that of learning through the silent reading of a book. No visible proof is readily available that the reader has actually learned anything. If learning has taken place, however, it will manifest itself in knowledge obtained or through some future behavior of the individual.

It can be hypothesized that when knowledge patterns develop or changes in behavior occur, learning has taken place. Also, when knowledge is lacking or no change in behavior takes place, learning has not occurred. It then becomes perfectly possible, for example, for the student to read an assignment in a textbook and learn very little or perhaps nothing.

Learning readiness

When is it possible for a person to learn? Can a small baby learn to walk before he learns to crawl? Can the student learn the intricate designs of calculus before he learns the multiplication tables? What are the necessary qualifications for learning to take place? It would seem to be obvious that in the two examples listed, the complex process cannot happen before the simple. It is necessary for the person to be ready to learn.

There are many experiences or activities that take place in the life of an individual. From the moment of birth certain needs of the baby have resulted in certain actions and experiences that, when they change the future behavior of the baby, fall into the realm of learned behavior. From this background of vague experience every individual draws certain specific experiences into the sharp focus of the present instant, arranges these experiences in a new manner, and then is able to learn. One may think of the vast areas of past experience as if one were viewing a scene through a wide-angle lens, slightly out of focus. By switching to a telephoto-lens view and seeing only a small part of this wide fuzzy background in very sharp focus, the person may be said to have differentiated from a vast ground of experience a definite segment of the larger scene. This, then, is what is necessary for the person to learn. The small area in sharp focus can be called *figure;* the large area, slightly out of focus, can be called *ground.* (116) All the elements of learning must be in one's ground of experience in order to perceive a particular aspect in relation to the total so that a figure-and-ground relationship may exist and learning may take place.

A baby in the act of learning to walk reveals a complicated relationship of strength, balance, muscular dexterity, and co-ordination. Without all of these skills in their correct relationships, the baby will fall. The baby then must have all of these skills in his ground of experience. When the final learning takes place, the child assembles all of the skills in their correct figure-and-ground relationship as he walks.

The three-year-old child attempting to write with a pen is an example of the lack of learning readiness. The three-year-old is well able to hold and mark with a crayon. When he attempts, however, to use a pen, his poor muscular co-ordination usually results in the destruction of the point.

This concept of learning readiness also applies to the college student. The student who is unable to recognize and understand the words on the page of a textbook (reading comprehension) is not able to learn from it. One skill seems to depend on another. Nothing is learned in isolation. Every person is dependent upon his ground of experience for any new skill to be learned.

Perception

Man has many senses; sight, hearing, feeling or touch, taste, and smell are the ones most commonly known. Kinesthetic (motion or body feeling), the sense of heat or cold, and a sense of pressure are some of the more uncommonly or little known senses of man. Man receives impressions of the world through the physical senses. This process of receiving impressions through the various senses is known as perception.

Perception is not a simple process. If an African native, never having left the confines of his native village, were suddenly to be transported to an American airbase and see a jet bomber take off, he might be most confused, frightened, or amazed. Such a large "flying bird" is completely beyond his experience. A young child may ascribe human or animal characteristics to a land tank in order to explain its motion or actions. The tank is beyond the child's experience. Perception, through the senses, is a function of experience and learning.

A sudden movement, a frightening cry, and many other everyday experiences may be fear provoking, surprising, or mystifying until perspective (an understanding) is achieved. Such is the nature of perception.

Man can know nothing except through perception. Eyes cannot intelligently see, and ears cannot intelligently hear except through perception. The senses work co-operatively with the brain, nervous system, and learning process.

The process of learning depends upon perception. A need or drive must be perceived in order for the individual to attempt to satisfy the need or drive. Learning cannot take place until perception has occurred. Learning readiness depends upon perception. A figure concept must be differentiated from a ground relationship.

The influence of perception upon learning has been clearly demonstrated. A hungry or perhaps starving person can think of little but food. Even clouds are seen in the mind's eye as objects to eat. Experiments have shown that starving persons can see or think of little but food regardless of how little an object may look like food, or how desirable it may be made to concentrate upon something else. Other senses have been shown to react in a similar fashion in similar circumstances.

Learning depends upon drives, needs, the adjustment process, and emotions. The learnings that take place as a result of these forces depend upon learning readiness, which is in turn a function of perception. Learning becomes a function of the total organism.

DESCRIPTIVE THEORIES OF LEARNING

From the moment the child is born until the time of death, learning is taking place. One never stops learning. Every action that a person makes, every word that he says is learned or modified through learning. All behavior, then, can be said to be learned. Why does this learning take place? Does it happen fortuitously or is it all caused?

In proceeding from observations of learning to abstract learning theory (not completely validated by scientific study), one is proceeding from description to prediction. When learning is completely understood, it seems reasonable to expect that psychologists and teachers will be able to predict when learning is going to take place, and to explain how learning takes place. Until that time, students and teachers will have to work with the observable, proved facts and only hypothesize as to the precise causes of learning.

Trial-and-error learning

Trial-and-error learning might be termed to be learning by blundering on to the solution. (80:52) When a person has no experience with a given problem, the solution of that problem usually depends upon the random trial of different possible solutions until the correct one is found. For example, experiments have been carried out with cats in "problem" cages or boxes. In this type of a situation a hungry cat is put into a cage. Outside the cage, just out of the reach of the cat, is food. The hungry cat, naturally wishing to retrieve the food, at first sets up a howl trying to claw through the bars of the cage to obtain the food; then she paces about the cage, frustrated by her inability to get out; finally, by accident, the cat steps on the release lever, and the cage opens. When the cat has been put into the same box often enough, she learns that the pressing of the release lever opens the cage. As soon as she is placed in the box, she goes to the lever and releases the door. The cat has learned this skill by "blundering on to it." The same process takes place with the nail puzzle. Two nails are bent and secured together. Someone is given the problem of getting them apart. First, one tries to figure it out, looking at all sides of the puzzle. When that fails, one tries to pull them apart. Then, in complete frustration, one throws the nails down, and the resulting impact separates them. The puzzle has been solved not through any skill on the part of the person, but by chance, trial and error, or "blundering."

Whenever a person is presented with a new or unique problem, he often resorts to a process of trial and error. One possible solution after another is attempted until the right one is happened upon, by chance. When this occurs the person becomes aware of his "blundering success," and learning has taken place.

Trial-and-error learning is a relatively low-level type of explanation of particularly simple, problem-solving behavior. Complex learnings and difficult problems are seldom solved through trial and error. On rare occasions, however, even great learnings, such as vulcanization (Goodyear) or the electric-light bulb filament (Edison) have resulted from this process.

Conditioning

With the advent of experimental psychology, there came into prominence many people interested in the theory of learning. One of the first, and still considered one of the most prominent, was Ivan Petrovich Pavlov (1849–1936). During the time that Pavlov was the director of the Physiological Department of the Institute of Experimental Medicine, St. Petersburg, Russia, he and his assistants conducted a great number of experiments in that aspect of learning that he called "the conditioned reflex." Pavlov hypothesized that if a particular response could be expected from a particular stimulus then perhaps a substitute stimulus would, after learning, evoke the original response.

Pavlov was able to measure the salivation of a dog when meat powder was placed upon the dog's tongue. The meat powder was thus the original stimulus; the salivation was the original response. Pavlov then found that the ringing of a bell did not affect the salivation of the dog. The substitute stimulus, alone, had no effect upon the dog. He then simultaneously rang the bell and placed the meat powder on the dog's tongue. Soon the bell (substitute stimulus) without the meat powder (original stimulus) could evoke the original response (salivation). Pavlov called this process of learning the "conditioned reflex" or "conditioned response." The following diagram shows graphically what Pavlov was able to accomplish.

BEFORE CONDITIONING

ORIGINAL STIMULUS ——————————————→ ORIGINAL RESPONSE
(FOOD POWDER)   (SALIVATION)

SUBSTITUTE STIMULUS ——————————————→ NO VISIBLE RESPONSE
(BELL)

ORIGINAL STIMULUS + SUBSTITUTE STIMULUS ——————→ ORIGINAL RESPONSE
(FOOD POWDER)   (BELL)   (SALIVATION)

AFTER CONDITIONING

SUBSTITUTE STIMULUS ——————————————→ ORIGINAL RESPONSE
(BELL)   (SALIVATION)

The response of the dog to salivate to the bell was hypothesized by Pavlov to be a learned response. That is, the dog learned that at the same time or shortly after the bell rang he would be fed. The salivation became automatic with the bell. Pavlov hypothesized that this was not only true in animals but that it was the way that much of human learning took place.

Conditioning is what might be called common-sense learning. (80:350) As an example, little Johnnie Jones is caught stealing jam from the kitchen cupboard. His mother catches him and spanks him soundly. If John refrains from taking more jam, his mother compliments herself on a knowledge of practical psychology. Johnnie has been conditioned by the spanking to refrain from stealing. He has learned that if the jam is taken a spanking will result. This type of learning is often common in school and life situations. A student learns to react to bells, letter grades, and even words as substitute stimuli. The entire process of learning language, a symbolic process, is deeply dependent upon conditioning.

Pavlov opened an entire new area in the study of learning. Procedures for training students, for training animals, and even for modern advertising, owe much to the simple conditioned-reflex action.

Association

Long before the advent of experimental psychology, philosophers had been contemplating that a method by which learning takes place is the association of one experience with a similar or different one in the past.

Modern experimental psychologists, among them E. R. Guthrie (61), have transposed these philosophical conjectures into two basic laws of association. They hypothesized that a certain contiguity of similarity or contrast will cause learning, and, secondly, that a certain contiguity in space and time will also cause learning to take place.

Learning by association is therefore very similar to conditioning. Some authorities unite the processes of association and conditioning whereas others insist upon individual consideration of each concept. It is beyond the scope of this treatment of learning to enter into such a debate. To study a description and outline of associative learning is more rewarding for the student who is beginning psychology.

The first law of association, contiguity through similarity or contrast, can be illustrated by common everyday experiences. All persons have become aware of meeting new friends who look like old friends. These persons may become associated through learning. The Air Force, in teaching ship and plane identification to its pilots, utilizes the law of contiguity by contrast. By teaching the pilots to recognize a standard basic United States aircraft carrier, the airmen are taught to know one particular carrier by its differences from others. Using the placement of the island on the deck as an example, carrier A can be identified by the placement of the island farther forward than on carrier B.

Contiguity in time and space are very common types of learning experiences. Let us suppose that a person parked his car next to a brand new automobile that he admired very much. Chances are that when remembering where his car is parked, the new model will also come to mind. This is an example of space contiguity. Contiguity in time is exemplified by such experiences as meeting someone while leaving a motion-picture theater. When the theater or picture is recalled, often the person met also comes to mind.

Association is learning through relationships. College students often use these laws of contiguity in their study habits. For example, when learning the characteristics of a certain culture, the college student may arrange the terms so that their first letters spell some common word. Then by association of the first letters, the student is able to learn the entire list of words. Sometimes called a crutch or helper, this process is really learning by association. Memorized multiplication tables, poems or speeches, and even such complex learnings as the crosscultural similarities of various ethnic groups depend upon association.

Insight

A theory of learning that differs from previously discussed theories in basic orientation is that of insight or the Gestalt type of learning. Psychologists and educators who explain the Gestalt (a German word that means pattern or configuration) view of learning feel that nothing is learned in isolation. All learning draws from a background of experience. The arrangement of these experiences into new and unique patterns calls for more than association, conditioning, or trial-and-error learning; it calls for insight into the problem. This insight or "seeing through" of the problem seems to depend upon much higher-level mental processes than do other theories of learning. The Gestalt psychologist does not reject the idea of trial and error, association, or conditioned learning, but he does hypothesize that all action or response is more than the sum of its parts. Therefore, insight learning takes place only after trial and error and other experiences. The learner draws conclusions from each unsuccessful trial, and, finally, through insight or "seeing through" the problem, arrives at the correct response, not by chance but by a higher mental process.

Koffka (73) reports on an experiment with an ape in a cage with a stick. Outside the cage, out of reach of the ape, was a piece of fruit. At first the hungry ape saw no relationship between the two. He made trial-and-error attempts to get at the fruit without utilizing the stick. Finally, he picked up the stick and used it to get the prize. This was not random behavior, but "insightful" learning. By a process of insightful configuration the ape was able to see all of the component parts of the problem in a new relationship.

Further experiments showed that after the animal had learned to use the stick further insights could be demonstrated. The fruit was placed beyond the reach of either of two sticks placed in the cage. The ape, after much trial and error, and failure, appeared to be considering the problem. With no trial or error, no conditioning or association (in their pure forms), the animal walked over to the two sticks, joined them and retrieved the fruit. Similar experiments with other types of problems showed a pure response that was called insight.

Another example of this type of complex learning is that of the child first walking. As has been pointed out previously, the walking process is a complicated one of body action, balance, and strength. Although the child develops each of these skills somewhat separately, when he finally starts to walk, he puts them all together in a pattern different from any other that he has attempted. He "sees through" the problem of walking; the skills involved in walking have been made a part of a new relationship. Trial and error, conditioning, and even association are involved, but a reorganization of experience is also necessary.

Insight certainly carries over into the school situation. Many of our educational practices divide work into areas for individual study. The Gestalt psychologist would insist that the sum of the parts is greater than the whole, and therefore school subjects should be taken up in their totality rather than "stacked" one upon another such as building blocks. Many examples of this "stacking" exist in college programs. The student studying biology is introduced to the different parts of the human body, and sometimes it seems that he never learns that each depends upon the other and that together they make up the marvelous machine with which he as been living all his life. Parts and procedures must be seen in their totality. Insight thus relates and unifies all of learning into a meaningful approach to problem solving and behavior modification.

EXPLANATORY THEORIES OF LEARNING

A description, or varying descriptions, of learning is certainly a necessary beginning in the search for knowledge in the area of how and why man learns. Description alone, however, is not enough. It is one thing to be able to say, "man A has learned that maze"; it is another to be able to say, "man A has learned that maze *because.* . . ." This discussion analyzes two of the more recent theories that begin to explain the causation of learning.

Phenomenological approach

The phenomenological approach to learning (116) differs from other theories of learning that have been discussed primarily in the point of reference that is used. In the study of trial-and-error, of conditioning, of association, and of insight, the process, the reference point from which the investigation began, and even the reporting of data, were externally oriented. In the study of the phenomenological approach, the point of reference becomes internally oriented to the learner. This approach becomes an attempt, not only to describe learning, but to understand the reasons why the person is learning. Each person has a picture of himself that is internally oriented. This view of self may or may not be in accord with the view that others may have of one's self, but is a unique, internally oriented, self-picture or self-concept. The basis of a person's behavior is the environment as seen by the self (the phenomenal field). The self-picture or concept operates within a world or environment as seen through the senses (perceptions) of the self. The phenomenal field of the individual is the sum total of all of the person's previous experiences. Snygg and Combs have presented the original formulations of these concepts, and their approach was described (by themselves) as an "internal view of personality."

In a learning situation the individual draws from his field of experience (his ground) certain experiences that he differentiates from the entire ground, bringing them into sharp focus (figure). By doing this, and arranging them in some unique order or pattern, learning takes place.

So far this has been a description of the process that takes place. Why, then, does this change of behavior occur? To the individual, his self-concept is realistic and right. Whatever he does, according to Snygg and Combs, is to enhance or defend this self-picture. When a need arises for defense or enhancement of the self, the person, in order to satisfy this basic need, will change his behavior, and learning will take place. Learning takes place when a need arises; to satisfy the need something must be done. This activity involves learning.

An example will aid in the clarification of this approach. The student in college who has never excelled in high school, but whose self-picture includes ability to attend college and succeed, is one who may possibly be very highly motivated to succeed in a college situation. Whether adequate learning in college will take place in order to satisfy this defense of the self depends upon whether the person's concept of himself is realistic. If the person who desires success in college is not able, through lack of scholastic aptitude, to succeed at the level that he desires, he may very well become a very unhappy, frustrated, and depressed person. On the other hand, if his self-picture is realistic, the need for self-satisfaction will result in learning to satisfy this need. It then follows that the more realistic a person's self-picture is, the more likely he is to be a happy, satisfied person, well able to meet the learning situations required to enhance his self-picture.

Canalization

Gardner Murphy (98), in his work on personality, discusses a theory of learning that in many respects is related to others that have been described thus far. In the discussion that follows the reader will probably notice the resemblance of canalization to the phenomenological approach, to conditioning, and to association because canalization tends to explain learning as part of the adjustment process, and to describe it in a manner similar to conditioning, or association or both.

Canalization is, in reality, none of these theories. As described by Murphy, canalization is the process of learning in which the individual selects or develops specific methods or objects that lead to the satisfaction of needs. This canalization or channeling of behavior through learning is dependent upon two factors: the initial selection of a process or object, and the opportunities to utilize the selected process or object. (98:162)

People all over the world can be hungry. This feeling of hunger is general, but people are not all hungry for the same type of food. In China there is a hunger for rice, in Italy for spaghetti, and in the United States for beef steak. These are developed preferences. There is no hereditary cause for this behavior. The reason for such behavior is that people become familiar with a certain food, they become attached to it, they like it, and they want it.

A study (84) was conducted in which thirty Russian names were divided into two groups of fifteen. Fifteen of these Russian names were read to a group of students each night for six nights. Then the entire list was read, fifteen familiar names and fifteen unfamiliar. The students were asked to pick those names that they liked better and that were more euphonious. There was a distinct liking for the familiar names. Children indicate their canalized (channeled) likes and dislikes in their preferences for certain toys and dolls. Often it is not the most beautiful doll that the little girl wants, but the one that she has grown to like the most, through familiarity.

Canalization resembles the phenomenological approach to learning in that it attempts to explain learning through the satisfaction of needs. When one needs to know something, and it is possible within his experience to learn, learning will take place. Canalization actually states that one will learn only that which he needs to learn for the satisfaction of some need.

SUMMARY

It should be noted that in the preceding discussion no value judgments have been made as to the validity of any one theory. The authors have only attempted to classify learning theories into two categories: first, those of description, and second, those of explanation. It is certainly questionable as to whether or not there is one theory of learning. There seems to be much more evidence that man learns in many ways rather than in one way. No theory presented in this chapter is offered as the only answer to or explanation of learning. There are indications that every theory presented in the chapter has some validity in the learning process.

The authors do believe, however, that some of the investigations into how man learns have been of more significance than others. It may be said in review that the theories of conditioning, trial and error, insight, and association are discussed as those theories that try only to describe learning; the phenomenological approach and canalization theories attempt to explain why the phenomenon of learning takes place. The attempts to explain the causes of learning appear to be more meaningful concepts for students than those of description.

The close resemblance of the phenomenological approach and the canalization process, and the seemingly valid basis upon which the concept of self has been built, seem to indicate that learning does take place to satisfy the needs, drives, and motives of the individual. With this in mind, it seems logical to suggest that the student who desires to learn should attempt to understand himself, his drives, needs, and motives, and therefore create an atmosphere in which learning can take place. The learnings that take place throughout a person's life determine the type of person he will be. Personality, or the end product of the interaction of learning with the causes of behavior throughout life, is the next topic to be considered.

SUPPLEMENTARY SOURCES

Bugelski, B. R., *The Psychology of Learning.* New York: Henry Holt & Company, Inc., 1956.

Deese, James, *The Psychology of Learning.* New York: McGraw-Hill Book Company, Inc., 1952.

Kingsley, Howard L. (rev. by Ralph Garry), *Nature and Conditions of Learning* (2nd ed.). Englewood Cliffs, N. J.: Prentice-Hall, Inc., 1956.

Lindgren, Henry Clay, *Psychology of Personal and Social Adjustment.* New York: American Book Company, 1953.

Murphy, Gardner, *Personality, A Biosocial Approach to Origins and Structure.* New York: Harper & Brothers, 1947.

Pepinsky, Harold B., and Pauline N. Pepinsky, *Counseling Theory and Practice.* New York: The Ronald Press Company, 1954.

Prothro, E. Terry, and P. T. Teska, *Psychology, A Biosocial Study of Behavior.* Boston: Ginn and Company, 1950.

Personality, as it is used in popular speech, appears to have many meanings. Sometimes it seems to refer to personal appearance or manners; sometimes it seems to mean a set of forceful or dominant characteristics; it seems to indicate an ability to meet people and be socially at ease; sometimes it seems to indicate a quality that is "strong" or "lacking" ("no personality").

The word "personality" comes from the Latin *persona,* the name of the mask worn by actors on the Roman stage. The

Chapter 6

PERSONALITY

purpose of the mask was to indicate the sort of person being portrayed on the stage and to conceal the actual appearance and personality of the actor playing the role.

The psychologist is not only interested in looking at the outward appearance and overt behavior of an individual, he is also interested in understanding the underlying causes of the person's behavior. The psychologist is interested in looking behind the mask to see what kind of person is behind the front presented to the public.

Those workers most familiar with the study of personality have no easy time defining the term, and often they do not agree among themselves. The psychiatrist is apt to define personality largely as an aspect of the physical self; the psychoanalyst may speak of the id, the ego, and the superego. The neurologist, in his definition, will stress the importance of the nervous system. The clinical psychologist might talk of the organization of integrative processes in human behavior; the social psychologist views personality particularly as it is manifested in interpersonal relationships. The biochemist would define personality largely as a matter of chemistry, glands,

75

hormones, and metabolism. Probably the best definition would be one that attempts to encompass the knowledge of all these specialists in a generalized statement acceptable to all of them.

Such a generalized definition of personality would surely state that every person has a personality and that each personality is distinctive and individual. Personality is not only the impression one makes on others, but it is also one's knowledge of himself; it is a persistent disposition to follow certain patterns of life in making adjustments. Personality includes such things as traits, character, values, ethics, attitudes, abilities, drives, moral and philosophical beliefs, and emotional patterns—in fact the whole of what a person is in relation to the universe about him. Personality is more than the sum of its parts because it is an integration of all these things. It is never static; it constantly develops and changes. Such is the broad concept of personality that is the basis of the discussion in this chapter.

STRUCTURE OF PERSONALITY

Since personality is an individual's particular pattern of meeting and solving problems and adjusting to life it is important to examine the structure of personality. The term or concept of personality is basic to all of psychology and particularly to adjustment and adjustment processes. The primary concepts of this book and the important principles thus far presented in previous chapters all lead up to and prepare for an understanding of personality. Succeeding chapters in Part III are an analysis of significant aspects of personality, and Part IV is an attempt to apply an understanding of personality. The examination of the structure of personality, along with an understanding of the development, dimensions, and functioning of personality and an interpretation of the applications of personality, is pivotal.

Personality formation depends upon drives, motives, needs, emotions, and the individual's organization of these forces into a pattern of problem-solving behavior in life. Learning and differentiation processes are the methods with which the individual harnesses and directs these life forces. The concept of self and the self-picture is in a commanding, directing, or core position in the structure of personality. As the basic forces of life interact with learning processes in a guided fashion of self-development, personality grows in values, attitudes, roles, and the adjustment mechanisms or processes of life (a constant series of adjustments or problem-solving actions).

The interactions between and among all of the factors within personality are dynamic and interdependent. No factor can be seen as a single independent force. A schematic representation of the nature of these basic factors within personality can aid in obtaining an understanding of their relationships.

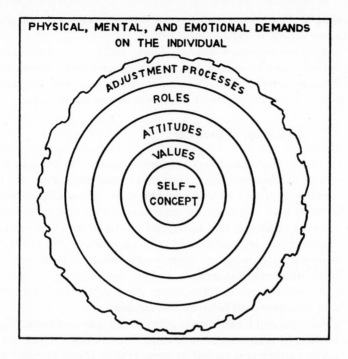

PHYSICAL, MENTAL, AND EMOTIONAL DEMANDS
ON THE INDIVIDUAL

ADJUSTMENT PROCESSES

ROLES

ATTITUDES

VALUES

SELF –
CONCEPT

Where the adjustment mechanisms and processes meet the environmental world of existence, personality is observed in action.

Some of the concepts involved in the diagram depicting personality structure have been previously presented; this diagram can aid in seeing these concepts in their totality and balance in personality. A discussion of the origins and development of personality, the self-concept or self-picture, values, attitudes, roles, and the interaction of personality and the environment will now provide a framework to understand and appreciate more fully the concept and structure of personality.

ORIGINS OF PERSONALITY

There is a popular conception that much human behavior is "natural" or instinctive, which would mean that by the hereditary process it was somehow implanted within us at the instant of conception. As psychologists have investigated these so-called instincts or "natural" forces, they have been forced to the conclusion that much behavior originally thought to be instinctive or natural is really learned.

The recognition that there were no simple and easy answers underlying human behavior and personality was at first disconcerting. As single causes or direct forces were ruled out of consideration, however, the science of psychology, human behavior, and personality began to develop.

Beginnings of behavior

Every personality is unique. Every human life begins with a unique physical organism with characteristics that have never been duplicated, and is born into an environment that no other human being has ever experienced in quite the same way. All behavior must come from one of two possible sources: it may be native; that is, depend on the inherited structure; or it may be learned; that is, determined by the experiences and pressures that are encountered in growing up. Some combination of these two factors, nature and nurture, must determine all behavior. This means that all behavior is determined and therefore, from the psychologists' point of view, all behavior is caused—all behavior has meaning.

In the newborn child, behavior is diffused and uncoordinated. The body acts as a whole in what appear to be random movements. Even this seemingly random movement is caused by some kind of stimulus, either internal or in the environment. Environmental stimulation may come from light, sound, or skin touch, and internal stimulation may come from hunger, pain, muscular fatigue, or the kinesthetic sense of body position and movement. Any stimulus causes a whole body reaction until the infant's nervous system begins to become organized.

When the child's eyes become focused, he begins to learn eye-and-hand coordination; then he begins to investigate his environment. He tests everything by grasping and later by trying to put everything into his mouth. This behavior has been called an exploratory or a curiosity "instinct." It is probably better to regard this behavior as a type of response to stimuli and the beginning of the differentiation of the things in his environment from each other and from himself.

Just as internal drives or needs and environmental (or social) stimulation lead to a generalized, diffuse type of responsive behavior, emotional reactions in the very young child are largely undifferentiated and might at times be called excitement due to overstimulation. Anything that threatens wholeness, physical freedom, or physical security or brings pleasure arouses a response. The nursing process illustrates this pleasure reaction since the infant begins to learn social behavior when he finds that by gurgling, cooing and grasping he can invite the caressing and patting that are pleasant stimuli.

Such are the beginnings of responses to stimuli which, as the environment becomes bigger and more differentiated, become the origin of much of habitual behavior patterns. As the child grows older the type of habitual responses he learns to make is determined by his emerging self-concept, or the evolving picture he has of himself and his personality. To investigate the determinants of personality and self-concept should help one understand personality as a background for the "self," and the "self" as a controlling force in personality.

In the beginning, the primary determinants of what one is to become are constitutional. These are the determinants that play upon a person by virtue of his inheritance. Such factors as the sex, race, skin color, body size and type, body, and particularly glandular, functions, the normality or abnormality of the physical self, physical attractiveness or the lack of it, and a myriad more will have a bearing on what kind of responses a child will receive in his early contacts with other people and with his groups.

The kind of personality the child develops is determined by everything in his environment that has significance for him and that exerts a force on him. Among the unnumbered factors are such things as the family he is born into, his position in the family constellation, the size of the family, its social and economic status, the religion he learns as a youth, the schools he attends, the neighborhood he grows up in—in fact, all the groups into which his environment thrusts him are strong determinants of his personality.

Probably equally determinant, although somewhat more remote as environmental factors, are the situations into which life thrusts an individual. The fact that a person is a New Englander, or a Southerner, or was born in the twentieth century, or during a war, or in time of peace, or during a period of economic stress or prosperity, or into a certain cultural heritage, and many other situational circumstances are determinants of personality.

Integration of personality

All of these untold factors underlying personality are interactive, cumulative, and integrative. The same factor in conjunction with one set of circumstances may have significance of one kind for one person but seemingly have a wholly different significance in another individual's special set of circumstances. One child born in poverty may be servile and passive; another from equally poor circumstances may be rebellious and destructive; whereas a third from like background may be fired with ambition and eagerness to improve his and others' lots. It is not so much the fact of poverty that is the determinant, it is the significance that the poverty, combined with all other influences, has for the individual—that is, the way that he sees his poverty in relation to his total self-concept.

The thing that may appear to be a handicap that defeats some individuals may be the very factor that is the spur to success in others. The very blessing that would be regarded by some as the advantage ensuring success may prove for another to be the debilitating, weakening influence that destines him to failure. No one entity can be isolated to be examined for its particular influence apart from the countless other determinants, and the casual observer of behavior is even less sure that he understands the meanings of a particular determinant for the person who is influenced.

An integrated personality is achieved by a person who has arrived at a reasonably consistent self-concept in which all drives and attributes of personality tend to work toward a harmonious set of goals, and in which there appears to be a maximum organization of this self-concept with a resulting minimum of friction in behavior. The student who has a self-concept of being a serious scholar and, at the same time, thinks of himself as a rousing rollicker at a party is probably having trouble integrating his personality. The individual who likes to see himself as scrupulously honest, but who cheats on his income-tax form, may be having personality trouble. Often a

SCHOOL AND COLLEGE RELATIONS

Many things make up the total personality of an individual

test of the integrated personality is the ability of the individual to suppress impulses to achieve immediate goals for the satisfactions derived from sustained effort toward the attainment of long-term goals. The urge that one has to indulge his selfish whim of the moment may conflict with his wish to be known as a socially conscious citizen. A certain lack of integration may be suspected in the man who states that his goal is to be a fine athlete and who obviously enjoys consuming as much food and drink as he can. The man who wants to make a real contribution to research and announces his intention to get rich quickly is surely not well integrated. A person may be said to have an integrated personality to the degree that goals are organized in a harmonious way so that there is a minimum of friction in the various aspects of behavior.

Integration in personality depends upon the development of consistent and meaningfully related values, attitudes, roles, and patterns of adjustment. As the individual meets and solves problems from the first moment of life these aspects of personality develop from both nature and nurture forces. Integration, or the lack of integration on a continuum and to a matter of degree, is the measure of the consistency and relatedness of personality.

SELF-CONCEPT AND PERSONALITY

What a person does or how he behaves is determined by his self-concept, or how he sees himself. If a woman thinks she is Cleopatra, she acts like Cleopatra, or at least according to her conception of the way Cleopatra would act. Her role and the techniques that she has differentiated or learned as being appropriate to her are consistent with her self-concept. The understanding of the self is the factor that makes various behaviors (or expressions of personality) become consistent, controllable, and to some extent predictable. Self-concept gives meaning to behavior. A child might be thought to be unbalanced if the observer did not understand that his behavior at a particular time is consistent with his self-concept of a space-ship pilot. The audience watching "People Are Funny" are not skeptical about the sanity of the people who take part in the show because they understand that the role in which these participants are seen is consistent with their concept of being "good sports."

Development of self-concept

Many of the adjectives that a child listens for and that are the cornerstone of his earliest conception of personality and his self-picture are based upon constitutional factors. The child hears that he is small or big, quiet or active, pretty or plain, healthy or sickly, a boy or a girl, or intelligent or slow. Each of these things, depending upon the kind of response he encounters from the people about him, he learns is "good" or "bad." As the individual's sphere of activities widens into the neighborhood, the school, and the community, his group memberships play an increasingly important part in the formation of self-concept and personality. He becomes more and more sensitive to others' judgments in his understanding of his self and the roles suitable to his self-concept. The influences of the group on his self-concept and the influences of his self-concept and appropriate roles upon the group are interactive.

The child soon learns that he is a "boy" (or that she is a "girl") and that as a boy his role, if he is to be admired, calls for a particular kind of behavior that is different from the behavior role for a girl. In a particular culture the role of a boy may be quite different from that in another culture; and from one neighborhood to another, or in a particular socio-economic group, or as a member of a particular religious faith. Of course, the same variety of roles for girls is determined by the groups in which girls find their roles.

One boy may find that his expected role in his particular social group is to learn early how to conduct himself at a dancing class, or with his piano teacher, or at very proper parties. Another boy from a different social context may learn that he wins approval of his group by conforming to the accepted behavior for boys of his group on the sandlot baseball diamond, or in the gang that charges up the alley after school to upset garbage cans or engage the rival gang in warfare. There have been several studies that indicate that the masculine and feminine roles of our culture are not biologically determined as much as they are determined by cultural modes. Children who do not conform to the expected behavior dictated by the group are quickly and usually ruthlessly taught to be ashamed of their deviant or different behavior.

The Negro child in an all-Negro community finds no particular significance in his skin color, but the Negro child in a non-Negro community learns to respond in a particular way to his contacts with the people of a different skin color. His "Negro-ness" becomes a part of his self-concept, and he tries roles with various kinds of groups to discover suitable modes of behaving.

The physically unattractive child notices very early in life that certain rewarding words she hears when her sister or playmate is discussed, such words as "pretty" or "lovely," are not used in reference to her. She comes to accept the role of "plain" or "ugly." She may withdraw from competition with the pretty girl or she may listen for words that will give her a cue as to the role in which she can successfully compete. She may come to learn that she gets approval by being "good," or "cheerful," or "bright." These attributes she takes into her self-concept. As long as she is not rebuffed by her groups she seeks acceptance and approval in roles appropriate to her values and attitudes that are an outgrowth of self-concept.

The boy with the "crew-cut" is making a declaration of the group to which he accords his allegiance and positive values, and to which he looks for approval and acceptance; so is the girl in Bermuda shorts and knee-length socks. The boy in blue-jeans and "ducktail" haircut says as much of his group affiliations, values, and attitudes as does the boy in prep-school "chinos" and "dirty bucks." The girl in the dark cashmere sweater, a tiny strand of pearls, and an Audrey Hepburn hairstyle has proclaimed her role as vividly as the girl in the yellow satin dress who is on her way to the sailors' bars on Saturday night has proclaimed hers to be a very different one.

Group memberships, primarily family, and other meaningful personal experiences develop attitudes within the individual, which, when fully accepted to the self, become values. Values then become an edge or external fringe of the core self-concept. Individuals frequently reveal this when they say "I couldn't do that! It simply wouldn't be me if I did." The person here has expressed a value judgment as a virtual expression of the self-picture or core of personality. Many aspects of the self are, of course, not expressed openly, consciously, or even fully known to the individual.

Conflicting roles

Frequently, a person finds himself in conflicting roles that are expressions of values, attitudes, and his self-picture. The boy who is an altar boy on Sunday and in the local poolroom six nights a week must vacillate between two radically different roles; so must the child who is passive and withdrawn in his family circle but who is accorded leadership by his peer group at school. The traveling salesman who tries to be a good husband and father when he is at home but who is on "the road" three weeks out of every four weeks must successfully switch his role as he changes his circumstances. The girl who is "the athletic type" and who loves her role as pitcher on the girls' softball team may find her role at the formal dance a bit frustrating and hard to manage.

Conflict in role is apt to take place when one changes his way of life drastically. Going to college is frequently accompanied by considerable conflict and anxiety when one leaves the role in his community, neighborhood, and high school or prep school, in which he has felt secure, understood, and accepted, and moves into a new situation in which he feels anonymous and unknown in a sea of unfamiliar faces. In the new situation he may have doubts as to whether he had better try to re-establish himself in the role with which he was familiar and practiced at home, or whether this is an opportunity to remake his personality and be known as a different kind of person; he may be very unsure as to what kind of role the new situation calls for. Every man or woman who has gone into the service has found that his role is drastically changed as a soldier or sailor, and again on taking up civilian life, it is necessary to find a new means of acceptance, usually with a new group.

The self-concept must undergo continual and sometimes violent changes as one progresses from childhood roles into adolescent roles, and in moving from adolescence into adulthood. When the student leaves school to become a worker, when the employee becomes a boss, when the bachelor or maiden becomes a marriage partner, when the childless spouse becomes a parent, and when the married are widowed are occasions that call for drastic readjustment of one's self-concept in establishing himself in acceptable roles with new groups.

Modifying the self-concept

The relation of the concept of one's self to one's environment has an important bearing on changes in self-concept. Once established, the self-concept tends to maintain itself. We hear someone say, "Good Heavens! Can't he see what he is doing? You'd think he would know better, but just try to tell him!" Such expressions suggest that the individual does not see his behavior as others see it. He does not see that it is inconsistent with the behavior approved by his groups for the particular situation. Unless an awareness of this discrepancy between the self-concept and the cultural demands occurs, the chances of change in self-concept are very slight. It is true that at a very early age a child develops a concept of himself as good or bad, important or unimportant, wanted or unwanted, but he can only make judgments about himself as others see him when he has developed the ability to put himself in another's place. This is an ability that normally comes with maturing.

The self-concept may change when one accepts views and understandings held by others and includes them in his self-concept. This may happen gradually, as in the adolescent's consciousness of being grown up. He is apt to be slow in regarding himself as adult, even though others, observing his general development, have become aware of the change. Thus, the adults around him are apt to become annoyed and wonder why the recently acquired adulthood does not result in more adult behavior. This gradual acceptance of a new concept, through repeated experiences, represents the most frequent type of behavior change in self-concept.

Changes may take place in self-concept when a person becomes involved in a relationship in which he is more or less completely accepted, as in the inter-relationships of a gang, a Boy Scout troop, a girls' club, a foster home, or a nonthreatening counseling situation. He is temporarily free from the burden of defending his self-concept; he is able to re-examine and re-define

*"As I see it a good deed is merely a means of satisfying
one's urge for self-approval."*

himself as he moves into the new situation; and he is able to learn new behavior patterns.

When the role is not consistent with the self-concept, an attempt is made to change the role. If a boy regards himself as a "good mixer," for example, his behavior at social affairs will reflect his self-concept and each experience at demonstrating his role as "good mixer" is satisfying. If for some reason, however, he finds that his attempts at playing his role are not accepted by his group, he begins to re-evaluate his concept of himself in social groups. He looks for new goals and tries his abilities in achieving them. In his floundering attempts to find a role for himself, he might decide to help the hostess with her work in the kitchen. A comment from her might suggest a rewarding role as being a "considerate" and "helpful" person. His concept of himself begins to change and he begins to look upon himself as the "considerate kind of person." At parties in the future, while someone else is being the life of the party in the living room, the "considerate one" can probably be found behaving consistently with his newly acquired role, opening a card table, distributing ash trays and napkins, carrying refreshments to the guests, and playing his accepted concept of being a real help to people.

The concept a person has of himself will determine the role that he feels called upon to play in a certain situation. The same person may find it rewarding to assume several roles in as many situations. The same person may be quiet and mannerly in the classroom, rude and impudent with his family, laughing and jovial with the corner gang, shy and embarrassed with the cast of the Sunday-school play, aggressive and capable on the basketball court, stammering and awkward at the family reunion, and boisterous and "smart-aleck" at a party where girls are present. The self-concept often modifies the role one feels is his in a particular environment. Some of these roles may be recognized as unsatisfactory and experimental, particularly after a trial has indicated a poor appraisal by the group. The role we play is intended to fill the need that is most readily satisfying.

The person who is sensitive to the reactions of people in his social groups and is secure enough to change his self-concept can adjust his behavior with facility. The adjusted behavior, if it is consistent with revised self-concept, enhances and strengthens it, contributing to the integration of the total personality—the well adjusted person.

ADJUSTMENT PROCESS

The human being is a continually adjusting organism; drives and needs set up tensions that the individual is constantly attempting to reduce. Some of these drives are innate or physiological, such as hunger, thirst, and the sex drive. Others, such as the need for acceptance by social groups, the need to be satisfied with one's self, or the need for approval, are induced and learned from the social and cultural context. A continual series of drives set up by stimuli, either constitutional or environmental, necessitates a continual series of attempts to relieve the tensions engendered by such drives. The effort to relieve these tensions is behavior. The individual is adjudged a success or failure in accordance with the degree to which these efforts comply with the standards accepted by the groups concerned.

Adjustment takes place when an individual's efforts to reduce tensions are thwarted by some obstacle he encounters as he strives to achieve his goal. If the thing that hinders access to his goal is something with which the individual is unfamiliar, he will try a variety of responses until through trial and error (or trial, error, and success), or some other method of problem solving, he achieves his goal. Some behavior, either reasonable and logical, or perhaps random and varied, usually results in a solution. The solution (overcoming the obstacle) reduces tension, and the goal is achieved. If he is not successful in overcoming the obstacle, or in circumventing it by a substitute method, a different goal will be substituted when the sustained tension can no longer be tolerated.

Everyone experiences sequences of the adjustment process many times every day. Such adjustive behavior on a level of rather transient motivation can be demonstrated through a return to the nail puzzle of the previous chapter. The puzzle itself is the stimulus. The desire to solve the puzzle and perhaps to be regarded by a friend as clever is the motive.

The person may examine it carefully first to see if he can, through insight, "think his way" to the solution. If he has a high level of competence, insight may result in a solution. If he has had previous experience with nail puzzles, or has seen them solved, he tries to solve it by remembering the solution he has experienced and patterns his attempts along the same lines. If this method is successful, the nails come apart, and the smile on his face as he hands back a disassembled puzzle attests to the fact that he has relieved tension and achieved his goal. If he has had no previous experience with nail puzzles, he may succeed eventually by trial and error or he may make random attempts at the solution. If he continues to twist the nails in the same manner that over and over again has failed to separate them his behavior is called nonadjustive.

If the nails refuse to come apart, he experiences frustration. He may attempt to pry them and, if the motivation is very strong, the words that he utters suggest that he is feeling considerable emotion.

Several modes of adjustment are open to him. He may eventually solve the puzzle either by insight, by trial and error, or by pure luck in his random attempts. If he is successful he will probably say, "Now let me see if I can do that again" and, by repeated experience, make the solution of the puzzle a matter of learning, almost of habit. If he fails, he may hand the puzzle back to his friend and turn his attention to other matters, pursuing an activity toward some other goal. If his motivation persists strongly but he can no longer tolerate the frustration, he may throw the puzzle to the floor and stamp on it or hammer it apart. If a direct solution cannot be found, a substitute solution will be successful to the extent that it relieves the original drive tension. These courses are adjustments to the immediate drive, but they would not be approved by his friend. Stamping the puzzle apart might relieve the original drive tension but the act would in turn set up other tensions, such as anxiety as to his friend's reaction, or perhaps fear of punishment for his destructive act. This example is, of course, an oversimplification of the adjustment process.

An example of a similar process, although of a more complex order, may be seen by returning to the example of the college freshman who asks himself, "Why am I in college?" Many stimuli have caused him to decide to enroll. Among these might be the wish to please his parents, the desire for acceptance by his college friends, the desire for admiration from his noncollege friends, the wish to master a field of endeavor, and many more. He may find obstacles blocking his attempts to reach his goal; these may be of three types: environmental (he does not have sufficient funds), personal defect (he has poor eyesight), or conflict with an antagonistic motive (he wants also to remain near his girl friend). If his motivation is strong enough, he can probably overcome these obstacles by such adaptive measures as

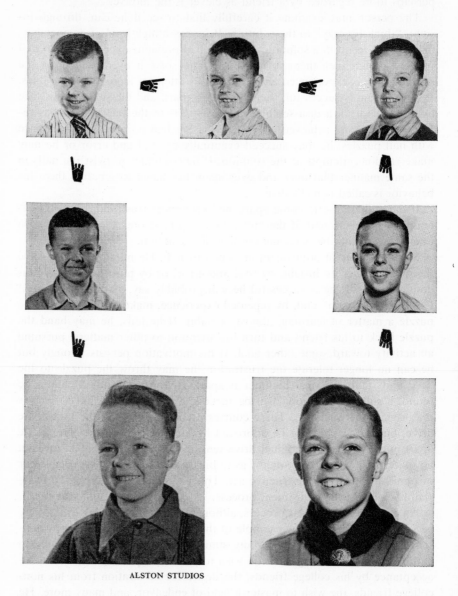

ALSTON STUDIOS

Significant changes in personality may often be revealed through a study of developmental patterns of growth

borrowing money and getting a job, having glasses fitted, and reconciling himself to seeing his girl only on week ends.

He no sooner starts attending classes, however, than he finds that there are constant obstacles confronting him in his desire to make good grades. His job may take up too much of his valuable time, or his previous school experience may not have resulted in his knowing how to organize his time efficiently (environmental), or he may learn that he does not have the scholastic aptitude that some of his classmates have (personal defect), or he may spend too much time socializing with his new friends (conflicting motives). The strength of his motivation and his experience in tolerating frustration will largely determine how successful he is in making adequate adjustment to the various obstacles he encounters. Persistent frustration may cause emotional reactions such as anxiety, fear, anger, or aggression. Depending upon his past experiences he will tend to make certain kinds of adjustments. He may relieve his tensions by withdrawing from school, giving up his original goal, and substituting another for it, perhaps by getting a full-time job. He may procrastinate until the situation is hopeless and new goals are forced upon him when he is dismissed from college. He may decide that if he is to succeed he must give up certain other pastimes and devote the time formerly spent in their pursuit to hard study, or he may realistically alter his self-concept to be more in keeping with a new realization of his strengths and weaknesses.

All adjustments or attempts at adjustment result from the effort to satisfy needs. The student who studies long and hard in order to succeed is probably trying to maintain his self-concept of being conscientious and dependable. The student who, for one reason or another, experiences little academic success may find that daily in the classroom his self-concept is threatened; he may resort to behavior that even he is at a loss to explain; for example, he may become cantankerous with his professors or his classmates, he may oversleep on the morning of an important examination, he may find that headaches and colds necessitate his frequent absence, or he may wonder why he deliberately cuts classes on the flimsiest of pretexts. Such behavior can be better understood if one looks for the need that he is attempting to meet. Perhaps the need is to defend his self-concept. The individual who has the ability to analyze his motives can possibly acknowledge the reasons for seemingly strange behavior, and having gained insight as to the needs he is attempting to fulfill by the unacceptable behavior he should be more competent in mastering and controlling his actions.

These examples oversimplify the acquisition of adjustive habits. Such habits are the result of constant responses to many complex situations. When a child learns that withdrawal from the attempt to reach his goal results in a reduction of tension, he may form a behavior habit of withdrawing when other frustrating situations are encountered. The child who avoids frustration and failure at school by feigning illness may experience headaches whenever a disagreeable prospect confronts him as an adult. The child who avoids strife with parents by being a model of virtue may become the self-righteous adult. Such personality traits are the results of his experience in reducing tensions by adjustive behavior.

The interaction of physiological drives, social drives, needs, emotions, and the adjustment process is the raw material from which personality is formed and also the area in which personality must function. In the problems of life as they are met and solved, as elements of the self-concept are created, the individual is reacting to life (adjusting) and forming patterns for future reactions (adjusting). Adjustment is therefore in one sense the expression of personality, but in a very real sense it is also an "origin of personality."

The first day of life (perhaps even before) begins this process of "personality-in-action," and "personality origination." The child faces needs, drives, and problems that must be solved. The adjustments and approaches to problem solving that are adopted or learned begin the process of personality formulation. Each day of life continues to add to the process of building personality.

Parents, environment, physical structure, problems to be solved, opportunities, deprivations, love, and even health and disease, as well as literally thousands of other factors, are all involved in the formation of personality. The process is cumulative and integrative rather than simply additive.

Since personality is cumulative and integrative, early life experiences become most significant. Childhood becomes the most important period of life insofar as the formation of personality is concerned. As problems are solved and approaches to life are adopted, the methods preferred may become part of the way of life of the individual. Changes in personality become progressively more difficult as the person grows older.

The purpose of this chapter, however, is not to enable students to change personality or adopt new personalities, but to understand and appreciate personality as a factor in life and future planning. It is in order, therefore, to seek out the dimensions or areas of operation of personality and patterns of adjustive behavior (or personality mechanisms).

ADJUSTIVE BEHAVIOR

The adjustive habits within personality most frequently employed to defend a developed pattern of behavior or to continue the growth of a self-satisfying self-concept are known as mechanisms of adjustment. These mechanisms of adjustment are utilized as the individual is called upon to function in various areas or as environmental demands are faced. Various authors in the field of psychology have used differing terminology. Many of the original understandings concerning adjustment mechanisms stem from Freud's early "mechanisms." Usage has modified certain terms, and unusual titles have been discarded. The present presentation is in the manner and terminology of Shaffer and Shoben. (113)

Defense mechanisms

Adjustments of this type are not usually deliberately acquired. They are apt to be more or less unconscious. Many of these behavior mechanisms overlap, and equally competent observers might not agree on the terminology or the degree to which one type or another is in play.

Compensation is frequently observed. The child who cannot experience success through academic achievement may become a show-off in class or a bully on the playground, or if compensation is directed into socially approved modes of expression, he may become an outstanding athlete. The person who is tempted by alcohol may become a militant prohibitionist. The person who has doubts about the competency of his own sex life may become a reforming prude as a compensatory measure.

Identification is a mechanism that is present to some extent in every well adjusted person; it is indeed one of the most frequent ways by which positive adjustments are made. One identifies with a hero, a movie star, a parent, an admired friend, or his fraternity brothers, and learns by imitation to manifest the behavior that is approved and admired.

Attention-getting devices are frequently resorted to by those who are unable to achieve the approval and attract the interest of individuals and groups around them. Children may demand attention by crying, by refusal to eat, by deliberate misbehavior, or by a myriad other kinds of behavior.

Rationalization is an attempt to make behavior that is inferior or unapproved appear to be consistent with socially approved standards. The boy who goes to a party when he should stay in his room and study tells himself that he needs the experience of the party as part of his social education. The girl who spends more than she can afford on a dress may convince herself that it is important to her college work because the lift it gives her in morale will show results in better grades on the next examination. The "sour-grapes" mechanism is a frequently encountered type of defensive rationalization. Commonly held notions are frequently rationalizations: for example, it is not scientifically true that there is a hair's breadth between genius and insanity, that if a girl is beautiful she is likely to be dumb, that the slow learner retains better than the fast learner. Such popular rationalizations are all fallacious.

Projection is a device in which one sees in another the characteristic motives of his own weaknesses and deficiencies. He believes all the fault to be in his environment or in those around him rather than in himself. The gossip delights in pointing the accusing finger at others because it obscures, to others, that she is experiencing the impulses she attributes to others and assures herself that she is not prone to these impulses. The student who is failing in his work is apt to project the cause of his failure to the prejudice of his teacher. Both rationalization and projection may become very serious maladjustments and are then apt to be called *delusions*.

Withdrawal

Withdrawal occurs when the individual has endured frustration to the point that he can no longer tolerate the tension it engenders. Everyone finds certain kinds of motives from which experience has taught him to withdraw, and this is perfectly normal. It is only when the pattern becomes so fixed that it interferes with normal social adequacy that it is regarded as a behavioral problem. The child who is developing a pattern of withdrawal as a means of adjusting is detected too seldom as a person who is not making positive adjustment patterns simply because it becomes his purpose to attract as little attention as possible. Such a person shuns the company of others, he prefers solitary pastimes to group activities, he looks on rather than participates. He is shy, bashful, blushes easily, and in stress may retreat behind a closed door. A habit pattern that exhibits a persistent tendency toward withdrawal indicates an urgent need for psychological help.

Although withdrawal tendencies are often extremely complex, there is considerable evidence that the most frequent cause is fear, which, when generalized, is called anxiety or an anxiety state. Such conditioning may be the result of cruel or abusive treatment in early childhood. Ridicule or repeated failure may induce the fear in any competitive situation so that the child retreats from all competition. Seclusiveness is the normal kind of behavior in the milder cases of withdrawal.

Negativism is a form of withdrawal in which the withdrawal manifests itself in open, vigorous rebellion against authority. This may be seen in the stubborn, "I'm-against-it" kind of person, the anarchist, the professional rebel, or in the delinquent, as a means of lashing back at the social groups that, in the eyes of the withdrawn person, have rejected him. Again it should be noted that a certain amount of this behavior is present in, and normal for, all individuals, particularly at certain periods of life. Everyone who has lived in the presence of children has witnessed the "no,-I-won't" period. The withdrawal of the adolescent from the bonds of family and "approved groups" chosen for him by his parents may be inferred by a period of seeming rebellion against conventional standards of such groups.

Fantasy is a phenomenon to which the withdrawn person is apt to be attracted. This often takes the form of daydreaming, which, so long as it is not substituted for real accomplishment or allowed to become a persistent preoccupation, has value as a recreation and as an imaginative, creative act that may culminate in practical activity. When daydreaming is constantly substituted for the more real satisfactions of actually overcoming inferiorities or meeting the realities of life, it may become a fixed maladjustment. Daydreams have been labeled the "conquering-hero" type, in which the individual imagines the glories accruing to him as the result of victorious deeds or of possessing the things he desires, and the "suffering hero" type, in which one receives pity or sympathy because he bravely continues in a heroic fashion despite insurmountable opposition and misunderstanding that eventually gives way to repentance when the cruel ones realize the error of their ways. When the daydreamer can be led to active attempts to realize his daydreams, the resulting satisfactions should preclude the need for further excessive daydreaming.

Regression is the attempt or tendency to experience again the satisfactions that resulted from a particular kind of behavior of an earlier age. The young child who is no longer the center of attention after the arrival of a sibling may wish to recapture the former attention by a regression to the uncontrolled toilet habits of his earliest infancy. College students who are suffering the loss of the protection of the home for the first time may suffer "homesickness," a regressive failure to adjust. Fairly innocuous examples of regression are evident in the perennial "college Joe" who leaves his dignity at home and indulges in adolescent behavior at homecoming in an attempt to recapture the satisfactions of an earlier period of his life, in which security and protection were not the least of the satisfactions. When regressive behavior is so persistent that the individual postpones mature responsible behavior it is regarded as a crippling adjustive pattern.

Phobias, which are unreasonable and persistent fears, and *repression,* which is the active forgetting of incidents, places, names, appointments, and so forth that threaten to arouse tension, are aspects of withdrawal.

Compulsive behavior is common to some extent with all people. The person who must search his pockets for his key after he closes a door that locks automatically even though he knows very well he has just checked to see if he had it before closing the door is displaying a harmless form of compulsive behavior. People who feel sustained tension frequently resort to a kind of repetition of behavior to reduce the tension they feel. Examples of behavior that may appear frequently and compulsively under stress or tension are: eating when not hungry, performing a particular part of housekeeping not especially needed (such as emptying ash trays), washing and polishing the car when more important work is waiting, or just taking a hot bath when there is a vague awareness of tension. Many students have a habitual pattern of activity to go through before serious study can be begun. This pattern may entail such compulsive business as sharpening pencils, tidying the desk and drawers, squaring loose papers into neat piles, manicuring the fingernails, combing the hair, and trying all the programs on the desk radio before any actual study takes place.

Compulsive behavior that is uncontrollable and of neurotic degree is often called a mania. Kleptomania (the urge to steal), pyromania (the urge to set something afire), and dipsomania (the urge to consume alcoholic drinks) are fairly frequent examples.

Functional ailments

Though they are too complex to discuss in this chapter and constitute a field of study in themselves, some neuroses and psychoses should be mentioned as a form of adjustive behavior; that is, adjusting by functional ailments. Such serious behavior disorders are essentially a breakdown of personality and frequently require long periods of psychotherapy, sometimes with a virtually hopeless prognosis.

SELF-APPRAISAL

An examination of the causes of behavior has pointed out that all behavior results from the basic need of the individual to maintain or enhance his "self" as he sees his "self." Values, attitudes, feelings, as well as objects or experiences may become goals or needs for the individual. The attempt to reach goals and to fulfill needs is the reason underlying action and the basic cause of behavior.

In Chapter 5 the study of learning indicated that behavior is modified by learning. Learning is a process of differentiation. This chapter has been designed to demonstrate how differentiation throughout life leads to a particular self-concept and personality that in turn influence all of behavior. Therefore, all actions are consistent with the concept of "self" as one attempts to attain his goals and to satisfy his basic needs.

Differentiation in critical thinking

The purpose of this book is to help the student to be able to think analytically in regard to his "self." This implies learning things about the "self" of which he has not been aware previously. Details of his "self" and of the world about him of which he has been unconscious or but vaguely conscious for the first time become sorted out of the "ground" and become "figure." Because the individual is aware of these details, he may consider them with some objectivity. Their meaning, if understood, tends to modify his concept of "self." His behavior tends to be consistent with a new self-concept.

One of the contributors to this book tells the story of a well-remembered morning during his undergraduate days when he was running his fastest across the campus so he would not again be late for his eight o'clock French class. All his evident hurry did not deter a professor, then unknown to him, from stopping him as they met on the campus walk. The point the professor made was that the headlong dash to class was unseemly and not in keeping with the dignity that the venerable gentleman liked to see in another adult.

True, the teller of the story was more than vaguely aware that he was of adult size, but he had not differentiated out of this awareness this element of behavior that ordinarily changes when the boy becomes a man. The professor's brief admonishment astonished this student, but it resulted in a rather sudden change in self-concept. He proceeded the rest of the way that morning and on following mornings at a pace consistent with his new concept of his "self" as an adult of some dignity.

The reader was earlier urged to ask himself, "Why am I in college?" The freshman who is confronted with such a question may rattle off a sequence of stereotyped answers that are a part of the rote learning of the American culture. The student who can be led to a critical examination of his reasons for enrolling may differentiate out of the vague "ground" the valid, honest reasons why he is now a freshman. Of the many reasons a person may have for continuing his education, there may be several that are influential factors in varying degrees. If these factors can be differentiated and taken into one's awareness and accepted as motives, then behavior may become consistent with this new consciousness of the "self."

For example, the student may be enrolled in college because he wants to adhere to the wishes of his parents; he may desire to live for a while on the benefits of other people's financing; he may wish to enjoy the status that is the reward of the college student; he may see college as the way to live the life of an intelligent citizen; he may accept education as the surest road to a higher income bracket; he may choose college as a means for remaining close to a girl friend or as a lucrative hunting ground for dates or a future marriage partner; or he may attend college simply as a device for forestalling the day of reaching a threatening decision or the day he will become a worker.

A long list of possible reasons could be compiled and somewhere in such a list the average college student should be able to differentiate out—to bring from the "ground" into "figure"—his real reasons for enrolling. When he can do this, he is capable of new self-understanding, and it follows that perhaps his new aspect of his new self-concept will result in behavior modified to be consistent with his revised picture of himself.

Process of critical thinking

By following a process of thinking through a typical ladder of abstraction, one may demonstrate the concept of critical thinking. The question is asked of a student, "Why did you come to college?" His prompt answer might be, "To get an education." Such an answer begs for critical pursuit by another question, "Why do you want an education?" Although the reasons may seem obvious at first consideration, different people want an education for differing reasons. If it is assumed that the subject answers, "So I can make lots of money," he might, if he is engaged in critical analysis, ask himself, "Why do I want lots of money?" Suppose his answer is that he has an unusual desire for money so he will be admired by other people. He is then confronted with a matter of values; how did he arrive at the belief that wealth demands respect? The pursuit of needs, motives, attitudes, and values thus goes on.

This is an oversimplified example of the process through which one attempts a critical self-analysis. It is in this kind of thinking that this book attempts to engage the student. In order to aid the process of honest and realistic analysis, certain information and data are provided in this and following chapters.

All normal people seem to be interested, even curious, concerning their own behavior as well as the behavior of others about them. Students in psychology or guidance courses frequently say they hope, during the course, that they will find out something about what makes them "tick" as they do. A study of personality and uncovering its origins and development should give the student more insight into his own behavior and the behavior of those about him. He should be helped toward a healthy, constructive attempt at dealing with the endless problems of human relationships with which life confronts him. These activities, when successfully carried on, provide a foundation for critical thinking. Meaningful conclusions or generalizations, on a higher abstract level, must then result in application in future problem solving. This, then, is the nature of critical thinking.

SUMMARY

Personality has been presented as a persistent and relatively consistent pattern of adjustments in living. The structure of personality involves the self-concept as a core with values, attitudes, roles, and adjustment processes as other essential elements. The self-concept serves as a controlling force within the structure of personality. Values, attitudes, and roles are developed as the individual reacts with his environment through the adjustment process. Such a system of personality stresses its dynamic nature and the various interrelationships of all of its constituent parts.

The origins of personality lie in the physical structure of the person and to a larger degree in the interaction of the organism with the environment (nurture). Personality is an integrated and related functioning of the individual solving his problems insofar as there is a compatibility of actions within the person.

Self-concept is a core element in personality. It is developed gradually as the person matures and adopts roles, attitudes, and values. Conflicting elements can lead to conflict within personality or the demand for constant modification of the self-concept. Changes in self-concept take place as the individual is able to examine his concept of self in an unthreatened, accepting atmosphere.

Personality develops out of an individual's efforts to adjust to life and at the same time it is the pattern of adjustment that an individual adapts or learns. There are many defensive and withdrawal types of "adjustment mechanisms" within personality. Compensation, identification, "attention-getting mechanisms," rationalization, negativism, phantasy, regression, phobias, aggression, and compulsive behavior were briefly described as examples of varied adjustment mechanisms.

Self-analysis and attempts to clarify the elements of an individual's self-concept are presented as methods of critical thinking. Personality change is not offered as a goal of the study of personality, but rather it is expected that, through a more thorough understanding of personality as a total factor, students can begin to enter into an examination of some of the major elements within personality. Self-analysis and self-understanding are offered as means to more effective living and future planning.

SUPPLEMENTARY SOURCES

Berg, Irwin A., "Personality Structure and Occupational Choice," *Personnel and Guidance Journal,* 32 (1953), pp. 151-154.

Bernard, Harold W., *Toward Better Personal Adjustment* (2nd ed.). New York: McGraw-Hill Book Company, Inc., 1957.

Jersild, Arthur T., *Child Psychology* (4th ed.). Englewood Cliffs, N. J.: Prentice-Hall, Inc., 1955.

———, *In Search of Self.* New York: Bureau of Publications, Teachers College, Columbia University, 1955.

Lehner, George F. J., and Ella Kube, *The Dynamics of Personal Adjustment.* Englewood Cliffs, N. J.: Prentice-Hall, Inc., 1955.

Lindgren, Henry Clay, *Psychology of Personal and Social Adjustment.* New York: American Book Company, 1953.

Murphy, Gardner, *Personality, A Biosocial Approach to Origins and Structure.* New York: Harper & Brothers, 1947.

Patty, William L., and Louise S. Johnson, *Personality and Adjustment.* New York: McGraw-Hill Book Company, Inc., 1953.

Pitt, William J., and Jacob A. Goldberg, *Psychology.* New York: McGraw-Hill Book Company, Inc., 1954.

Shaffer, Laurance F., and Edward J. Shoben, Jr., *The Psychology of Adjustment.* Boston: Houghton Mifflin Company, 1956.

Snygg, Donald, and Arthur W. Combs, *Individual Behavior.* New York: Harper & Brothers, 1949.

One of the characteristics of American young people is their desire to achieve "maturity" at ever-younger chronological ages. Sometimes this takes what seem to their elders to be ridiculous forms, such as a physician's report on the demands he receives from preadolescent and adolescent girls for information on how to improve their physiques. Newspaper columnists who purport to deal with the personal problems of readers are frequently asked by adolescents (and parents, too, astonishingly enough) at what age they

Chapter 7

PSYCHOLOGICAL AND
SOCIAL MATURITY

should begin to date or "go steady," and the evidence seems to indicate that the approved ages for such activities are becoming younger. We know, too, that the average age of marriage in this country has been declining steadily over the past decade or more. A corollary to this is the evidence that the mean age of mothers at the time of the birth of the first child is dropping. The State of Georgia recently has lowered the minimum age for voters to eighteen; considerable agitation for similar action has been evident in several recent election campaigns.

These items are cited to point up the interest in "earlier" maturity. An examination of the matter from the point of view of the psychologist and the sociologist presents an interesting paradox, for their objective studies of our culture in general, and of the adolescent and young-adult periods of life specifically, indicate that historically we have in the United States tended to lengthen the process of maturing.

Every state in the Union now requires that all young people attend school until the age of sixteen, with some states specifying the equivalent of twelve years of schooling as a

99

minimum. The number, both real and proportional, of high-school graduates moving on to further education either in college or technical school
is growing at a rate that dismays educators and politicians alike. Another
indication of this advancing trend in maturity is found in the laws of most
states, which regulate the minimum age at which persons may begin full-
time work. Thus, it is seen that the age at which young people complete
the period of preparation for adult living, that is, finish formal education
and become economically independent, has consistently become higher
while the individual person seeks maturity at an ever-decreasing age level.

MEANING OF MATURITY

The paradox and conflict between the culture and the individual on the
meaning of maturity raise the problem of determining how those who use
the term "maturity" define it. Primarily, we are interested in the meaning
that the psychologist has in mind when he speaks of the maturity of the
individual. In one fashion he refers to a *physiological process* that he labels "maturation"; in another sense *social development* or "maturation" is
implied.

Physiological maturation

Physiological maturation is concerned with the developmental process of
growth. This process arises out of the individual's physical and physiological need to achieve "completion" in the growth process. (95) Studies of
the physical growth of body organs and systems show that the unborn
child, within a few weeks after conception (when it is called the embryo)
possesses a nervous system, muscles, sense organs, and glands that develop separately with no connection among them. Later, through physiological growth and maturation processes, the nervous system sends down
nerves to the muscles, and still later the sense organs connect with the
nervous system. Some connections between muscles and sense organs are
made as early as three months after conception. (29) Other connections
(as with eyes and ears, for example) do not appear until about the seventh
month.

Although most of the reflexes and elementary forms of behavior are
ready for use at the time of birth, other patterns, not needed so early, develop more slowly. Casual observation of infants will show that they are
unable to follow moving objects with their eyes until several weeks after
birth. The ability to sit up, crawl, and walk must wait until nerves, muscles, and bone structures have matured. These activities, as well as more
complex behavior, depend in large measure on the slower-maturing brain

or cerebral cortex, most of the maturation of which is completed by the age of two years, but Smith (115) has shown that some cerebral-cortex maturation goes on until the individual is from ten to fifteen years old. All of us are conscious of the late-maturing aspects of one of the glandular systems of the body. The sex glands do not mature until the age of puberty, when the secondary sex characteristics become pronounced, and the capacity to produce offspring becomes active. Along with the bodily changes come changes in behavior and motivation, resulting from the secretion of sex hormones into the blood stream. The entire physical organism we know as a human being is subject to varying rates of maturation in all areas of physical growth until physiological maturity is reached.

Social maturation

Physiological maturation is of great significance to the individual and to the psychologist, but it is only one of the aspects of maturity that concern us. The second consideration is that of *sociological* maturation, or socialization. Here too, we are dealing with a process, one which begins at birth and involves the external forces that mold the human being. Each person has an heredity that is physiological, and he experiences an environment that is primarily social in nature. There are, of course, physical aspects to the environment that help determine what one will become—factors such as nutrition, climate, geographical locale, and the like. But in the twentieth century, such factors are relatively less important than the social environment in which the person lives.

The young person is largely the product of the experiences that have happened to him. Particularly, he is the product of the experiences he has had with other people. This becomes more obvious when we study individuals who have come from social environments markedly different from our own. Margaret Mead, whose studies of the peoples of some of the Pacific Islands have contributed greatly to our understanding of the role of the social environment, points the matter up as follows:

> One reason why the theory of Race has been given such wide acceptance is just because the inhabitants of Hamburg are not like the inhabitants of Plymouth or Naples, and the man in the street, who hadn't spent his life checking up on the social processes by which babies become adults, just couldn't believe that these groups of people could have turned out to be so different, if they had started out—as babies—with the same kind of gifts and the same kind of limitations. In America, as we watched one wave of immigration after another hit our shores, it was much easier to refer startling differences between the Southern Italians and the Poles to their "blood" than it was to realize that not only the Italians and the Poles but even we ourselves have been shaped by our social environment—that the language one speaks, the religion one professes, the code of ethics by which one judges and is

judged, one's taste for wine or beer or vodka, or one's preference for paprika or snails or French-fried dragon-flies can all be referred to the culture within which one is brought up. It is hard to believe that the same children who can eat food seasoned so highly with red pepper that it burns our tongues for hours after would have indignantly repudiated that "horrid highly-spiced foreign food" if they had been adopted at birth by people who ate tasteless food. But we know—on the basis of modern anthropological findings—that this is true, that it is not blood, but upbringing which determines all of these ways of behaving.(89:19)

In infancy the person is almost completely subject to the desires, demands, whims, and examples of adults, particularly those in his immediate family. As he grows in his capacity to reason and take responsibility for his own actions, he gradually moves away from the immediate control of his family. But never is he able completely to escape from the learning that he has experienced in his early years. The human being begins as a helpless infant with no social skills, no social habits, no social likes or dislikes, no conscience, no sense of right and wrong, and no social motives. He is, in social experience, a blank page, on which life will make impressions of bewildering variety and varying intensities. He ends as an adult, more or less self-sufficient, accountable in society's eyes for his own actions, with a greater or lesser degree of skill in dealing with other people, with a habit pattern of responses or personality that is seen by others as typical of him, but that include patterns of thought that only he can know. He has developed a conscience or a value system, which is one way of saying that he has ideas of what behavior is right for him, and what is wrong. He works, but his motivation may not be clear, even to himself; perhaps his work gives him deep personal satisfaction, as well as money with which to purchase additional satisfactions; perhaps work is only a means to an end, an unpleasant necessity by which he obtains the time and opportunity to engage in more gratifying activities. He is married, and again, he may not know quite why; and he has children, and again, the motivations for desiring children, who are often annoying, expensive, and frustrating, are likely to be mysterious to him. He will, in other words, have matured.

THE MATURING PERSON

Some adults are considered by themselves, by those who know them intimately, and by casual acquaintances, as "mature." Others are considered, by all or some of the same judges, to be "immature." What is meant? First of all, the mature person recognizes and conforms to a degree to social regulations and society's control devices. This is primarily a matter of self-regulation; the mature person abides by the rules because he accepts the wisdom and the necessity for doing so both for the good of society and for his own well-being and happiness. The norms or standards of the group to which he belongs become the standards or norms by which his conduct is measured.

In all societies there are certain over-all general norms of conduct which are accepted throughout the total national group. Other group norms are more local and less fundamental. Still others are confined to neighborhoods or even to families. Every individual's conduct in the end is a product of the way he sorts out and accepts or rejects these various group norms. His standards and values, in fact, come to reflect in adulthood the groups which he has accepted or rejected, since harmony within oneself is attainable only as one achieves some harmony in group associations which are meaningful to him. (75:148)

Yet, as the maturing young person is expected to accept and conform to the behavior standards of the groups to which he belongs, it is hoped that he will not completely become a conformist in all aspects of living. It is desirable that a measure of spontaneity and creativity will characterize him. An independence of mind and outreaching beyond the standardized and the routine are qualities that the adolescent is also encouraged to develop. Here again, the paradoxical nature of the process of maturing is present. The dual aspects of conformity and independence bear further examination. One consideration has to do with the adjustment relationships of the maturing person with his family, his age and sex peers, and those of his age group of the opposite sex.

Adjustment and maturity

Emancipation from the home as an aspect of maturity within personality should usually begin in the preadolescent years through contact with playmates, the school, and other groups. The more independence the boy or girl between six and twelve has developed, the easier will be the inevitable break from the home in later adolescence. The initial efforts of the child to free himself from the overprotection of and the overattachment to his parents may be feeble and incomplete, but as he advances in the adolescent years to an ever-widening range of friends and acquaintances with new interests, the healthy-minded boy or girl will make an even greater effort to emancipate himself. His efforts at freedom, however, are very likely to be met with resistance on the part of parents, which in turn will be met by similar resistance on the part of the child. This situation causes misunderstanding, anger, and sorrow between parents and children. Parents frequently begin at this period, even though for years they may have allowed the child to have much of his own way in minor matters, to invoke the traditional parental authority. This in turn may lead to dishonesty and deceit by the child in an effort to escape censure. Parents often reveal their own emotional immaturity by resorting to rage, weeping, and violence at the behavior of their adolescent children. This makes it difficult if not impossible to establish rapport within the family at a critical time. Should the parental repression be successful, the child either fails to develop freedom with a matching sense of responsibility for his own actions or seeks an outlet in some form of highly emotional or neurotic behavior. "It often happens that emotional maladjustment is rooted in the child or youth who is considered a model of deportment, kindliness, and obedience." (140: 406) Yet the maturing person, moving toward ever-greater independence, does not, indeed cannot, fail to conform to the standards and examples of earlier years in the family circle.

The centering of one's emotional attention upon members of one's own sex or upon older people is typically a childish reaction. Neither of these interests is an adequate basis for an adult adjustment, although both may form the basis for many secondary emotional attachments throughout life. The physical and emotional changes of puberty usually arouse a great interest in sex, which may find expression in an exaggerated awareness of one's own bodily development or that of other people. This sort of interest is typical of early adolescence. During this period both boys and girls normally do a great deal of experimenting in emotional relationships. This need not necessarily be sexual experimentation, although it is not unusual for this to be part of the process. An interest in all members of the opposite sex is strong in early adolescence, but tends to be replaced gradually by a concentration upon individual members. Thus, a person moves toward the eventual selection of a mate, centering his interest on one person to the exclusion of other possible love stimuli about him. During the years when these changes are in progress, the adolescent may get into more or less serious emotional difficulties; certainly, it is a trying time for his family and intimates, but no trouble can be as serious as the failure of the normal developments to take place.

The process of evolvement of heterosexual relationships, the manner in which the person deals with the problems of adolescence, and the attitudes he takes into dating and courtship are functions of personality that will have been conditioned largely by the formal and informal learning that have taken place during early adolescent years. Behavior will, in other words, be that which conforms by and large to the demands of conscience and prior expectation. Having said this, it is essential also to say that it is at the same time imperative that the individual should become more and more free to choose and to act on his own responsibility, but the alternatives that he sees as available to him are those that will enable him to act in accord with his own background of experience.

As Young states: "Responsibility means the ability and willingness to take the consequences of one's acts. It implies that the person is a free moral agent, capable of being deterred or controlled by consideration of social sanctions, legal and moral." (140:409) Freedom means the absence of, or exemption from, restraint by the power or control of others. In our society it implies self-determination of marriage, vocation, religion, and politics. It should not, however, be confused with license or absence of responsibility. Freedom from parents is therefore not merely a matter of getting away from home ties through uncontrolled indulgence of emotions and desires. The young person who sets out upon this course will discover that his "freedom" enmeshes him in difficulties and problems. The process of growing up in adolescence is predicated upon what happens in earlier years. The problem of attitudes, habits, and personality in adolescence and adulthood cannot be dissociated from what has gone before. As the child develops there needs to be a growth toward independence, discrimination, and a sense of responsibility for his choices and acts—that is, freedom to grow must be provided gradually over a period of years. Too often, childish dependence continues into adolescence or early maturity, and then the individual, when confronted with problems demanding his own decisions, meets them with failures or half measures.

Emotions and maturity

Another relevant approach to the concept of maturity is that of "emotional maturity." Franz Alexander lists as the essence of the mature state of mind the conquest of insecurity and the ability to take oneself for granted. (2:1-4) The adolescent is characterized by an excessive competitiveness, a necessity to prove himself to be an adult. When he falls short of his goal, he feels inadequate and insecure, and seeks some method by which he may compensate for his failure. This frequently takes the form of aggressive competitiveness. The mature person has tested himself and knows his capacities; therefore, he has less need to be concerned with himself and can turn his attention to other factors in his environment. Alexander also stipulates that the emotionally mature person is flexible and adaptable. He can accept his own limitations realistically, and does not expect more of life than it is likely to provide him.

A discussion of emotional maturity would be incomplete without some attention to the matter of the individual's relationships to other people. As a child one is primarily oriented to members of his immediate family. As he matures, he increases his capacity to take part in the activities of groups without trying either to dominate them or to withdraw from them. At the same time he must not depend so extremely upon his social group that he is constantly concerned with what others will say and think about him, his work, appearance, clothes, and ideas. A part of the individual's orientation to others, especially in the adolescent years, should be an increasing tolerance toward people different from himself and his group—other nationalities, races, and social classes. The child tends to be tolerant because he is ignorant and insensitive to social stimuli; the adult is tolerant because of knowledge, understanding, and compassion. The adolescent is often characterized by intolerance that must be overcome. (33)

A significant aspect of emotional maturity is the manner in which the person reacts to stressful situations. Children typically have little power to inhibit their responses. They are highly emotional, and have little capacity to differentiate responses according to the degree of the long-range significance of the experiences confronting them. Thus, a momentary frustration may elicit an emotional reaction virtually identical with that resulting from a deprivation that would mean a permanent or long-time unhappiness. The child's methods of expressing his emotions, moreover, are often potentially harmful to himself physically. The development of a mature emotional life involves the control and direction of modes of expressing emotion. Objectivity must be combined with emotional integrity within the person so that his normal reaction is basically intellectual and rational as well as emotional.

Most of the attributes of maturity given so far have dealt to a greater or lesser degree with the need of the individual to control himself, to withhold action and expression, to sublimate his reactions and himself to the social requirements and social sensitivities of others. Jersild protests that this is only part of the picture, that maturing involves additional, more positive factors of fulfillment. (67) Included in his listing are these items:

> One mark of maturity . . . is a kind of inner freedom—freedom to feel, freedom to experience—in an intimate, personal way life's sorrows and its joys, the force and meaning of threats and thwartings from without and the impact of impulses and strivings from within . . . (p. 193)
>
> The concept of being free to feel involves also the concept of being responsible for one's feelings. The one who is free to feel does not necessarily allow himself unlimited freedom in the expression of feeling . . . An important aspect of the ability to feel is the capacity for concern about what others feel . . . (p. 193)
>
> One important—and perhaps the most important—feature of growth toward emotional maturity during adolescence is an increased capacity for concern about the feelings of others and an increased capacity for sharing emotional experiences with others. . . . (p. 194)
>
> The ability to appreciate and respect the feelings of others and to share emotional experiences with them gives the adolescent a great advantage in dealing with the problems of his life. . . . If the adolescent can see some of his problems as things to be shared, and his experiences with other persons as something mutual rather than something one-sided, he may be spared much of the turmoil that comes when he tries to solve his problems and to make his decisions solely with a view to exploiting others or to protecting himself from being exploited by them. . . . (p. 196)
>
> One mark of a rather high level of emotional maturity is an ability to see

people as real persons. A mature person can perceive and appreciate the humanity of those about him. He does not expect the good person to be a perfect saint or the bad person to be an all-out sinner. The mature person has learned, at least to some degree, not to perceive an individual's appearance or his actions entirely from the point of view of his own need to find a hero to worship or a scapegoat to blame. . . . (p. 197)

EVALUATION OF MATURITY

Understanding maturity is, of course, only a first step. How does one go about determining if he is mature, or if his associates are mature? Self-evaluation can help one to determine his own degree of maturity, and several useful devices are also available for external measurement.

Self-evaluation

For the individual anxious to evaluate himself in terms of the present level of his maturity and to ascertain further goals and objectives toward which he may reasonably aspire, there needs to be available a summary listing of the significant factors generally considered to be involved in personal maturity. Many lists and aspects of maturity or normality have been offered. Maslow and Mittlemann discuss "normality," and to a large degree this is similar to the present discussion of maturity. (85:14-15) An adapted presentation of their view of normality can aid the individual concerned with the assessment of "maturity."

1. *Security*. The sense that life provides positive opportunities, rather than a continuous series of threats; that one is unthreatened in his occupational, social, and family activities.
2. *Realistic self-evaluation*. A feeling of one's own value and worthwhileness that is in line with achievements and potential; an acceptance that one has limitations that contribute to individuality, and that some of one's desires are socially and personally unacceptable.
3. *Satisfying emotional life*. The formation of strong and lasting emotional relationships with others; control of the expression of emotions within socially and personally acceptable limits; an ability to understand and accept the emotional expression of others; and the maintenance of a relatively consistent level of serenity and well-being.
4. *Accepting and flexible outlook*. An ability to sustain and accept the inevitable shocks of life, such as illness and reversals; and the capacity to change if external circumstances cannot be altered. (This has been called "co-operation with the inevitable.")
5. *Healthy acceptance of bodily activities*. Acceptance of bodily func-

tions but not preoccupation with them; ability to derive satisfaction from physical things such as exercise, eating, and sleeping; sexual adequacy and gratification without fear or guilt; and the ability to withstand, at least temporarily, deprivation of any of the physical satisfactions.

6. *Integrated personality.* Well-rounded versatile interests; a conscience that is neither too flexible nor inflexible in terms of the standards of one's normal group; and a consistency of response that typifies one's self to other people.

7. *Adequate life goals.* Realistic goals that are achievable and compatible; ability to persist in striving for goals; and goals that are socially as well as personally beneficial.

8. *Ability to profit from experience.* The accumulation of knowledge and skills; and an elasticity and absence of rigidity in one's approach to life's tasks; the avoidance of responses that experience indicates to be overly hazardous; and the utilization of the best-known methods for handling problem situations.

9. *Satisfactory group participation.* The individual regulates his conduct by the folk ways of the group; he is not greatly unlike other members in ways that the group considers important; he accepts group ambitions and group limitations; and he is interested and involved in the affairs of others in the group.

10. *Independence and emancipation from the group.* Although considering himself a group member, the individual maintains his own integrity by cultivating originality and individuality and some independence of group opinions—particularly the right to dissent; he is not dominated by a need for flattery, reassurance or group approval; and he is tolerant of cultural differences.

External evaluations

The previous list of elements of maturity or normality may prove extremely useful to the self-concerned person, in that it provides a tool for what might be termed an informal self-evaluation. It is, of course, not possible for the individual to be completely objective in evaluating his own capacities, qualities, and personality traits. It is, therefore, helpful to have available additional kinds of information concerning one's maturity level. An approach to this type of evaluation is the so-called *personality rating scale* by means of which other people rate the subject on a variety of traits based on their observations of him in social, business or school, and personal relationships. Scales of this type are frequently used by colleges and businesses in attempting to determine which applicants should be admitted or hired. The judgments of former teachers, co-workers, employers, and supervisors concerning applicants often provide significant information that supplements achievement and employment records. An example of a widely read rating scale is that furnished by many secondary schools to colleges as part of the credentials on graduates applying for admission to colleges. It consists of a series of traits, with a linear scale beside each on which the rater (usually teacher, guidance counselor, or principal) checks how highly he considers the subject to rank.

Although this sort of rating scale affords at best a very modest and informal indication of the individual's personality, including aspects of maturity therein, it can be helpful for rough appraisal or screening purposes; particularly is this true if several ratings, each by a different observer, are obtained, and consistent patterns of response are indicated.

A more elaborate approach to the problem of rating the personal characteristics of others is represented by the Vineland Social Maturity Scale. Modeled on the approach of Binet to the measurement of mental age, the Vineland Scale provides a series of descriptions of behavior, each series representing activities typical of the normal person at particular age levels. "The items are arranged in order of increasing average difficulty, and represent progressive maturation in self-help, self-direction, locomotion, occupation, communication, and social relations. This maturation in social inde-

BOSTON UNIVERSITY PHOTO SERVICE

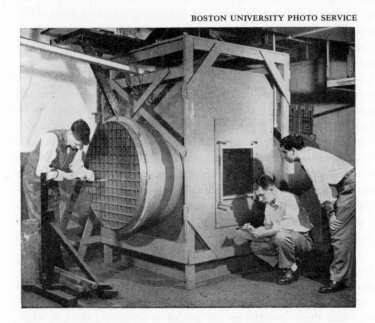

Maturity involves the ability to work well with others

pendence may be taken as a measure of progressive development in social competence." (134:1-2) The scale calls for judgment by trained testers based on direct observation of the subject and on interrogation of persons who know the examinee's behavior patterns well.

Standardized measures

A different approach to the problem of measuring maturity as an aspect of personality is represented by a number of "adjustment inventories" that require the subject to respond to a series of statements and questions that probe his preferences, typical reactions, and emotional responses. The replies are then given standardized value ratings by the examiner, enabling him to arrive at numerical descriptions of the subject in terms of such traits as general activity, ascendance, submission, sociability, emotional stability, morale, objectivity, friendliness, health level, thoughtfulness, home adjustment, personal relations, and masculinity or femininity. The Personality Inventory, by R. G. Bernreuter, yields scores for neurotic tendency, self-sufficiency, introversion or extroversion, dominance, submission, confidence, and sociability. The California Test of Personality contains 180 questions to which the subject must respond with either "yes" or "no." On the basis of the subject's answers, he is rated for self-reliance, sense of personal worth, sense of personal freedom, sense of belonging, freedom from withdrawing tendencies, freedom from nervous symptoms, freedom from antisocial tendencies, and social standards, social skills, family relations, school relations, and community relations.

Obviously, questionnaires of this type can yield valid results only if the subject is completely honest and as objective about himself as possible. As indicated previously, it is very nearly impossible for human beings to be so, particularly if one recognizes that the results obtained may be a consideration in whether he gets a desired job or is promoted in a military organization, or is admitted to a special program in school. This matter of the difficulty in obtaining valid responses poses one of the major problems involved in using the adjustment or personality inventory device. Other objections to the use of inventory devices result from the disagreements prevalent among psychologists on the relevance and significance of the traits purported to be measured, the sometimes questionable methods used in attempting to validate the items used, and the tendency of users to overgeneralize from the results obtained. Despite these criticisms, the personality or maturity inventory may be of some value in calling attention to personality tendencies when used with discretion on the part of all concerned. Most often these inventories are useful as screening devices when large groups are assessed on particular traits. The extreme scores of either a high or low nature are usually significant.

MATURITY IN LIFE

The maturing young person who has considered maturity in terms of more or less abstract principles and has also attempted to determine the level of his own maturity may still be somewhat at a loss to see ways in which he may look forward to the application of the concepts of maturity in his own future life. In a word, he is concerned with the *pragmatic* value of the preceding discussion: How may the principles and formulations be useful and valuable in real-life situations that will be faced in the future?

Young adults look forward to many and varied new experiences in the years immediately before them. Additional schooling, military service, courtship leading to marriage, the choosing of, training for, and entry into a life occupation, and the final break of close daily ties with parents, all are in prospect for those in the middle and late teen years. Each of these experiences will involve the making of decisions and the building of new manners of behaving and thinking. Hence the emphasis in this book, and in the courses that will use it, upon critical thinking based solidly on accurate information and realistic self-analysis.

Among the variety of future experiences awaiting them, young people usually are most deeply concerned with two factors that are virtually universal in our society. Because most people marry, and most people undertake some sort of remunerative employment, and because success in these aspects of living involves so greatly the personality and maturity traits of the individuals involved, a discussion of the mature personality in these relationships should prove meaningful.

The following pages of this chapter, then, will involve the reader in an analysis of some of the factors of maturity that contribute significantly to success in two endeavors of life: marriage and occupation. These were chosen to exemplify the application pragmatically of the "mature personality in action" chiefly because of their universality and their overriding importance among the concerns most young people hold. The discerning student will see not only descriptions of mature behavior here, but also suggestions for the critical examination of other phases of life in which he will in the future be involved.

Marriage

How successful the young person will be in the processes of courtship and marriage-building will depend very largely on the personality or maturity that he brings to these endeavors. The individual who is ready, in terms of maturity, will have passed beyond childish behavior patterns, will have strong heterosexual interests, will have achieved a relative emancipation from parents, and become an integral member of his own age group. He will have tested and evaluated his capacities and interests, and will have a good idea of what he can and cannot reasonably expect to achieve from life. He will have examined and weighed the major values and objectives of life. As a result of his analysis of himself, he will have developed a self-confidence that will act as an inoculation against emotionally immature action.

In general, the personality that is most nearly ready for the new activities and responsibilities of courtship and marriage is that which most nearly approaches the concept of mature personality already developed. Particularly worthy of emphasis in connection with the most intimate of human relationships are the following major factors.

Feelings of dominance or dependence. The mature person will not be driven by an inner need to dominate or hurt other people because of his own feelings of rejection or insufficiency. Instructive at this point is the case study of Jack and Barbara Gordon reported by Levy and Munroe in their excellent book *The Happy Family.* Briefly, it is the story of a "self-made" man who married an ambitious girl of a higher social class. Jack, the successful businessman and politician, was made to feel inferior and incompetent by his talented, strong-willed, society-bred wife who wanted, sincerely, to do all that she could to further her husband's career. But . . .

> . . . His pride in having come so far was changed to shame that he had not come all the way. Barbara's breeding made him conscious of his own crudities, made him feel a little uneasy and gauche. Jack's protective attitude toward his wife was his method of handling his uncomfortable feeling that he was not quite equal to her. Protection is a sign of strength. We can only protect those weaker than ourselves. Jack could accept Barbara's perfection so long as she was dependent upon him. . . . His picture of Barbara as an exquisite, helpless, feminine creature was necessary to his natural desire for masculine superiority. (78:159-160)

A strong need to dominate (which in the example cited took the form of a desire to protect the "helpless female"), obviously, can be a destructive factor in marriage. So, however, can its opposite: an insatiable hunger for emotional support, or *overdependence.* The mature person will find that he fits somewhere between the extremes of overdependence and the need to dominate. He will feel adquate and at ease with others, consciously prepared to make the variety of new adjustments that each new life experience requires. Every social relationship, particularly one as intimate as marriage, requires numerous compromises; the person who is so set in his patterns of behavior or perception that he cannot compromise will almost inevitably fail to find security or happiness in marriage.

Emancipation from home relationships. An emancipated relationship with his family should be part of every young person's readiness for marriage. If he is forced to continue the parent-and-child relationship over into the years of courtship and marriage, he will find himself beset with the often humorously-treated but not-so-funny "in-law" problem. (This has a close relationship to dominance-and-dependence needs, of course). Those who are able to achieve their emancipation most successfully and with a minimum of resentment and antagonism on both sides are those who have acquired a high degree of insight into the personalities of their parents. Children fill an important place in their family's need for affection and belongingness. Much of their parents' motivation for twenty or more years has been the drive to satisfy the needs and desires of their children. Marriage marks, in the parents' minds, definitely and finally, the end of this sort of relationship, and unless both parents and offspring are ready to face the next stage of life, frustration is certain to result. Although it may often be true that a large measure of difficulty at this stage is the responsibility of parents who are not prepared to let their children achieve independence, the younger generation will find that they can help materially by working conscientiously during the years of adolescence to demonstrate their own adequacy in handling their lives. Respect and attention to the advice of parents, whose experience, after all, has been more extensive than the adolescent's, will usually be productive not only of a better understanding of immediate problems, but of improved parental and in-law relationships. But at best, the process of weaning is a troublesome one. The person who faces life realistically will anticipate occasional difficulties, realizing that maturation must take place on the part of both parents and youths. The ability of the youth to deal successfully with this phase of maturation may be considered one of the criteria of his readiness for marriage.

Knowledge of other people. The young adult who comes to the courtship period with a wide and varied background of experience with people, particularly those of the opposite sex, is likely to be somewhat better prepared for marriage than one whose contacts have been limited. The modern school furnishes many opportunities in classroom, extracurricular activities, and social life, for young people to become absorbed in common interests and enterprises. Employment situations may contribute to a broadened acquaintanceship. All such opportunities should be grasped, for experience with people in various relationships brings an understanding and tolerance that are vital to a mature readiness for marriage. As youths observe friends and acquaintances diversely reacting to common experiences, they become more realistic about themselves and other people. The naïve, the wide-eyed innocent, the overly cynical, and those baffled by the "mystery" of the opposite sex are the immature who have not actively endeavored to gain a broadened perspective for living with other people. The mature person is able to evaluate others, including the other sex, realistically.

Factors of marital happiness. The young adult who is interested in a mature approach to marriage will do well to examine some of the studies of psychologists on marital success. A variety of criteria have been employed by different investigators for adjudging success or failure in marriage. Dr. L. M. Terman used the scores that 792 husbands and wives made on a marital success scale (125) to find what factors made for an individual's success in marriage, finding that the following factors correlated positively with marital happiness:

(a) marital happiness of parents
(b) happiness of childhood
(c) absence of conflict with parents
(d) firm but not harsh discipline in the home
(e) strong attachment to father and mother
(f) frank attitude of parents toward early sex curiosity
(g) relative mental ability (husband some but not much superior)
(h) absence of frequent and severe childhood punishment
(i) absence of disgust and aversion toward sex in premarital attitude toward the subject.

Burgess and Cottrell (21:349) made a statistical and case-history study of 526 marriages, finding that:

(1) Contrary to popular opinion, American wives make the major adjustment in marriage.
(2) Affectional relationships in childhood, typically of the son for the mother and the daughter for the father, condition the love-object choice of the adult.
(3) The socialization of the person, as indicated by his participation in social life and social institutions, is significant for adjustment in marriage.
(4) With the majority of couples, problems of sexual adjustment in marriage appear to be a resultant not so much of biological factors as of psychological characteristics and of cultural conditioning of attitudes toward sex.
(5) Prediction before marriage of marital adjustment is feasible. . . .

These writers found that those who had the highest scores on premarital background items (such as those given above, from Terman), that is, those who seemed to have the most factors favorable to a successful marriage, actually did have more successful marriages. It appears, then, that it is possible to predict with some reliability the chances of success in marriage if certain factors are taken into account. The individual desiring to know himself more fully might well include information about his chances for marital happiness in his self-analysis data collection.

Expectations. Finally, in connection with maturity and marriage, a word needs to be said concerning the expectation that young people bring to marriage. There is widespread agreement among marriage counselors that adolescent dreams, nourished by movies, television, radio, and fiction, when applied to courtship and marriage problems, are responsible for wrecking many potentially happy marriages. The idea that marriage is an accomplished fact once the ceremony is finished and that the couple will live happily ever after is a fantasy promoted by scores of story and movie endings. Its immaturity is obvious. The same attitude would be considered ridiculous in other life situations.

It is trite but true to say that one receives from marriage about what he puts into it. No successful intimate relationship between two people just happens; it is a result of effort by both partners. The earmark of mature love is to desire the happiness of one's mate. The immature person, involved wholly with himself and his own concerns, is anxious to receive, and never to give. He does not perceive his mate as a person with needs and feelings, but will use the mate to enhance his own ego or as a screen onto which he can project his own difficulties. A mature marriage partner will want to contribute to building a family emotional climate that will be most helpful to the other's development and contentment.

Vocational maturity

The vocationally mature person has been defined as "one interested in from one to four specific occupations, one of which ultimately agrees with the reality of measured interests, aptitudes, and ability." In contrast, the vocationally immature person is vague, uncertain, general, and unrealistic in occupational planning. (101:254) Yet, as indicated earlier, maturity, whether emotional, marital, physical, or psychological, does not suddenly overtake the individual. Vocational maturity too, is a process—one that takes place over a period of years. (57) Indeed, research currently emphasizes the concept of "vocational development" in order to avoid giving an impression of instantaneousness, and to point up the unfolding, developmental nature of the vocational choice and adjustment process. (124)

The individual is born with certain physical tendencies or potentialities. He finds himself in an environment that contains demands for tendencies and potentialities with which he interacts in his daily living. As he has experiences and makes use of the resources of his environment, bringing his own tendencies and potentialities to bear upon them, he is performing developmental tasks that hopefully will aid him in moving toward vocational maturity. Strong has used this concept of the interaction of the individual and his environment to explain the development of vocational interests. Interest is seen as an interaction and expression of a person's adjustment to his environment. (119:682) As a person's experiences and opportunities expand, he is, either consciously or (more frequently) unconsciously, exploring himself and the world with the ultimate objective of finding a vocational situation in which he can be comfortable and contented, and in which he can make a socially useful contribution.

A variety of factors and experiences are involved in the process. Fantasies are significant in the vocational preferences of preadolescents, after which interests, aptitudes, values, and external reality factors come into play. One study (17) concluded that four characteristics of individuals and four characteristics of occupations determine occupational entry: (a) the individual's occupational information, technical qualifications, social-role characteristics, and reward-value hierarchy; (b) the occupation's formal opportunities or demands, functional or technical requirements, nonfunctional or social requirements, and amount and types of rewards.

The process of reaching a vocational choice has been described as essentially one of compromise, in which *preferences for* particular occupations are weighed against *expectations of* being able to enter the occupations. The compromise is continually being modified as new information becomes available, and changes in self-concept occur. Thus, it is "a series of inter-related decisions taking place in an extended developmental process." (122) Basically, the process described is one of learning for the individual. He is striving to discover ways in which he can meet his needs, satisfy his values, find outlets for his interests, and use his aptitudes. If he is successful, and finds an occupation that gives the satisfaction of "rewarded use of abilities, the approved meeting of needs, the accepted manifestation of interests, and the social realization of values . . . the result is then an integrated person, whose personal resources are harmoniously allied, attuned to the cultural resources of his environment, and adequate for the developmental tasks with which he must cope." (122) If, on the other hand, learning takes place in a situation that leads to failure—to conflicts between what one wants to do and what one can do, or to the development of abilities that have only marginal acceptance in one's social world—then the result will be "a poorly integrated person who is ill-equipped to fit into his environment and to meet the requirements of society." (122)

From this point of view, the wisdom of—indeed, the necessity for—the maturing person to have available accurate information about occupations, and realistic data about himself, becomes obvious. He needs an opportunity to get occupational information, and to consider it in the light of information about himself. He needs opportunities to test various ways of meeting his needs and achieving his values. He may utilize semi-reality situations such as school clubs, or the reality of a job, or in his own thinking try out his abilities and his interests, and evaluate them. Only as he has such information, analyzes it carefully, and tests it to the best of his ability, can he reasonably hope to achieve vocational maturity.

Vocational maturity is therefore similar to marital maturity and to maturity in other areas of life. The environmental factors will change constantly as the individual meets new problems. The process involved in achieving and maintaining maturity is similar; maturity depends upon the adjustment of the self within the demands of the environment.

SUMMARY

This chapter deals with the process of maturing, the description of mature behavior and thought, and the application of the concept of maturity to life situations. The opposed points of view of adults and young people with regard to the length of time the process of maturing should require are presented as a major concern of contemporary American society. The implications of the two viewpoints are examined as they involve economic, educational, family, and legal questions. Maturation is defined as essentially a process, *beginning at birth, by which the human organism is molded to a pattern of behavior, thought, and response that is unique within limits, yet acceptable to the social group of which one is a member. The persuasive influence of interpersonal relationships in determining the direction that the developing personality will take is emphasized.*

The necessity for the maturing person to free himself from a too-great dependence upon home and family ties, and the very common difficulties in doing so, are cited as relevant concerns of the adolescent period. Equally significant is the establishment of satisfying heterosexual relationships in anticipation of marriage and family life. The balance within the individual of the personal freedom to be independent in action and thought and yet to be responsive to the needs and demands of society and the total environment is seen to be the most significant aspect of maturity. The balance between freedom and responsibility needs to be present in all areas of life, for each person.

Maturity from the standpoint of emotional reaction and control offers further insight into the problems facing young people. The outward manifestations of emotional stability are not only involved but the internalized traits concerned with one's feelings, capacity for concern and compassion toward others, and recognition of the essential humanity of others are also significant.

The young person anxious to weigh and evaluate his own maturity is offered the opportunity to examine himself in terms of standardized descriptions of "the mature person," to have other people rate him by means of personality rating scales, and to make use of data provided by so-called personality tests and inventories. The dimensions of psychological and social maturity presented were:

1. *Security*
2. *Realistic self-evaluation*
3. *Satisfying emotional life*
4. *Accepting and flexible outlook*
5. *Healthy acceptance of bodily activities*
6. *Integrated personality*
7. *Adequate life goals*
8. *Ability to profit from experience*
9. *Satisfactory group membership*
10. *Independence and emancipation from the group*

Finally, an examination of the meaning of maturity is made in terms of its application to two of life's problems. The mature person in marriage and the mature person in a vocation have been chosen as examples of "maturity in action" because they are of greatest concern for most young people in late-adolescent and early-adult years. In each case, the importance of systematic and realistic self-analysis and self-evaluation is emphasized as the most effective way by which the reader may utilize in his own development the concepts presented.

SUPPLEMENTARY SOURCES

Cole, Luella, *Psychology of Adolescence* (4th ed.). New York: Rinehart & Company, Inc., 1954.

Jersild, Arthur T., *Child Psychology* (4th ed.). Englewood Cliffs, N. J.: Prentice-Hall, Inc., 1955.

————, *In Search of Self*. New York: Bureau of Publications, Teachers College, Columbia University, 1955.

Landis, Paul H., *Adolescence and Youth*. New York: McGraw-Hill Book Company, Inc., 1947.

Levy, John, and Ruth Munroe, *The Happy Family*. New York: Alfred A. Knopf, Inc., 1938.

Mead, Margaret, *Male and Female*. New York: William Morrow & Company, 1949.

Morgan, Clifford T., *Introduction to Psychology*. New York: McGraw-Hill Book Company, Inc., 1956.

Young, Kimball, *Personality and Problems of Adjustment* (2nd ed.). New York: Appleton-Century-Crofts, Inc., 1952.

Counseling is invaluable in setting and reaching goals

Part III

PROCESS OF
SELF-ANALYSIS AND
SELF-UNDERSTANDING

Part III takes the student into a process of self-analysis and self-appraisal. "Individual Differences" opens Part III so that students may begin to appreciate that the process of self-analysis and self-appraisal is unique for each person.

The chapters that follow allow each student to examine himself carefully in many fields. Areas of study include vocational interest, aptitude, intelligence, scholastic aptitude, and other related factors.

Chapter 13, the "Process of Self-Analysis," gives each student an opportunity to unify his self-analysis learnings and to present such information in an orderly fashion. Appendix C, the Self-Analysis Student Workbook, focuses for students the material of the chapters in a personal, private way. The "personal application" sections of the workbook allow each student to study examples in the text material from a personal view. The "self-analysis essay" draws these personal sections together.

*M*ost *individuals* excel at some activities and are poor in others. Some persons are outstanding scholars but mediocre athletes; others make fine journalists but poor mechanics; and still others succeed as scientists who would have failed as salesmen. Such is the nature of individual differences. It is just as incorrect to think that everyone has the same mental characteristics (that is, intelligence, aptitude, interest, and personality) as it is to think that all individuals possess the same physical characteristics (such as height and weight) and

Chapter 8

INDIVIDUAL DIFFERENCES

physical prowess (such as running, jumping, and throwing).

Psychologists have devised some comparatively accurate instruments for measuring individual differences. They are in the process now of constantly refining these measuring devices with a view toward achieving greater and greater accuracy. The range of their interest is well expressed by Cronbach in his book *Essentials of Psychological Testing.*

> The testing movement in Europe and America stands as a prime example of social science in action, since it touches on vital questions in all phases of life. What is character, and what type of children have good character? What personality make-up promises that an adolescent will be a stable, effective adult? How can we tell which six-year-olds are ready to begin learning to read? Is this young man a good prospect for training in watchmaking, or should he go into a different vocation—say, steamfitting or patternmaking? Such are the problems to which testing and research on individual differences direct their efforts. (39:3)

This statement raises questions dealing directly with the variability of human behavior. It suggests that not only does human behavior vary, but that this variability is meaningful

123

and important for the individual and for the society in which he lives.

Democracy is intrinsically related to this very notion of individual differences, if freedom of expression is considered a necessary corollary of a democratically conceived society. A society that is autocratic in nature, contrary to popular belief, is the society that considers its members (the masses) as equals. That is to say, all men are created equal, and woe be to the one who gets out of line! On the contrary, a democratically oriented society recognizes the principle that individuals differ, and attempts to make allowances for them.

Perhaps the accompanying illustration will serve to clarify this.

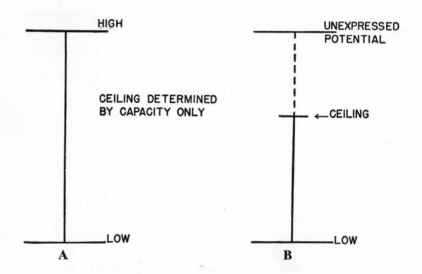

Figures A and B would place creative thinking ability on a continuum ranging from low to high. Figure A suggests that individuals in a democratic society vary in this respect and that this variability is allowed full expression. Figure B suggests that although the same range of differences exists in an autocratic society, limits are set on the extent to which this characteristic is allowed expression. Hence, this latter group is forced to think alike, a false way of making all individuals equal.

In our society it is possible to give the individual information about himself, and, on the basis of that information, the individual (within rational limits) is allowed to make his own decisions. In autocratic societies the state makes the selection and the decision. The former would appear to offer greater opportunities for individual satisfaction and independence, since the individual must assume the responsibility for his decision.

HISTORICAL PERSPECTIVE

Plato (108:632) was one of the first to note and recognize the importance of individual differences. In Book II of the *Republic* he states, "I am myself reminded that we are not all alike; there are diversities of natures among us which are adapted to different occupations."

Plato's views of social and political theory were founded on this very concept of individual differences. He failed to realize, however, the extent of these differences, and as a result his concept of individual differences was a narrow and restrictive one. Plato had everyone falling into one of three intellectual classes, the philosopher, the soldier, and the craftsman. Such a classification scheme obviously fails to consider the wide range of differences possible within a given class.

The ancient Hebrews had some rather interesting notions of individual differences. According to Drazin (47:105) the Hebrews not only knew that such differences existed among the pupils but also endeavored to classify them. They said, for example, "There are four types among pupils: swift to hear and swift to lose—his gain is cancelled by his loss; slow to hear and slow to lose—his loss is cancelled by his gain; swift to hear and slow to lose—this is a happy lot; slow to hear and swift to lose—this is an evil lot." The ancient Hebrews relied almost exclusively on memory or retention as the method of education. This is reflected in their classification scheme. It is interesting to note that the student who remembers quickly ("swift to hear") and does not forget ("slow to lose") is considered a "happy lot." The "dull" student who remembers only after much difficulty ("slow to hear") and forgets quickly ("swift to lose") is considered an "evil lot." Much the same stigma is attached to the slow learner in some schools today.

Chronologically, the significant recognition of individual differences was brought to a focus in 1796. It was in this year that Maskelyne, the royal astronomer at the Greenwich observatory, dismissed his assistant Kinnebrook. The dismissal was due to a discrepancy in Kinnebrook's observations of the times of stellar transits as compared to the observations of his chief, Maskelyne. These observations depended to a large extent upon the sensory acuity (eyes and ears) of the individual observer. In 1816, Bessel, a German astronomer, read of the Kinnebrook incident and considered the possibility of a discrepancy between observers as being a result of individual differences in reaction time rather than the observer's incompetence. To prove his point, Bessel set about determining the "personal equation" of different observers. The personal equation or error of each observer was determined by recording the differences in seconds between the estimates of two trained observers. Bessel was surprised to learn that not only did the estimates of two observers differ, but that reported estimates made by the same observer varied from time to time. Individuals differed then, not only from one another, but also within each other. This would suggest that there are *intra-* as well as *inter-*individual differences.

First the astronomers and then the psychologists became concerned with the nature and extent of these differences. Their methods for studying them varied from the dubious findings of chance observation to the comparative sanctity of the experimental laboratory. News of the existence and signifi- cance of individual differences became widespread. The measurement of individual differences came to dominate the time and energy of investigators throughout the European continent.

Until the turn of the twentieth century, psychologists studying individual differences were primarily concerned with the measurement of simple and isolated "bits" of behavior, that is, the sensory-motor activities such as the speed of reaction time, auditory and visual discriminations, the sensations of smell and touch, pain, motor discrimination and co-ordination tasks. It was not until this century that they turned their attention to the measurement of the more complex behaviors of intelligence, aptitude, interest and person- ality.

It is not the intent of this chapter to deal exhaustively with the develop- ment of the testing movement. It is impossible, however, not to mention names such as Sir Francis Galton, who exhaustively measured a wide range of individual characteristics and devised statistical techniques for dealing with them; James McKeen Cattell, the father of American mental testing; Alfred Binet, a French psychologist who was one of the first investigators to measure intelligence successfully; and Lewis N. Terman, a Stanford Uni- versity professor who took Binet's intelligence test and refined and adapted it to American use.

The advent of World War I was responsible for the development of men- tal testing, as it is known in America today. The mass enlistment of over one and a half million men necessitated the creation of a screening or classi- fication device that would provide reliable intellectual discrimination. Such an instrument had to be easy to administer, had to be "given" to large num- bers at one sitting, and had to be quickly and accurately scored. These re- quirements were met, and thus began group and mass psychological testing.

The individuals, events, and forces that we have just mentioned helped to give impetus to the widespread concern regarding the nature and extent of individual differences.

ASPECTS OF INDIVIDUALITY

In any classroom situation, it is evident that classmates differ from one an- other intellectually. Some students appear to grasp material faster than others, or to arrive at a solution of a complex problem quickly and accurately. The school or college grading system of A, B, C, D, or F illustrates the principle of individual differences, for what this grading system is implying is that students must differ in their capacity to achieve. Otherwise, all students would receive the same grade!

Capacity to achieve and intelligence are related but not synonymous terms. Individuals differ intellectually from A to F or, in terms of I.Q., from 0 to 200 plus. Students are prone to think of themselves as intellectual equals, and therefore differences in achievement are seen as reflections of differences in interest and motivation rather than basic ability. Lindgren (80) refers to this notion as the "anyone-can-be-intelligent myth," and Topps (132) warns "you cannot always do it if you try!"

Individual differences do not, however, follow an "either-or" classification. That is to say, an individual's performance on any test is not either "high or low," "poor or average," or "average or superior." As the discussion that follows will indicate, all such differences are continuous ones. The difference between a grade of A and B is usually an arbitrary one, since the instructor is the one who decides "where the A's end and the B's begin." His "cutting line" is almost always drawn on the basis of some outside criteria, however, so that it is not simply a matter of drawing a line of demarcation. People in general like to think in terms of classifications and categories; it seems to make things easier to understand. It shall become increasingly more evident that psychological characteristics are not so easily and neatly filed.

Hence, while differences in intelligence exist, intelligence needs to be thought of as a continuing factor. Differences in intelligence are matters of degree rather than absolute "either-or" classifications. This would imply that there are degrees of "average" and of "brightness" rather than the curt label that students tend to attach to their acquaintances and classmates: "he's dumb," "she's just plain average," or "he's a bright student."

The infinite variety of vocational and avocational tasks in which individuals participate is generally related to aptitude and interest. This is a notion that tends to be easily accepted and recognized by the population at large, such as: Jim is a good mechanic but a poor carpenter; Mary enjoys typing but loathes bookkeeping; Mike makes a good physician but a poor business man. Such statements imply that the strengths and weaknesses, the likes and dislikes of any individual for a particular task will vary indeterminately. People are more receptive toward accepting this concept because it is less apt to pose an emotional threat, for there is little that a person can do toward defending himself if he is labeled intellectually "stupid." When talking in terms of aptitudes, however, if the individual is chastised in one area, he can usually find consolation in another area in which he feels he is capable. "I may not be as good a pianist as she, but she's no match for me in typing class."

Aptitude and interest are considered to be related but not synonymous terms. In general, aptitude refers to the potential ability an individual possesses for a given kind of activity, and interest, the preference or liking for that particular activity. When both aptitude and interest are found to be high in a particular area, a comparatively high measure of success is usually attained. Individual differences in both aptitude and interest suggest the wide variety of experiences, both success and failure, to which the individual has access. It becomes the task of psychological measurement to improve the probability of those occurrences of experiences that are successful and intrinsically more satisfying to the individual.

Of all the characteristics of humanity, the principle of individual differences is nowhere more apparent than in the consideration of the concept of personality. The infinite variety of behavior that characterizes each individual and makes him a person, unique and distinct from other persons, is referred to as personality. Although individuals are capable of a wide variety of external behavior and internal experience, the way in which these behaviors and experiences are organized tends to be unique for each individual. It is this organization that makes one individual different from an-

STEPHEN GROHE

Aptitudes, abilities, and interests must be carefully correlated

other, and it is the same organization that makes the individual's behavior consistent. For example, Mary's personality is different from Janie's; Mary's personality is also subject to fluctuation and change due to maturation and experience; and Mary is not Mary today, however, and Janie tomorrow. There is an element of consistency here that allows for variation and change. Personality must always be regarded, then, in light of the dual aspect of individual differences, namely, differences "within" as well as differences "between."

The variability of individual performance is regarded as an intra-individual difference. The individual does not always perform a particular task in exactly the same way. It is well to keep in mind, however, that although there is some inconsistency in the response from time to time, the variation is small, except under extreme circumstances. Physical factors tend to have some effect on the individual's behavior, especially in a group testing situation. The effect, however, is generally only minimal. Shifts in motivation, interest, and physical condition all seem to affect the consistency of individual performance on psychological tests. Extreme fluctuations in individual behavior must be regarded as the exception rather than the rule.

Psychological tests are constructed on the premises that (a) individuals *are* different, (b) these differences are measurable, and (c) knowledge of these differences is useful and important.

If all individuals possessed identical psychological characteristics, there would be little point in measuring them, since each individual would be equal to every task. It should make little difference as to who became a doctor, lawyer, auto mechanic, baker, teacher, minister, mason, or carpenter. It would be simply a case of choosing an occupation entirely at random. If one were to plot a curve typifying the way in which human characteristics would distribute themselves, the relationship shown in the accompanying figure would be recorded.

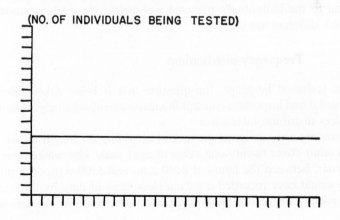

(NO. OF INDIVIDUALS BEING TESTED)

Rather than a curve, a straight line parallel to the baseline is drawn. This suggests that all individuals are equal in the characteristic that is being measured. The need for measuring devices under these circumstances does not exist, since the capabilities and performance of one individual would be typical of the population as a whole.

If it were not possible to measure individual differences, everything that the individual did would be a matter of trial and error or the product of a subjective or intuitive kind of evaluation. The early pioneers in psychological testing have proved beyond question that it is possible to measure certain mental characteristics by the presentation of a variety of materials (problem-solving tasks, reading and vocabulary items, inventories, incomplete sentences). By observing and recording the extent and nature of the changes in behavior that these tasks effect, it is possible to make certain predictions and diagnoses that attain an accuracy not attributable to chance.

By the designing of instruments that will test the extent and direction of these differences it is possible to make certain predictions regarding academic and vocational success and failure, diagnose educational and emotional difficulties (reading, mental retardation, underachievement, emotional stability), and evaluate the effectiveness of educational and industrial training programs.

This unit will especially attempt to familiarize the student with some very simple and basic concepts of measurement. It is hoped that this will serve to facilitate the interpretation and understanding of the student's performance on a wide variety of psychological tests.

SELECTED MEASUREMENT PRINCIPLES

Granting that individual differences exist, and that the quantitative analysis of these differences is vital to the society in which the individual functions and vital to the individual's personal well-being, the curious student may ask "How different are we?"

Frequency distributions

In more technical language, the question that is being asked relates to a fundamental and important concept in measurement—namely, how do these differences distribute themselves?

If a student were assigned the task of obtaining the height measurements of each adult (over twenty-one years of age) male who walked past a certain corner, between the hours of 8:00 a.m. and 5:00 p.m. on a particular day, he would have recorded a meaningless mass of data by the end of the day. A page of his record book might look something like the following:

HEIGHT (ADULT MALES)

Names	Feet	Inches
Smith	5	6
Brown	4	11
Green	6	4
Kelly	5	10
Jones	5	9
O'Brien	5	1
Mello	6	2
Anderson	5	5
Lepska	5	11
Cohen	5	8

In analyzing this data, the student now notes that of the first ten heights recorded, the shortest adult male was 4′ 11″, while the tallest was 6′ 4″. This gives the student a measure of the two extremes. The distribution, although much too small to make very reliable generalizations, suggests a clustering of measures somewhere between the two extremes, and a gradual tapering off at both ends of the distribution. Most physical and psychological characteristics distribute themselves in a similar manner, namely, the grouping or "bunching" of scores near the center of a distribution of scores and a gradual symmetrical "tapering off" at the extremes. This phenomenon of "grouping and tapering off" is referred to in measurement terms as a *normal distribution*. The normal curve is frequently used to portray the characteristics of a normal distribution in graphic terms.

If the hypothetical student mentioned above decided to plot all of the heights recorded during the day on a sheet of graph paper, he would simply plot height against frequency (number of adult males) as follows:

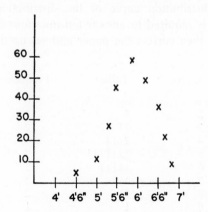

The height distribution of a sample of adult males

Moving from left to right, the first plot means that only one person has a height of 4' 6", while at the 5-foot mark, ten adult marks are recorded. The height having the greatest frequency is near the 6-foot mark and is about 5' 10". This indicates, then, that most of the adult males who walked by this corner were around 5' 10" tall.

The reader is now asked to connect each of the points plotted above. Does this curve possess the characteristics of a normal distribution?

The perfect normal distribution curve can be obtained only when an extremely large number of measurements concerning a particular trait or characteristic are available. It is a theoretical distribution, then, since infinite measures are not obtainable.

On the assumption that it would be possible to record the height measurements of all American males, the distribution of measures would approach the perfect normal curve, as illustrated here:

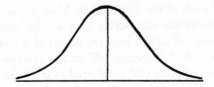

Most distributions, however, only approximate the normal curve. Therefore, the plotting of most distributions will result in somewhat unsymmetrical or "off-center" or irregular or "bumpy" curves.

A frequency distribution based on examination results typifies the approximate normal distribution curve of the distribution. If a class of twenty-five students is required to answer ten questions in a science quiz, the instructor would then correct the paper and set up the following tally sheet:

Raw scores	Tallies	Frequency
1		0
2	1	1
3	11	2
4	1111	4
5	1111111	7
6	11111	5
7	111	3
8	11	2
9	1	1

Each raw score represents the number of items answered correctly in the quiz. The instructor then simply records or tallies the number of students receiving a particular raw score. It then becomes a simple matter to add the tallies and obtain the frequency distribution for the science-quiz results of these twenty-five freshmen.

As the instructor's tally sheet is examined, the frequency column indicates that no one received a perfect score of ten correct answers, and no one got less than two correct answers. Most of the students' scores cluster near the center of the distribution. The frequency column suggests that if this distribution were plotted on a graph it would not be entirely symmetrical. One would also expect to find some "bumps" in this curve. Despite the "unevenness" of this distribution, it has all the characteristics of the normal curve. Individual differences tend to "spread out," then, according to the shape of the normal curve. Individual performance is evaluated according to its location in the distribution. Since it is not possible to use calipers or a yardstick in the measurement of human characteristics, the normal curve thus provides a rationale for measurement.

Measures of central tendency

When raw scores or measures have been obtained and arranged in a distribution or plotted in detail on a graph, the group of individuals measured or tested has been described. This kind of description is a time-consuming and wearisome task. As in all areas of mathematics, other methods are available and are frequently used to express the characteristics of a group. A "short cut" or special measure of the distribution frequently used is the central tendency of the group. Measures of central tendency, as the name would imply, do just that—namely, describe the central point in the distribution, that is, tendency toward the center or average. These measures are thus used to typify the group as a whole. There are three measures of central tendency most commonly employed:

1. *Mean =* the arithmetical average—that is, the sum of all scores divided by their number.
2. *Median =* the midpoint in a distribution—that is, that point on either side of which 50 per cent of the cases lie.
3. *Mode =* score of greatest frequency—that is, the score in a distribution appearing the greatest number of times.

In the following distribution of scores, 7,6,6,6,5,4,3,3,2,1,1, the **mean, median,** and **mode** are easily obtained.

Since the *mean* is obtained by simply adding all the scores and dividing by the number of scores, the following formula would be applicable:

$$\text{Mean} = \frac{\text{sum of scores}}{\text{total number of cases}} = \frac{44}{11} = 4$$

The *median score* is also found to be 4 since it is the middlemost score.

The *mode* is a measure of central tendency that is rarely used, since it is least accurate in measure. It is used only when a quick estimate of the central tendency of a large distribution of scores is needed. By quickly checking the scores in the above distribution, the mode (that is, the score that appears the greatest number of times) is easily found to be 6.

Measures of central tendency represent one device for obtaining a description of scores. There are other techniques for obtaining more accurate descriptions of a particular distribution of scores, but they are, however, comparatively more complex and not deemed essential to an introductory consideration of the principles of measurement.

Norms and norm groups

If a carpenter reported the length of a new and unfinished room as being sixteen the first question that the potential home owner would ask would be, "Sixteen what? Feet? Yards? Inches? Meters?"

The number "sixteen" is meaningless unless the carpenter reports the "standard" of measurement he is using. If the carpenter had reported the length of the room as being sixteen feet, the potential customer would have a reasonable notion as to the actual length of the room. It is only through the use of commonly accepted standards, such as feet and inches, that a person is able to interpret measures as being "too long," "too short," or "about right."

Similarly, in the field of mental testing, a test score alone is meaningless, and is made meaningful only through the use of *standards* or *norms*. A *norm* is synonymous with the term standard, and provides the test interpreter with a kind of yardstick for evaluation. When norms are available, the individual is able to judge, fairly accurately, as to "how high" or "how low" his test performance falls.

Norms are obtained in psychological testing by administering a particular test to a large sample of individuals, similar to those for whom the test was designed. If the test utilized is purported to measure scholastic aptitude, the large sample will obviously be made up of individuals in a "scholastic" situation, such as "freshmen entering college," or "graduate students." Similarly, the norms for a test of mechanical aptitude are obtained by administering the test to a large sample of individuals working in mechanics. These large samples are referred to as *norm groups,* since the performance of these groups will be used as the norm or standard to evaluate the performance of other individuals.

Norm groups are based on a large number of individuals who are assumed to be representative of the total population for whom the test was devised. This is done since it would be impossible and impractical to test

the total population (for example, all the college freshmen in the U.S.A.).
It becomes apparent, however, that the larger the population sample, the
more representative it becomes of the total population, resulting in the
increased reliability of the norms.

Hence, after a test has been standardized (administered to a norm
group), the scores of the norm group are rearranged to form a frequency
distribution. The individual who later takes the test can then compare his
performance with the representative group. He will then have a reliable
estimate as to how far above or below average his performance places him
with regard to the norm group.

After taking an intelligence test, a student finds that he has a raw score
(total number correct) of 50. He is given a table of norms, and finds the
following:

Norm group	Mean or average score
Non-high school graduate	32
High school graduate	40
Freshman entering college	50
Medical school student	65

This table of norms suggests that the student above is superior, intellectually, to both non-high school and high school graduates. When his score
of 50 is compared with the mean for freshmen entering college, it is noted
that this student is just average himself. When his score is compared with
the mean score for medical school students, it is seen that his score falls
considerably below the average. This is due, of course, to the fact that he
is now being compared to a highly selected intellectual group.

It must be noted that, if the student mentioned above is a high school
graduate, contemplating college, then the "freshman entering college" norms
would be most applicable. It would be meaningless to interpret this student's test performance on the basis of any other norms. The most appropriate norms available must always be used. A potential plumber would
compare his scores with those of plumbers successfully employed in that
line of work, just as a high school senior considering an engineering education would compare his scores with freshmen entering engineering school.
The norm group selected, then, must be meaningfully related to the testee.
If this is not done, any interpretations made will be invalid, and in some
instances ridiculous. A norm group needs to be large enough also in order
to approximate a normal curve of distribution or the data will be meaningless in most instances.

Derived scores

The raw score of 50 mentioned above becomes meaningful only upon comparison with the performance of others. The student was able to evaluate

his score in terms of a general classification of "above average" or "below average." He was unable, however, to determine just how far "above" or "below" average his score placed him. By converting a raw score to a *derived score,* the individual is able to do this—that is, to locate himself more precisely in a distribution of scores.

Percentiles. A type of derived score most frequently used is the percentile. The percentile score simply states the percentage of persons or cases in a given norm group that falls below a particular score. The percentile score gives the individual an accurate measure of his relative standing in a large distribution of scores. A percentile indicates where on the normal curve of distribution the student's score is located. Raw scores are converted to percentile scores by means of conversion tables. If a raw score of 20 is found to place a student on the 5th percentile, this would mean that 5 per cent of the persons taking this test obtain scores lower than this. Similarly, 33 per cent of the cases fall below the 33rd percentile, 50 per cent of the cases fall below the 50th percentile, and 78 per cent of the cases fall below the 78th percentile, and so on. It is to be noted that the 50th percentile is the median or middlemost score and as such represents the "average." Because psychological tests are susceptible to some degree of error, allowances must always be made for the imperfection of the measuring instruments. It is to be noted, therefore, that in the majority of cases, any score falling between the 40th and 60th percentiles falls within the median or average range.

After taking a scholastic aptitude test, a college candidate may find that he has obtained a raw score of 21 on this test. He may then obtain the following conversion table:

SCHOLASTIC APTITUDE TEST

(Norms of freshmen entering college)

Number of correct items	Percentile score
78	99
64	90
58	80
54	70
50	60
46	50
41	40
36	30
28	20
21	10
12	1

The candidate's raw score of 21 is comparable to a percentile score of 10. A 10th percentile score would mean that 10 per cent of freshmen entering college obtain scores lower than this. Interpreted another way, 90 per cent of freshmen entering college do better on this test than the above candidate did. The prognosis in this case for a successful freshman year would appear to be a very poor one.

Age scores. Age scores indicate the average performance of persons of each age. A pupil with a reading achievement age of ten years is able to read as well as the average ten-year-old pupil. An eight-year-old pupil reading at the ten-year level is obviously accelerated in this respect. Age scores are frequently used at the elementary and junior-high-school level, and become less applicable at higher levels.

Grade scores. Grade scores indicate the average performance of children in each grade. In securing the grade score, the pupil's raw score is converted into an average grade status, instead of an age position. The pupil who obtains a reading grade of 4.0 is comparable in his reading skill to the average fourth grader. He may be accelerated or retarded in this respect depending upon his grade placement at the time of the test.

Mental age and I.Q. A type of derived score that takes into account two variables at the same time is the intelligence quotient or I.Q. Here the individual's performance on a mental test is expressed in terms of "mental age." The mental age, like the age score, is defined as the age for which a given score is the average.

Although the mental age measures the pupil's performance, a measure of his brightness in relation to normal expectation for his age is helpful. Such a measure is referred to as the intelligence quotient. The I.Q. is the ratio of mental age to chronological age (a person's age from birth). Thus:

$$\text{I.Q.} = \frac{\text{mental age}}{\text{chronological age}} \times 100 = \frac{\text{MA}}{\text{CA}} \times 100$$

The I.Q. is computed by simply making substitutions into the formula above. The mental-age score is based on the individual's test performance. The number 100 is introduced into the formula purely as a matter of expediency, since it serves to eliminate fractions and decimal points.

DANGERS IN TEST INTERPRETATION

The student must not lose sight of the fact that test scores are not absolute measures. Intra-individual differences become evident in the relative nature of test performances. If the imperfections of psychological testing instruments and the assumptions made regarding norm groups are considered, one sees that the validity and reliability of psychological measures may vary and therefore should be examined.

Perhaps a brief discussion of the principles underlying the use of norm groups will serve to demonstrate the fallibility of standardized test scores.

College-freshmen norm tables are based on "a certain number" of scores of college freshmen who have taken that particular test. This sample is assumed to be a typical cross-section of the total college-freshmen population. Is this assumption justified? The true norm group would be the total population of college freshmen, which, of course, cannot be obtained. Since the usual norm is based on a sampling of the total college-freshmen population it is only an estimate of the true norm group. All tests are based on norms obtained in this way for reasons of expediency and practicality. Statisticians are able to compute the limits within which the norm group appears to be representative of a total group. It is not necessary at this point to understand the mathematical logic involved or the formula used to accept the fact that some psychological tests yield extremely accurate results, but the relative nature of most human characteristics makes standardized measurement still an "approximate" rather than "exact" scientific tool.

Self-concept and test interpretation

Unless an individual's performance on a test "fits into" his concept of self, he may reject certain or all measures of ability, aptitude, interest, or of other things. He may soon forget his test scores, or make excuses for them, such as, "I wasn't feeling well when I took those tests." The individual finds ways of defending himself when the situation becomes threatening. Test scores become meaningful and important only when the individual is ready to accept and assimilate them into his frame of reference. Many individuals have pictures of the kind of persons they think they are, but they are uncertain as to how much is fact and how much is fiction. A person's relative performance on a test gives him a measure of one aspect of reality because he can determine his performance in comparison with that of other students. The test interpreter is able to give the student information relative to an aspect of self as it approaches reality, that is to say, a picture of the kind of person the student is, despite the fact that this may sometimes be at variance with the picture or image the student has of himself.

To be truly effective, however, test interpretation operates on two assumptions: first, that the student has an understanding of the mechanics of measurement as discussed in this chapter; and, secondly, that he is genuinely ready and willing to discuss, consider, and assimilate the implications of the findings of measurement.

A counselor may interpret test scores and discuss some of their implications with the student, if the student so requests. The student may "keep" or "throw out" test data in accordance with the dictates of his self-concept. Frequently, the student is not aware of this "filtering-out" process. He rationalizes or represses unconsciously. This acceptance or rejection of information of a highly personal nature is a function of the extent to which the individual perceives it as a threat to the existence of his concept of self.

It is the task of the skilled counselor to "know" when the student is "ready" for test interpretation. Frequently, a discussion of test results will serve as the basis for a consideration of other and more pertinent aspects of the self-concept.

Decision making

Some students labor under the false illusion that if they take enough tests they will then know what they are supposed to do. Test results cannot make decisions for a person. They furnish the testee with additional information about himself, but test scores in and of themselves do not supply answers— only relative facts or data. It remains to the discretion and the responsibility of the student to supply those answers for himself. Test scores, then, supplement the individual's knowledge of himself and serve as additional sources and cues from which the individual can draw in arriving at sensible and sound decisions or solutions.

The results of a scholastic aptitude test may give the student some notion as to his chances for success in college. On the basis of his test performance, his chances, in statistical terms, may be poor, fair or excellent. The test does not, however, answer the question, "Will I succeed in college?" This is a decision the student must make for himself. His decision may be a sound one or a poor one. It is hoped that the availability of test data will add to his fund of self-knowledge and thereby increase the probability of his making a judgment that will have successful consequences for him.

Tests of special aptitudes and interests generally do not "point" to one specific vocation. Rather, they help to eliminate certain vocational areas and encourage the investigation of others. Educational and vocational tests are usually broad in their implications. Such nontest factors as parental pressure, sex, religious affiliation, nationality, ethnic group, socioeconomic needs and cultural ethics will help swing the pendulum of temporary indecision in one direction or the other.

It should become increasingly apparent to the reader, as he progresses, that test scores are an important but incomplete source of material from which predictions, decisions, and solutions evolve. The existence of significant but unmeasured factors in human behavior and experience suggest that test scores are but one aspect of the total pattern.

SUMMARY

Chapter 8, "Individual Differences," deals with the quantitative aspect of self-analysis and understanding. Through a study of measurement an individual can begin to understand and appreciate how each person is different from every other person. Similarities of appearance, ability, and interest, and other factors may cause a person to believe that he is the same as others, but from a factual view of biological science and psychology he should know that there are no two persons exactly alike. The many complexities of society allow for the unique contributions of many persons. If it is possible to measure individual differences (within reasonable degrees) an individual might then begin to know his or her own strengths and weaknesses and therefore to plan more effectively for the future.

It is hoped that through the acquisition of basic skills and tools, the student will be better able to appraise his strengths and limitations and thereby increase his chances of making sound educational and vocational plans. By comparing his test performance with the performance of similar students on the same test, and "seeing" his performance as a "point" in a distribution of scores having the contours of a normal curve, the student will find that he now possesses skills and knowledge that are fundamental to an understanding of individual differences.

When one begins to appraise himself realistically in the light of objective data, examines his strong points and weak ones, accepts them and makes positive and constructive plans in light of them, he is achieving a primary goal of education—namely, the understanding of himself and the world around him by means of critical thinking.

SUPPLEMENTARY SOURCES

Anastasi, Anne, *Psychological Testing*. New York: The Macmillan Company, 1954.

———, and John P. Foley, Jr., *Differential Psychology, Individual and Group Differences in Behavior*. New York: The Macmillan Company, 1949.

Cronbach, Lee J., *Essentials of Psychological Testing*. New York: Harper & Brothers, 1949.

———, and Goldine C. Gleser, *Psychological Tests and Personnel Decisions*. Urbana, Illinois: The University of Illinois Press, 1957.

Lindgren, Henry Clay, *Psychology of Personal and Social Adjustment*. New York: American Book Company, 1953.

Munn, Norman L., *Psychology* (3rd ed.). Boston: Houghton Mifflin Company, 1956.

Thorndike, Robert L., and Elizabeth Hagen, *Measurement and Evaluation in Psychology and Education*. New York: John Wiley & Sons, Inc., 1955.

nterest is perhaps the most easily seen of all personality factors, and therefore is an early reference point in the process of self-analysis. Interests tell much about personality. Not only do the type of activities enjoyed by a person indicate what kind of a person he is, but they also tell something about his values and goals. The boy who would rather continue skating than hurry home to a meal seems to be getting a good deal of pleasure from his pastime, and he may also be spurred on by the hope of becoming a national champion. The girl

Chapter 9

VOCATIONAL INTEREST

who chooses to attend Red Cross First Aid classes instead of meeting her friends at the corner drugstore may be the kind of girl who sincerely wants to help others, and may also be thinking of nursing as her future career. The boy who earns his own spending money and spends it all on buying his friends ice cream or sodas no doubt has different values and goals from the boy who spends all of his hard-earned money on model airplanes. The individual is generally interested in the things that he considers important and of personal value. He is prepared to spend his time upon that which gives him the most personal pleasure and satisfaction. Looking at interests may furnish a key to the understanding of a personality; some of the old proverbs and sayings illustrate this idea well. "By his deeds ye shall know him" or, "Actions speak louder than words," "Sow a habit, reap a character" are phrases that indicate a common belief that activities tell about personality. Because interests are visible and fairly simple to examine they form a good beginning for study in the process of directed and conscious self-analysis.

    Educational and vocational planning demands that stu-

dents recognize the importance of interests and give particular attention to
the later development of activity interests into patterns of vocational interests. As a psychological principle in education this idea is comparatively
recent, but the idea has been simply accepted for generations. The satisfaction of a job well done, such as the medieval craftsman is said to have felt
in his work, was recognized by other artisans and his customers as the outcome of his love of his work, and an indication of his genuine interest.
Whether it was working on a great cathedral, hand stitching a saddle, blow-
ing glass or shoeing a horse, his pride in accomplishment was closely associated with his interest. The most successful man in those days was usually
the man most happy at his work. In our complex modern times this fact is
still recognized. In order to succeed in a position or a job a person needs
to have a vocational interest in that field of work. To be a successful carpenter a man must like working with wood, he must enjoy measuring,
sawing, planning and finishing. To be a successful pharmacist a man must
like mixing drugs, interpreting formulas and also be interested in studying
the ever-increasing research on new drugs. To be a successful artist a person must enjoy painting in the media of his choice, or sketching in pencil
or charcoal, depicting life or still life as he sees it, and also regard his work
as the best means of conveying his ideas and feelings to others. More simply
expressed then, a vocational interest may arise from a liking for or enjoyment in particular kinds of work activities and it thus becomes an expression of personality.

At this point it is worth while to note and compare some definitions of
the general term interest, of which vocational interest is a derivative. Dictionary definitions of interest read something like this:

1. A force that motivates activity.
2. A mental set that urges a person on in a certain direction.
3. A tendency to select one activity in preference to another.
4. A liking for some activity.

G. Frederic Kuder, one of the well known researchers into the theory of
interest, who is the author of the much used Kuder Preference Record, describes interest as an attitude toward an activity or response to emotions.
Walter V. Bingham describes interest as "a tendency to engage in an activity as opportunity offers, to concentrate attention on it, and to prolong
it because of the satisfaction it yields." (15:62) In keeping with this idea
that the degree of satisfaction obtained determines the persistence of the
interest, Donald E. Super of Columbia University gives an interesting theory
of the origin and dynamics of interest. His approach (122) seems to suggest a division into four parts:

(a) A person experiences a need or drive, that may be of biological origin, but as expressed earlier, the drive through learning becomes a motive.

(b) A tension results from this motive that seeks release through activity.

(c) The activity perceived as offering release is the interest.

(d) Special abilities, general abilities, opportunities and the nature of the need itself, make certain types of activities more satisfying than others, so that the specific interest changes from time to time, but the basic interest persists.

A very simple example of this theory would be:

(a) A need such as hunger or thirst, set up by a biological or physical condition, exists.

(b) An unpleasant feeling of emptiness or dryness causing tension results.

(c) The activity of eating or drinking meets the need, and tension is relaxed.

(d) Food and drink are the perceived "interests" that satisfy the need. Various types of food and drink can bring about satisfaction in different people.

VOCATIONAL INTEREST AND PERSONALITY

Interests are as much part of the total person as the physical appearance. We frequently indicate acceptance of this fact, for when describing a friend we often add, "he has mechanical interests," or "she is very artistic" or maybe we say "sports are his main interest" or "he's a real bookworm." Such phrases are even linked with physical description in such a way that the listener is able to identify the person quite easily. More frequently we may say "I have forgotten the fellow's name, but you know him—he's the chap who is always talking about sailing." As different stages in life are reached, interests alter, develop, or persist just as physical attributes do.

Interests may be common to the group or unique to the individual but the fact remains that interests are significant parts of personality. In personal relationships the presence or absence of common interest between individuals is a pertinent factor. Either as an aid in conversation in early acquaintance, or as a foundation for more permanent friendship, common interests aid good human relations. They also form attractions between individuals in group relations and are basic factors in group dynamics. Much of life is founded on common interests, springing from common needs, but the satisfaction of those needs can be met in a variety of ways, and this leads to individual patterns of interests. During developmental growth each individual evolves for himself a behavioral pattern best suited to his own individual needs. Individuality in interests thus develops along with the development of the self, and it helps to create variety and vitality in each personality.

A general underlying basic need causes the individual to develop ways of obtaining satisfactions that become in turn deep and broad personal preferences referred to as basic interest patterns. These basic interests tend to persist and become a vital function of personality; they become the general manner in which the individual is likely to react in different situations. As new situations are presented and new opportunities occur this "basic interest" has a variety of expressions that change from time to time, and these are generally referred to as "specific interests." For example, an individual may develop a basic pattern of interest due to his need for belonging: at the age of seven this is seen in a specific interest in gang games of the cowboy and Indian type; at fourteen his interest is expressed as a member of his high school band; and then at nineteen his specific interest is working with the young people's group at his church. Although these specific interests at different ages result in different activities, they are only reactions to the opportunities for socially acceptable behaviors that are part of a basic interest in being with people in order to satisfy the underlying need of belonging.

Other basic needs cause various basic interest patterns to develop. The needs for affection, independence, for feelings of personal worth, and for security are a few of the basic needs that set up tensions in the human body and mind that result in efforts on the part of the individual to find means of satisfying himself. The child who has feelings of insecurity may develop an interest in reading; in the realm of fiction he can forget the threatening situations of real life. This specific reading interest may or may not persist. If it does continue, it does so because a satisfying pattern of behavior evolves that gives the child a socially acceptable method of fleeing from reality. Other opportunities, however, within his scholastic and social experiences may offer alternative means of satisfying this same basic need. His interest in reading may seem to disappear, an interest in drama either in the form of going to plays or joining acting groups may develop, or interests in art or music may become absorbing. Any one or all of these would offer realms in which the threatening situations of real life could be avoided or forgotten. Thus, this behavior pattern of evading situations where feelings of insecurity are most threatening and seeking and finding other situations apart from reality forms the basic interest pattern in this instance; specific interests are the different activities through which, from time to time, the individual is able to meet the underlying need. The specific interests vary according to the opportunities presented and the socially acceptable forms of behavior available to the individual.

INTERESTS AND VOCATIONAL CHOICE

Specific interest patterns tend to develop just as general behavior patterns do through experience and learning. During this developmental stage, social needs, social pressures, and social expectancies play important parts in the selection of interests. The environmental factors and personality needs thus become interwoven determining agents, both with and without any appreciation of their effects by the individual. As man is placed in society as an interacting human being, and not as a solitary animal, he is greatly dependent upon others for the means of satisfying both his physical and his social needs. The specific interests that each man develops and takes unto himself tend to be those best suited to his own individual and unique place in society, yet these same interests are also dependent upon satisfactory interpersonal relationships, and thus are closely related to his personality development. Recent research into the reasons behind vocational choice suggests that a person's choice of occupation may be definitely related to his basic personality needs. If such be the case, it is even more likely that the selection of interests is also closely related to the same area of personality needs. It has been observed that persons engaged in similar occupations tend to have similar interests.

Stages of vocational interest development

Vocational interests pass through many phases that affect the process of vocational choice. Eli Ginzberg and his associates (57), in their study of occupational choice, found that the process of occupational choice appeared to pass through three consecutive periods that they described as fantasy, tentative, and final. Vocational interests pass through quite similar periods. A child becomes fascinated by the local traffic policeman and is sure he will be a policeman when he grows up. He takes an airplane ride one day, and from that time decides he will become a pilot. A child's interests are variable, and easily affected by the adults with whom he comes in contact. His vocational choices are often far removed from reality. He has no concept of when or how his ambition will be accomplished, as it is sufficient for him that it is "not today," but "sometime." He is content to enjoy the fantasy. With the growth of knowledge and more experiences both at home and at school, the child becomes absorbed in pleasure-giving activities. His vocational choice then becomes linked with specific interests based on these pleasure-producing activities. Ginzberg calls this "function pleasure." The young person wants to be a road worker so that he can drive the steam roller and make the road smooth. He wants to be a painter so that he may put paint on the fence. Later, however, there is a distinct shift in interests showing concern for the results and rewards of work. The eight-year-old says he wants to be a doctor, so that he can help his family if any-one is sick. At this time interests are very strongly influenced by school learning. Horizons are extended by reading stories and by being exposed to new experiences. There is a tendency to be spectacular and grandiose or adventuresome in making vocational choices at this stage. Still, choices are not linked with reality, the child has no concept of the means to the end, nor is he conscious of any inappropriateness in his choice.

Gradually, with intellectual growth, vocational interests are affected by knowledge of the world outside the immediate surroundings. Childhood gives way to adolescence, and many factors now influence interests. Identi-fication with a much-admired adult, the father, uncle, or aunt, a favorite teacher, or some outstanding sports figure may be the particular influence. At this time parents begin to show concern about vocational interests and vocational choice. Some parents become directive, making educational plans for their offspring without careful consideration of their child's in-terests and abilities. The young adolescent becomes aware of the time ele-ment, and thoughts about the kind of person he wants to become enter his mind. Interests at this time will begin to indicate the goals and values that the individual is beginning to build. This image of the future person plays a significant part in changing vocational interests. Tentative choices now have to be made, for it becomes necessary at this time to select high school courses and make plans for further education.

Expressed interests

The fact that an individual expresses interest in certain activities may prove, upon deeper investigation, to be misleading. The essential element in interest is that the individual gains personal satisfaction only through the investment of effort. It is significant that true interests necessitate participa-tion and action; they cannot be entirely passive. Expressed interests are frequently the outcome of an awareness of social pressures. These types of interests are expressed because they are often demanded by the society in which we live. A person may say he is interested in politics, but if he does not read the political news regularly or follow political-party development critically or contribute financially or personally to political causes—his ex-pression of interest is merely lip service—saying what he thinks he is ex-pected to say. Another individual may say he is very interested in drama, but if he does not try to see some new plays, read plays for enjoyment, choose plays for his radio listening or select plays for his television pro-grams, sometimes participate in community play productions, or take part in summer stock, then his expression of interest in drama is perfunctory, with little real meaning. Expressed interests are thus often poor foundations for making vocational choices.

Maturity and vocational interest

Every time the individual is exposed to a learning situation, every time he partakes of education, the experience causes a change in the self-picture. As Arthur T. Jersild says, "The learner has not put a new patch on himself, the whole fabric of the self has to a degree been changed." (68:100) Experience and learning may bring a new concept of potentials and powers or a new understanding of limitations. This process of the changing self is an important part of maturity. Vocational interests can only be taken as criteria on which to base vocational choice when a realistic self-concept has been established, and a mature image of the self is beginning to take shape. Most psychologists today recognize that there is a direct relationship between an individual's self-concept and his vocational interests. Maturity in one area affects the realism of the other area. Thus this process of self-analysis, beginning with a look at vocational interests, can be a most significant factor in achieving a realistic self-concept. The young man who sees himself as a future famous surgeon without looking at his intelligence, scholastic aptitudes, specific skills, interests, personality, and health in a realistic manner is showing his immaturity and revealing his unrealistic self-concept. The mature mind faces facts and relates the past, present and the future within a framework of reality.

MEASURING VOCATIONAL INTERESTS

Many check lists, questionnaires and preference records have been developed to measure interests. Some of the most commonly used are:

1. The Kuder Preference Record (74)
2. The Strong Vocational Interest Blank (120)
3. The California Occupational Interest Inventory (102)

Kuder Preference Record

The Kuder Preference Record is one of the most commonly encountered interest inventories. It is suitable for use with both high school and college groups, and is comparatively simple to take and easy to score. The questions are arranged as an inventory, with each item presenting three choices. By a system of marking the activity liked most, and the one liked the least,

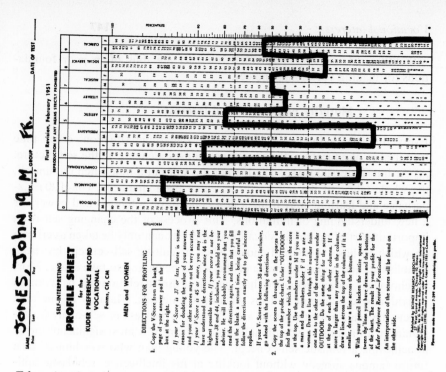

Educational and vocational planning demands that students recognize the importance of interests and their relationships to aptitudes and abilities.

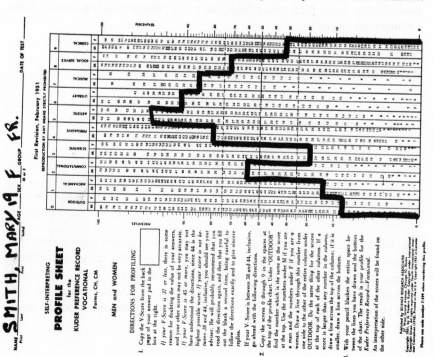

scores are obtained in different interest areas. These results may be compared with general population, male and female, norms. Extensive research has been carried out with this inventory in measuring professions. Consequently, it is possible to compare results with the scores of typical interest patterns in specific fields of work. Ten main interest areas are used in this inventory: outdoor, mechanical, computational, scientific, persuasive, artistic, literary, musical, social service, and clerical. (For detailed descriptions of these areas, see Appendix B.)

Strong Vocational Interest Blank

The Strong Vocational Interest Blank has different forms for men and women, and is used both individually and in groups. It is more complex to score than other interest measures but it gives more specific results. There are some four hundred and twenty items to which responses must be made. It has been found that the person making these responses tends to treat items that are important to him in the same way, again and again. Thus, a dominant interest persists. Results are tabulated to give indications of interests in contrasted areas: social or intellectual; scientific or linguistic; mechanical or commercial. The interest patterns of thirty-nine male occupations and eighteen female occupations have been derived and are used in basic comparisons. The inventory is based on the fact that Strong found that successful people in the same occupational field indicated similarity of interests and also patterns of interest that contrasted with those of the general population. Results are claimed to indicate whether, granted the necessary ability and requisite training, a person will probably enjoy that kind of work and find himself among associates with tastes and likings similar to his own.

UNDERSTANDING VOCATIONAL INTEREST

Interest inventories are not the only way of assessing possible vocational interests. Although interest does not necessarily mean that an appropriate ability coincides, it has been found that individuals generally tend to enjoy doing things they do well. It is often worth while, however, to look into a few other areas that may indicate the presence of an interest that has not been either expressed or measured.

Many hobbies can indicate interest areas. Some hobbies such as making airplane models, cabinet making, building "hot-rods" and constructing radios suggest mechanical interests. Activities such as gardening, raising pets, or collecting wild flowers might be classed as outdoor interests. Social activities also can be recognized as interest pointers. The boy who belongs to the opera club, or the glee club, or plays in a local dance band does not need an interest measure to discover his musical interest. It is wise, however, to view a hobby or leisure-time activity in some detail to see what interest it does represent. Photography might indicate an outdoor interest, or a scientific interest in developing pictures, or an interest in people, depending on the emphasis placed on the various activities it involves.

Although students are generally concerned with earning money by part-time or summer work, the fact that an individual chooses a certain type of work may have significance and suggest a type of interest. Work as a counselor in a children's camp or as a waitress, or part-time nurses' aide, may indicate some degree of social-service interest. Working as a cashier in the supermarket may show some computational interest. If the job was enjoyed and done efficiently it is fairly safe to conclude that the experience and the activities proved to be interesting.

Another area indicating vocational interests may be the school subjects that were liked and in which good grades were obtained. It is, however, better to take good grades in a particular subject to indicate some interest but not necessarily high interest. Research has generally served to show only that a more positive correlation exists between grades and ability than between grades and interests.

The clear-cut differentiation of interests into patterns may mislead students to believe that the interpretation of a vocational interest inventory merely means selecting an occupation in the area of high interest. However, it is not quite so simple. The results are often a complicated picture, with high, low, and average scores. All scores are important and must be considered in relation to each other.

Interest patterns

The typical pattern of interests for engineers on the Kuder Preference Record, for instance, will include high interest scores in mechanical, computational, and scientific areas, but the interrelationship of these is important in pointing up different types of engineering within the whole engineering field. For example, an industrial engineer would probably be highest in the scientific area, computational would come next, and then mechanical, whereas an electrical engineer might be highest in the scientific area, with mechanical second and computational next. Editors usually show high interest scores in the literary, persuasive, and social-service areas, but there are varieties of editors. There are news editors, sports editors, art editors —to name but a few to complicate the picture. In this consideration it is worth noting that several occupations in unrelated fields can share similar interests. High literary and persuasive interests are shared by lawyers and teachers. It must be realized that no one interest can be used to select an occupation in which the individual can be sure of success. The utilization of the results involves determining the individual's basic interest pattern, his specific interests, his opportunities, his ability, aptitudes, and personality. These factors must then be correlated with the requirements of the occupations and other occupational data. A trained counselor is needed to ensure that all aspects of the problem receive adequate consideration.

If a person is interested in engineering he needs to know his mathematical ability, whether he has any engineering aptitude, and if his personality is such that he is likely to get along well in the profession. He needs to investigate the placement possibilities of the engineering field. He must find out where he can get the necessary training and how much it will cost. In terms of his answers to all of these questions, and their alignment with his interest pattern, the individual will be able to make an evaluation of his vocational choice of the engineering field.

Vocational interest and ability

Another important factor to be considered in interpreting vocational interest patterns is ability. Many students seem to think that if they are sufficiently interested in doing something they are bound to be successful. Enough interest, they maintain, is the only essential for success. Is this really so, however? Can a man without legs walk ten miles, no matter how much he is interested in reaching the destination? Can a woman become a Hollywood star without beauty or other attributes, no matter how great her desire? Can a man read a story in Spanish, however interested he is in the story, if he does not know the language? Are there not always other factors as well as interest that must be present to ensure success? Among these other factors that are necessary for success in any occupation is "ability." We can express it in oversimplified form as:

$$\text{Interest} + \text{ability} = \text{success}$$
$$\text{Interest} - \text{ability} = \text{failure}$$

A high interest in music does not necessarily mean success in a musical career. Ability to play an instrument or use the voice must also be present. A high interest in creative writing without the ability to use words or write will only result in mediocre work. Another assumption accepted by students is that, given the interest, ability is bound to be present. This too has been found untrue. Ability is not synonymous with interest, nor is it dependent upon it. No definite correlation has at present been established between the two. Much research has been attempted, but in all of the research the evidence points to the fact that there is a much greater positive correlation between intelligence and ability than between interest and ability. In other words, it has been found that ability without interest is more likely to succeed than interest without ability. Interest can act as a spur and a motivation for learning and practicing skills and lead to a greater measure of success when ability is present, but interest alone is not a guarantee for success.

Research has shown that levels of ability and vocational interest are factors that must be considered jointly if vocational success is desired. During World War II the Army developed the Army General Classification Test. (7) This test was designed to measure verbal ability, numerical reasoning, and spatial relations. The results of this test furnished the Army with a general classification of an individual's intellectual level or ability. The test results were then compared with civilian occupations. It was found that there were definite levels of ability or ranges of test scores that were valid for particular occupations. From these results, an occupational distribution by percentiles that enables anyone to investigate occupational levels or ranges was set up.

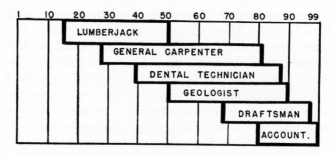

OCCUPATIONAL DISTRIBUTIONS
BY
PERCENTILES

(MIDDLE FIFTY PER CENT OF OCCUPATIONAL DISTRIBUTIONS)

Almost every occupation demands a particular level of ability that the worker must have to function effectively. Vocational interest alone, as stated earlier, is not enough. A subway motorman or an airline pilot must possess certain visual acuity and muscular co-ordination. An information clerk in a large railroad terminal or a "simultaneous translator" at the United Nations must possess certain verbal facility. Persons who have interest in succeeding in an occupation should be asked these questions: "Are the required abilities also present?" and "Do the abilities exist at the desired intellectual level?" These are complicated queries that involve not only a study of vocational interest but also a detailed and careful consideration of numerous other factors. It is essential that not only intelligence, scholastic aptitude, special skills, and personality traits be considered, but that time, money, family influences, cultural factors, and other individually significant areas also receive due thought when vocational interest appears to point toward a particular occupational choice.

SUMMARY

Vocational interest expresses the individual's likes or dislikes for particular activities or areas of life. Individuals do that which they like—that which gives satisfaction. To analyze interests is to begin to analyze the individual and to begin to know the person "behind" the interest.

The theory of dynamics of interests explains interests as the results of deep drives or needs. Interests are the behavior patterns showing how the individual reacts to situations and how he obtains satisfactions.

The simplest definition of an interest is: the liking of an activity or area of life. A vocational interest narrows the interest to an occupational area. Interest involves nothing but a "liking"; ability, aptitude, intelligence, personality, and other factors cannot be inferred from or dependent upon an interest.

The development of interest is closely related to the growth of self-concept; basic interests generally persist, whereas specific interests change from time to time. Experience, environment, the family, other people, and the school all play their parts in influencing interests.

Various "inventories" have been developed that provide for a comparison of an individual's likes and dislikes with those of other people. A simple checking of approval, disapproval, or preference can provide for a quantitative comparison with other individuals.

Interest does not necessarily mean ability is present—without the required skills, ability, and other essentials, interest is rather like possessing a car without gasoline, engine, tires, wheels, and a steering mechanism. Ability must first be considered. Additional factors such as aptitude, special skills, personality traits, family influences, time, and money should also be considered. Only when all factors are clearly seen can a judgment be made or a vocational interest become significant.

SUPPLEMENTARY SOURCES

Anastasi, Anne, *Psychological Testing*. New York: The Macmillan Company, 1954.

Beilin, Harry, "The Application of General Developmental Principles to the Vocational Area," *Journal of Counseling Psychology*, 2 (1955), pp. 53-57.

Bingham, Walter V., *Aptitudes and Aptitude Testing*. New York: Harper & Brothers, 1937.

Ginzberg, Eli, and associates, *Occupational Choice*. New York: Columbia University Press, 1951.

Meadows, Lloyd, "Toward a Theory of Vocational Choice," *Journal of Counseling Psychology*, 2 (1955), pp. 108-112.

Roe, Anne, *The Psychology of Occupations*. New York: John Wiley & Sons, Inc., 1956.

Strong, Edward K., *Vocational Interest, Eighteen Years After College*. Minneapolis: University of Minnesota Press, 1955.

Super, Donald E., *Appraising Vocational Fitness*. New York: Harper & Brothers, 1949.

———, *The Dynamics of Vocational Adjustment*. New York: Harper & Brothers, 1949.

———, *The Psychology of Careers*. New York: Harper & Brothers, 1957.

An *aptitude* is a potential capacity to learn. An aptitude test attempts to predict level of success in a particular, fairly narrow area after the necessary training has been acquired. An aptitude is not a skill; skill means a current ability to achieve one level of performance at the present time; aptitude means the likelihood of being able to achieve a higher level of performance after additional training has been acquired. Skill or ability is a present level of performance; aptitude is an index of what higher level may be reached in the future after

Chapter 10

CONCEPT OF APTITUDES

appropriate training. The distinction is an important one.

As an example, assume that Farmer Brock had a deposit of gravel on his ground. Since it was on the surface, he always had known about its existence. From time to time he used small amounts of it on and about his farm. He felt that he was fortunate in having this on his property, for he could use it whenever he needed gravel, and he did not have to pay some-one else for it.

Brock asked the county soil-conservation agent what further use could be made of the deposit and if there was enough to dig commercially. The agent and a geologist made a careful survey of the bounds and extent of the supply, using test borings and an estimation process that had proved reasonably correct in other similar situations. They estimated that there certainly was enough for commercial exploitation; Brock would not be likely to ruin the business of the big sand-washing plant down at the county seat, but the income would be better than selling butter and eggs. The agent said that after a modest investment in equipment and an access road, and with careful management, the gravel should keep the Brock

155

household financially rather comfortable for the rest of their lives.

A general understanding of aptitude can be interpreted from the case of Farmer Brock, even though this example lacks the complexities involved in the evaluation of human personality. The gravel represents aptitude. The deposit had been present long before its owner thought of developing it. The amounts he had used about the farmyard represent ability, that portion of an aptitude that is currently being used. The bulk of the deposit was the potential usable for the development. This development or training with which an aptitude can be exploited to its maximum is symbolized by the access road and digging equipment. When measuring the deposit the agent and the geologist used an estimation process (an aptitude test) that had proved reasonably accurate in similar situations. In predicting a certain level of production, the agent assumed good management on Brock's part, but still could not guarantee results. Aptitude tests predict on similar bases, but can deal only with the likelihood of success and they are not an automatic guarantee. Too many other factors are involved that cannot be counted on at the time of prediction.

SOURCES OF APTITUDES

Aptitudes are derived from the complex interrelationship between heredity and environment; exactly which of these determines what and to what extent is as yet unknown. It is clear, however, that heredity does set the broad limits within which the personality can develop. Stimulation of the environment determines how much of the hereditary potential will be developed. The environment must stimulate intellectually and physically, while at the same time protecting the original "investment" from physical or mental deterioration.

This complicated intertwining of causes continues to affect man throughout his entire length of life. Some aspects of personality are chiefly determined by heredity, such as sex, hair, and eye color. From our varying environments we learn language and our value structures. Aptitudes as aspects of the personality are themselves molded by the interplay of both hereditary and environmental forces. Through the childhood ages, aptitudes seem to be too plastic and changeable to be measured by current methods; during early adolescence aptitudes seem to settle into patterns unique with each individual. Since the pattern of an individual's aptitudes is fairly well established by later adolescence, it is doubtful that it can be materially changed during college ages. Inquiry into the sources of aptitudes is therefore not of significant value in self-analysis. The problem becomes one of measurement and exploitation, using to the utmost the potential within the individual.

As an example, Farmer Brock did not concern himself with how the gravel arrived at his property. Perhaps glaciation pushed it from the north; perhaps it was deposited by a prehistoric river. No matter how it arrived, it was there. Mr. Brock knew that he could not change history. But he could rejoice that he could use the deposit for his own benefit. In a similar manner, exploring the sources of aptitudes is of little value now, when the pattern of aptitudes can be changed very little. Scientists in fields of eugenics, education, and medicine do study the interaction between heredity and environment for the purpose of influencing the process in early youth while it is still plastic. To these researchers, the question is, "How can we help make better individuals and a better society?" For the student engaging now in self-analysis, the important question will be, "What are my current abilities, and can I profit from further training in these areas?"

Discussion of heredity and environment implies that the persons resulting from these diverse interacting forces will be different from each other. Even identical twins, who have identical genetic bases, have different friends, read different books, and from these differing environments develop separate patterns of aptitudes. If this is true in cases of identical genetic background, it is even more true in the more usual cases in which hereditary bases, too, are much more diverse. These differences exist both within each individual and among individuals. It is seldom that superior aptitudes in many areas are present in any one person. Each individual seems better at some tasks than at others. Just as there is no *superman,* there are no *supermen.* No group of individuals is superior to another in a particular aptitude, unless that group has been previously selected on the basis of this or some similar factor.

Differences exist in a random manner throughout the general population. Mechanical aptitude exists to a great degree in a few people, to some degree in many, and to a slight degree in a few. It is a question of "How much?" rather than "Does he have it or not?" Aptitudes exist in the general population on the basis of a continuum, or a normal distribution. Farmer Brock owned a certain amount of gravel. It was a larger deposit than some owners had, but smaller than that of others. The geologist predicted that there was enough to dig commercially, but not enough to compete seriously with a large producer. One person may have aptitude that is sufficient for a hobby, another person may have aptitude that is sufficient to plan a life's work, and another person may have aptitude that is sufficient to enable him to become a leader in the field. All three persons (and those who fall between) possess the potential; the difference is in "How much?" and "How much compared with what group?"

Farmer Brock has helped to introduce the various facts and concepts associated with aptitudes and aptitude "use." Aptitudes are a part of personality and its functioning in college and life. It is now necessary to examine in an organized fashion the particular aptitudes with which students must deal.

CLASSIFICATION OF APTITUDES

This classification is intended to clarify the problem for students now engaging in self-analysis. Other groupings have been made, but that which follows seems most appropriate for its current intended use.

Specific aptitudes

Specific aptitudes are those defined at the beginning of this chapter as potential capacities to learn. These exist in fairly well defined areas, but are not necessarily unitary. In fact, current research indicates that there is some amount of overlap between the so-called specific aptitudes.

Verbal aptitude is the understanding of concepts expressed in words. Persons who can deal well with increasingly abstract ideas expressed in language symbols are described as having verbal reasoning aptitude. This is one aptitude that is a partial predictor of success in almost all academic programs. (44)

Numerical aptitude tests measure the understanding of numerical relationships. Arithmetical problems are used to test the student's ability to manipulate quantitative materials. Numerical aptitude is necessary in mathematics and physical-science programs, and in occupational fields such as accounting, toolmaking, and engineering. (44)

Abstract reasoning is a nonverbal index of reasoning ability. Verbal reasoning requires the effective understanding of concepts expressed in language (word) symbols, whereas abstract reasoning is the understanding of ideas when expressed in symbols other than words. These symbols are often diagrams and the student must recognize the principles upon which a series of diagrams change. This aptitude would apply to fields requiring perception of relations between objects (rather than between numbers or words), such as engineering, architecture, and art. These three aptitudes, verbal, numerical, and abstract reasoning, comprise one concept of general intelligence. (44)

Spatial visualization requires judgment of sizes, shapes, and other relationships of objects in space. This has been called three-dimensional thinking and spatial-relations aptitude. Carpenters, sheet-metal workers, draftsmen, dress designers, artists, and engineers are required to make these judgments in their work.

Manual aptitude involves the co-ordination of fingers, hands, arms, and eyes for the successful completion of tasks. There may be two related aptitudes here, one involving finger dexterity for fine work, the other being the use of arm and hand for more gross work. In general, manual aptitude is more related to physical co-ordination and handling operations than to understanding and deciding.

Mechanical aptitude refers to a grouping of factors that tend to predict success in mechanical work. The understanding of mechanical principles and visualization of objects in three dimensions are components of this aptitude. Both of these require mental processes more than physical action.

Clerical aptitude refers to several factors, but chiefly perceptual speed. This is measured by speed and accuracy in recognizing similarities or differences between numbers and letters. Analysis of additional factors contributing to success in clerical occupations shows that intelligence and fluency in language and arithmetic should be included. However, as "specific aptitude" is defined in this chapter, perceptual speed in number-and-verbal symbols is clerical aptitude.

Art aptitude, apart from creative skill in art, seems to be based mainly in esthetic judgment. This is recognition of unity in composition. Although esthetic judgment can be modified by experience, it is considered basically a hereditary trait. Four additional factors related to success in art are high-level intelligence, creative imagination, spatial perception, and manual dexterity.

Musical aptitude parallels that for art. The basic abilities seem to be sensory capacities, mainly hereditary. The essential senses of pitch, rhythm, and time can be improved by training, but their establishment is physical. Intelligence, manual skill, and creative imagination are also necessary for success in music.

Vocational aptitudes

Vocational aptitudes are those that enable success in particular professions or jobs. But "vocational aptitude" is a misleading term. It does not agree with the definition of aptitude given at the beginning of the chapter: a capacity or potential *in a fairly narrow area* to benefit from further training. Success in almost any vocation requires a combination of specific aptitudes. The accountant requires scholastic aptitude, particularly in quantitative thinking, and clerical aptitude. A tool-and-die maker must have scholastic, manual, mechanical, and spatial aptitudes. Thus, it is correct to define a "vocational aptitude" as a particular assembly of specific aptitudes, composed according to the requirements of the vocation. Combinations of specific aptitudes are used in all vocations, seldom one aptitude alone. The generally popular notion that people have "aptitude" for a certain few specific jobs and none for others is incorrect. It is more likely that the level of each person's specific aptitudes, along with his motivation, interest and other factors, can be combined into many different patterns that would indicate qualification for many different vocations.

Researchers are constantly locating the patterns of criteria that predict likelihood of success in various occupations. Most of the occupations so far studied, however, are those that require long training periods—the professions. This research is based on the assumption that these fields require highly qualified personnel. Thus, when criteria are so strict, it is simple to eliminate potential failures before the training program is begun rather than to allow potential failures to enter and later drop out after much frustration and loss in time and money investment.

The professions of law, medicine, nursing, and teaching each have patterns of specific aptitudes, tests of which can predict, within limits, likely success in their respective training programs. With such long training programs, scholastic aptitude is understandably weighted heavily by all. The other component specific aptitudes are determined by the needs of the profession.

MEASUREMENT OF APTITUDES

Aptitudes can be measured by direct processes, but this is an inefficient method. As an example, an engineering school can admit three times as many freshmen as it expects to graduate, then can dismiss the lowest students after one year. The school has directly measured the aptitudes of these students to do the work of an engineering curriculum. This result is not considered worth its costs in discouragement, lost time, and crowded classrooms. Aptitudes can be evaluated by indirect methods, and even though these tests may lack the accuracy of the more direct approach, their predictions are sufficiently correct to be used in counseling and screening procedures.

Need for aptitude tests

The likelihood of a student's being successful as a freshman in college can be predicted. This evaluation is based partly on aptitude-test scores. Thus, before choosing a vocation, the student can be advised of his chances for success in selected fields. If one field or level seems an inappropriate choice, the process of measurement and comparison can be continued until more compatible matches are found. The use of aptitude tests in counseling keeps the element of choice in a student's hand. He is probably not told that he is prohibited from entering a field of his choice even though the bulk of evidence is against his being successful. He is informed of his chances; he may attempt the program if he wishes.

Let us assume that the school of the student's choice uses a series of entry examinations. This battery of tests predicts a probable degree of success in this school. If admission is granted or denied partly on the basis of this test battery, the battery is being used as a screen to weed out potential failures. Whether the screening is used for college entrance, job selection, or entrance into an advanced program of ROTC, the principle remains the same. In screening procedures, the power of acceptance or rejection is in the hands of the screening agency—college, employer, or Army.

In all applications of aptitude tests, the agency evaluating the results can do no more than predict chances of success or failure. No results of aptitude testing can guarantee absolutely a particular outcome. Some test results can be used to quantify chances to the extent that it is possible to say that with the performance on this battery the testee has 5 chances in 100 of completing flight training. The student pilot being tested may be one of the 5 out of the 100 who have this same score who will complete training successfully, but this minute chance may be too small to plan for. The predictive value of aptitude tests is constantly being refined, but the process is such an intricate one that progress is slow.

Several assumptions underlying aptitude testing must be set forth: aptitudes can be measured; there is value in being able to measure aptitudes; and, once established, aptitudes are relatively unchanging. The first two of these assumptions have been touched upon and will receive no further comment; the third is used when predictions are to be made. If aptitudes were to change, either "rise" or "fall," after a prediction had been made, the prediction would be useless. There is reason to believe, as discussed earlier in this chapter, that aptitudes change little after early adolescence. For this reason the use of appropriate aptitude tests, even as low as the eighth-grade and ninth-grade levels, is a valid procedure. (44)

Whether "aptitude" is defined as a potential in a fairly narrow area (such as clerical aptitude) or as the likelihood of success in a vocation (such as "aptitude" for law), the process of developing appropriate tests is much the same. The steps are functional analysis, selection of test items, development of a scoring method, trial administration, and analysis of results (validation).

Types of aptitude tests

This discussion of types of aptitude tests parallels the section entitled "Classification of Aptitudes." The outlines in the two sections are in agreement. More complete descriptions of these tests are given in the student psychological test glossary included in Appendix B. These examples of tests used to measure specific aptitudes are intended to be representative only.

Verbal aptitude is mainly verbal intelligence, and as such is measured by many "scholastic aptitude" tests. The Ohio State University Psychological Examination for freshmen (OSU) is used for screening purposes by many colleges. A somewhat similar test is the verbal section of the College Entrance Examination Board's scholastic aptitude test. In the Differential Aptitude Test the verbal reasoning score is an index of this understanding of concepts expressed in word symbols.

Numerical aptitude is the understanding of numerical relationships. The second score of the Differential Aptitude Test, numerical ability, is designed to measure this facility in manipulating quantitative materials. Other mathematical and quantitative reasoning tests also measure this particular aptitude.

Abstract reasoning is a nonverbal expression of reasoning proficiency. Several tests attempt to measure this understanding of concepts expressed in designs, among them the abstract reasoning score of the Differential Aptitude Test (D. A. T.).

Spatial visualization. The Minnesota Paper Form Board is principally a test of spatial visualization. The student must visualize how parts of diagrams will fit together when turned, revolved, and assembled. This is testing the psychological processes involved and not the actual manual handling of materials. The space relations test of the D. A. T. is a similar measure, but is composed of other kinds of items.

THE PSYCHOLOGICAL CORPORATION

Careful testing can reveal aptitudes with accuracy

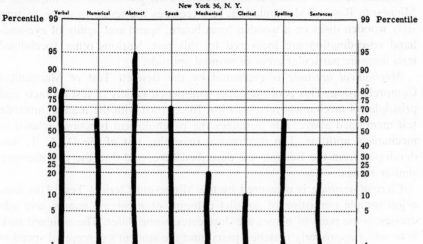

Reproduced with Permission of The Pychological Corporation

Aptitudes can be measured. The performance of an individual can be compared with others. Comparisons may be expressed in many varied ways.

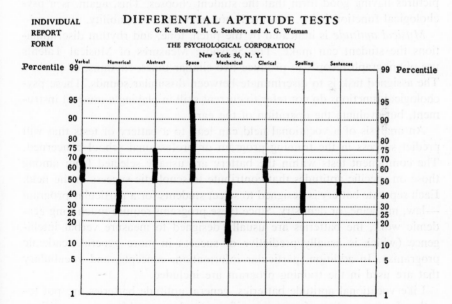

Reproduced with Permission of The Pychological Corporation

Manual aptitude usually is measured with the job-sample technique. The Minnesota Rate of Manipulation Test requires the testee to place or turn sixty wooden disks on a wooden form board. Speed and agility of eye-and-hand co-ordination are measured by this test. Various other specialized tests measure particular areas of manual aptitude.

Mechanical aptitude is evaluated by the Bennett Test of Mechanical Comprehension. This is of the paper-and-pencil variety of test on facts and principles of mechanical relationships. In contrast with the manual aptitude test mentioned above, this examines the psychological functions related to mechanical aptitude. The mechanical reasoning test of the D. A. T. was developed from the Bennett test described here, and thus the two measure similar things.

Clerical aptitude is measured by the Minnesota Clerical Test. This uses a job sample consisting of parallel columns of numbers, names, and addresses; some pairs of names are duplicates, some differ. The assigned task is to select improperly matched pairs, and the student's perceptual speed is measured by the number of correct discriminations made. A somewhat similar result is obtained on the clerical speed and accuracy subtest of the D. A. T.

Art aptitude is often interpreted to be esthetic judgment. In Meier's Art Judgment Test, the student is asked which picture in each of 100 pairs he prefers. Degree of esthetic judgment is indicated by the proportion of the pictures having good form that the student chooses. This, again, is a psychological function being measured, not painting or art ability.

Musical aptitude is indicated by the pitch, tone, and rhythm discriminations the student can make. The Seashore Measures of Musical Talents use phonograph records to produce two similar tones, rhythms, or pitches. The assigned task is to discriminate between dissimilar sounds. These psychological functions do not refer to current skill in playing a musical instrument, but evaluate the operation of the ear.

An analysis of a vocational field can lead to a battery of tests that will predict success in the training program or professional school concerned. The component tests within the battery are usually selected from among those on specific aptitudes that contribute to scholastic success in the field. Each separate battery is designed to select students for a particular program —law, medicine, or dentistry. Since these programs require much long academic work, the batteries are usually designed to measure verbal intelligence (which is usually predictive of success in more general academic programs). In addition, particular information, concepts, and vocabulary that are used in the training program are included.

Like vocational aptitude batteries, general aptitude batteries are put together from grouping of many specific aptitude tests. After a general battery has been administered to large numbers of people who are in many different occupations or school settings, a series of norms for these many particular occupations or grade levels is devised. When a person is given the battery, his pattern of scores can be compared with those patterns already established by others in either occupational or grade norms, or both.

General aptitude batteries are thus composed of tests of specific aptitudes, probably a wider range of aptitudes than are included in any single vocational aptitude battery. The performance of an individual can be compared to that of others currently working or studying in many different fields. The occupational fields for which the student would seem to have most aptitude would be those in which his pattern of test results agreed most closely with patterns established by workers in those fields.

In comparison with giving a series of separate specific aptitude tests, and trying to devise a pattern of aptitudes from these results, a pattern from a general aptitude test has many advantages. In administration time and effort the cost is somewhat lower. Of chief value is the existence of unified norms—based on large comparable groups of students and vocational groups instead of a separate group for each aptitude test. Examples of general aptitude batteries are the Differential Aptitude Test, Multiple Aptitude Test, and the Flanagan Aptitude Classification Test. (44, 96, 50)

APTITUDES, ABILITIES, AND INTERESTS

Among the concepts of aptitudes, interests, and abilities exist many interrelationships. These three factors are defined here and their intertwinings are discussed.

Aptitude is a learning potential; an undervalued capacity that can be developed by training is an aptitude. Current skill, such as reading speed, is not aptitude. The concept of aptitude is expressed in terms of a higher level of performance than has been reached. If an individual can benefit from further training in an area, he is said to have aptitude in that field.

Abilities are skills. They are a result of past training that has produced a certain current level of performance. This current skill may be of little significance in terms of what the individual's potential may be. A current level of performance may be near the individual's ceiling, or he may have additional unused potential.

Interest is the appeal of and liking for something. An interesting task should stimulate one to begin and be enjoyable while it is being done, and completion should produce a feeling of satisfaction. Interest in something should maintain effort; the interested person will want to explore beyond the required limits.

With these statements of definition, their interrelations can be illustrated. In Farmer Brock's backyard there was a deposit of gravel. He knew of its presence and even used some about the barnyard. Exploration indicated that more was present beneath the ground and available for the digging.

That portion of the gravel that Brock used about the farmyard can be called ability. From past experience he knew that some gravel would be usable about the farm. He had dug some and used it at various times in the past. But, as estimates indicated, that level of use was by no means near what the deposit was capable of producing; the deposit had much more potential for future use. This concept looks to the future: what further level of performance is likely if the proper training is acquired? The concept of ability looks backward. It is a measure of what current level of skill has been reached after past training. Aptitude refers to the next step: how much more training can be absorbed? Ability can be interpreted as that portion of an aptitude that has so far been developed by training and results in a current level of performance. Aptitude tests try to determine how much unused capacity remains.

This unused capacity is developed through training, but only if the individual is interested enough to do so. Farmer Brock was not compelled to exploit his gravel pit. To develop the deposit he had to be interested enough in the probable results to invest money in the digging equipment. He was not required to do this. But unless he did so, the gravel would remain undeveloped—used only to a minute extent. In a like manner, aptitudes can reach full development only through the interest of their owners.

In another sense, interest and aptitudes are further related. Whereas aptitudes tend to settle into patterns by adolescence, and generally little change in them occurs after the end of that period, interests may keep changing throughout life. Interests are thought to be means through which man supplies his basic needs. As such, these means can vary to some extent so long as the needs are met. Aptitudes change little in pattern. Physical or mental injury can decrease these potentials, or they may remain almost unused if unexploited, but little can be done to increase aptitude, and our concern is one of the identification and full development of these existing potentials.

AN EXAMPLE OF CAREER PLANNING

When Farmer Brock spoke with the soil-conservation agent he was wondering about a new career. When he asked the agent if his gravel deposit was big enough to dig commercially, he was asking if his current ability had enough aptitude behind it to build a career.

Al Morris was doing the same thing as Farmer Brock when he went to the Counseling Center. He wondered if he could become a civil engineer. In talking over his background with the counselor, he stated that he was twenty-one, single, and a high-school graduate. His high-school grades in science had been low, math was average, but English, social studies, and shop classes had been above average. Al said that he knew this record was not outstanding, but he hoped his practical experience would help him in engineering school. After high school he had worked on construction, then entered the Army engineers. There he had been trained as a heavy-equipment operator (bulldozers, graders) but had also done some estimating before becoming supply sergeant for his company.

From the background and goals that Al had discussed thus far, the counselor selected a series of tests that seemed most appropriate. Broad ones were first selected, including a battery of general aptitude tests, then one of scholastic aptitude, and an interest inventory. Others could be used later, depending on what need was indicated from the results of these, and more discussion.

Al's performance on these tests is listed below:

Test	*Percentile*	*Norm*
Ohio State Psychological Examination (Form 23)	62nd	National college freshmen
Co-operative Reading Comprehension (Form C2T)	45th	National college freshmen
Differential Aptitude Test (Form A)		12th-grade boys
Verbal reasoning	91st	
Numerical ability	64th	
Abstract reasoning	86th	
Space relations	23rd	
Mechanical reasoning	62nd	
Clerical speed and accuracy	37th	
Language usage		
1. Spelling	81st	
2. Sentences	88th	
Kuder Preference Record (Form CH)		General male population
Outdoor	24th	
Mechanical	75th	
Computational	55th	
Scientific	18th	
Persuasive	78th	
Artistic	15th	
Literary	95th	
Musical	25th	
Social service	85th	
Clerical	15th	

These test results seemed to indicate that Al had aptitudes that would help him to succeed in college, but that he was probably a poor risk for an engineering program. High mathematical and spatial-relations aptitude are required for success in engineering schools. In these areas on the D. A. T., Al's performance was average for male high-school seniors, but would be below average for students entering an engineering school. His stronger aptitude seemed to be both in language and abstract thinking, and in recognizing correct grammar (OSU and D. A. T.). These stronger and weaker aptitudes seemed to form a rough parallel with his high-school record so far as areas are concerned. However, the OSU, C2T, and D. A. T. results all indicated that he was probably working below his potential while in high school.

In discussing these results with Al, the counselor wanted to see how Al's other hobbies or part-time work experience might help to complete the picture. Al was not surprised with the explanation of his test performance; he had always liked to read and felt that the reading requirements in high-school English and social studies were the reasons he had done any work at all in those courses. The remainder of his high-school career had been "mainly social." During junior high he had entered the Scouts and spent two summers at camp, plus one as a counselor. Out of this experience he worked one summer as a playground director during his last summer in high school. He had enjoyed all of this, but thought these were only "pocket-money" jobs without any relation to his life's work.

Before entering the service, he had worked in construction because "the money was good, and laborers were needed." In service he had eventually "bucked" for the supply job because it looked "soft." As supply man he liked seeing satisfied "customers" more than taking care of his stocks of equipment. His chief hobby overseas was reading. When the local library no longer interested him, he took two U.S.A.F.I. courses (American novel and United States history) to get new books.

This information gave some background to Al's test results, and both together helped the counselor to suggest some alternate goals. Al seemed to have a fair chance for success in college, but probably not in an engineering program. His higher aptitudes would be better applied in fields requiring more use of language in written and spoken form. This grouping of aptitudes was supported by both measured and hobby interest in reading. The part-time work experience and the persuasive and social-service interests could suggest some applications of Al's stronger aptitudes. Some of these combinations might be in teaching, either of English or social studies, or more directly dealing with books as a librarian or conceivably as a book salesman or dealer. If Al had creative-writing ability, more possibilities would be present.

At this point, the counselor's role was to discuss the interpretation of these facts with Al—facts from all of his work experience, high-shool program, service time, hobbies, goals, and others not introduced in this report. There were many possibilities in line with Al's potentials, but the final decisions had to be in Al's hands.

SUMMARY

Aptitudes are a basic concept within the framework of self-analysis and self-understanding. This chapter has attempted to define that concept and to show how and why aptitudes differ from one person to another. A classification has been given, and the measurement of aptitudes outlined. The relationships among aptitudes, interests, and abilities have been discussed, and one application of the concept summarized through an example of the use of psychological tests in planning a career.

Aptitudes are potentials that can be developed by training. They exist to varying degrees in everyone. The individual can usually decide for himself whether he will exploit them to their maximum, or whether he is satisfied with a lower level of performance. Aptitudes can be developed if "develop" is defined as "make the most use of." Employers are interested in the present ability of prospective employees and how much they can progress in the future. With interest, help, and training, aptitudes can be used to their maximum potentials.

People differ in aptitudes for the same reasons that they differ in interest, in shoe sizes, and in tones of voice. They differ because these examples are all determined by the intricate latticework of hereditary and environmental forces. Everyone receives skin, we all have hearts, and we all begin with the same number of teeth; these are implanted in everyone evenly on a qualitative basis. Aptitudes likewise occur in all people, but with quantitative differences. A few people have superior aptitude in spatial visualization, many have some aptitude, and a few persons have little aptitude. Aptitudes seem to occur in a normal distribution throughout the population, rather than in equal distribution.

An aptitude pattern is the general level of various aptitudes possessed by an individual and the manner in which they combine. If the specific aptitudes are conceived of as being represented by vertical lines of various heights, the aptitude pattern would be represented by the level and shape of this profile.

Vocational success requires the complete co-ordination of all forces —abilities, aptitudes, interests, motivation, and other factors. Maximum realization of potential can occur only when one's interests, skills, aptitudes, and opportunities all point in the same direction. Career planning is successful when all these influences are mobilized together.

SUPPLEMENTARY SOURCES

Anastasi, Anne, *Psychological Testing*. New York: The Macmillan Company, 1954.

Bingham, Walter Van Dyke, *Aptitudes and Aptitude Testing*. New York: Harper & Brothers, 1937.

Hahn, Milton E., and Malcolm S. MacLean, *Counseling Psychology* (2nd ed.). New York: McGraw-Hill Book Company, Inc., 1955.

Munn, Norman L., *Psychology* (3rd ed.). Boston: Houghton Mifflin Company, 1956.

Super, Donald E., *Appraising Vocational Fitness*. New York: Harper & Brothers, 1949.

———, *The Psychology of Careers*. New York: Harper & Brothers, 1957.

Terman, L. M., and M. H. Oden, *The Gifted Child Grows Up*. Stanford, California: Stanford University Press, 1947.

It *soon* becomes apparent, after the examining of even surface problems of behavior, that an adequate definition of intelligence must be broad and inclusive enough to include all behavior classifiable as "intelligent." Such behavior as manual skills, scholastic aptitude, speed, variability of response, and capacity to adapt and manipulate one's environment, are frequently considered to be aspects of intelligent behavior. On the other hand, a definition that becomes so all-inclusive as to possess vague limits of demarcation in terms of

Chapter 11

INTELLIGENCE AND SCHOLASTIC APTITUDE

what constitutes intellectual and nonintellectual behavior fails to serve its function. The better known definitions of intelligence are summarized by Mursell (100:70) and some of them are presented below:

> "Intelligence is a general capacity of the individual consciously to adjust his thinking to new requirements." (Sterns, 1914)
>
> "Intelligence is the ability to learn." (Buckingham: *Intelligence and its Measurement,* 1921)
>
> "An individual possesses intelligence insofar as he has learned or can learn to adjust himself to his environment." (Colvin: *Intelligence and its Measurement,* 1921)
>
> "An individual is intelligent in direct proportion as he is able to carry on abstract thinking." (Terman: *Intelligence and its Measurement,* 1921)

All of these definitions stress higher mental powers and ability to learn, adapt, and adjust. One may ask, however, which one of these definitions is best. They all appear to be behavior descriptions and nothing more. The authors cited above are simply describing the manifestations of intelligence without directly discussing intelligence itself. Intelligence appears to be the underlying "something" that makes the person behave according to the descriptions offered in the definitions cited above. But just what, then, *is* this thing called intelligence? Is it a distinct entity? If so, what are its components, and where is it located? Is it associated with particular areas of the brain? Is intelligence something a person inherits from his parents or is it largely the product of experience?

Defenders of the importance of hereditary influences refer to the results of experiments in selective breeding and family similarity in intelligence, particularly in the case of identical twins. But even here, it is difficult to isolate environmental factors entirely. Although the evidence suggests that the old adage, "like father, like son" is in many respects true, it is difficult to attribute this entirely to heredity, since father and son usually share common environments, and hence their learning experiences tend to be quite similar. Although there are a number of genetic studies that point to the importance of heredity in determining both the limits of learning and intelligence, the findings of research are again far from conclusive. A commonly held notion logically argues that heredity "sets" the intellectual limits, and the environment determines how much of this intelligence is used.

Bischof (16:4) challenges both the importance and logic of the question, "Which is more important: heredity or environment?" He asks:

> Would it not be just as fruitful to ask a student to clap his hands together once and then ask him, which hand made the noise? Was it the right hand or the left hand? It matters not which, but how much noise resulted. How hard did the student *want* to clap? Are his hands bigger than those of another student? Could he clap just as hard on each and every occasion? All these questions coming out of our hand-clapping analogy may equally well be asked about intelligence and especially the *measurement of intelligence.*

Bischof feels that questions regarding the nature of individual differences in intelligence are much more meaningful and promising than concern for the nature-nurture controversy.

The fact remains that both the contributions of heredity and environment are important in the determination of all behavior, intellectual and otherwise. It is physically impossible to make a clapping noise by using the right or the left hand alone. Both are needed. Similarly, the human organism cannot and does not function in a vacuum. It is constantly interacting with the environment. Both are essential conditions to life itself. To consider one factor in isolation from the other becomes meaningless in both practice and theory.

The variety of definitions and nebulous findings of research may serve to confuse the reader in his search for the definition of intelligence; yet herein lies a clue as to its nature. One psychologist defined intelligence as "that which an intelligence test measures." While this definition may sound somewhat absurd, it does have a ring of truth attached to it. *Intelligence is a relative concept.* Whatever else it might be, the way in which one defines intelligence depends in large measure upon what he intends to do with it. The exact definition used, then, depends primarily upon the objective of the definer. The author of an intelligence test will define intelligence in terms of concepts that are measurable with a view toward making accurate diagnosis, recommendations, and predictions. Intelligence as "that which an intelligence test measures" takes on significance as a definition then, since it points to the uncertainty, relativity, and function of this important concept. Similarly, the theoretician will define intelligence in terms that help to explain behavior and promote research, with a view toward gaining a greater understanding of its nature.

Intelligence is not unlike electricity in many respects. For many years now, people have been using electricity in innumerable ways—for consumption, for production, and for research. It is possible to measure electricity with great accuracy. Yet despite its utility and amenability to a variety of sensitive measuring devices, the precise nature of electricity is difficult to comprehend. It has no visible shape or form. One assumes its existence only by inference. The individual does not perceive electricity directly (except through shock), but only its manifestations. Press a button and the room lights up, turn a switch and the motor starts. Similarly, intelligence is found to be a useful if intangible concept; no one is certain as to what it is, but within limits, indirect measures are obtainable. In addition, psychologists and educators are able to make some reasonably accurate predictions with it, and people are using it all the time (even if it is not as often as some other people would like).

Intelligence, then, is a useful, practical concept referring to a group of complex mental processes. There is no single definition of intelligence. The matter of definition is related to the extent and purposes of the definer. Definitions of intelligence appear to contain some common denominators, however, such as the ability to solve problems with regard to the complexity of the task to be learned and flexibility of response. The task to be solved or learned may be a social, academic, or mechanical one. Herein is the difficulty and confusion of definition. The common denominators are necessarily broad and inclusive. As a result, some authors stress one aspect of intelligence and ignore others. This matter of differing emphasis is dependent upon the particular bias of the author. Despite efforts to define intelligence narrowly, it becomes increasingly apparent that breadth and depth of definition are indispensable, since intelligence appears to be an intrinsic aspect of all our behavior.

Intelligence, as a concept of the individual coping with his environment, has been a concern for speculation for many years. The exact nature of intelligence, though debatable, has not precluded varying theories of intelligence from being developed. The next section examines two major theories.

THEORIES OF INTELLIGENCE

Two psychologists of international prominence, Spearman and Thurstone, have proposed two widely accepted, if somewhat conflicting, theories of intelligence.

"G" factor theory

Spearman (117) thought of intelligence as being a general ability, a common factor in a wide variety of special aptitudes. He referred to this general ability as "G" and to special aptitudes or specific abilities as "S." This is perhaps best illustrated by Bischof's diagram. (16:7)

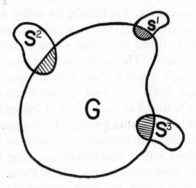

This diagram suggests that specific abilities have varying amounts of G (general capacity) and S (factors peculiar to each of them). The shaded portions above represent areas of similarity or relatedness between the specific and general factor. The unshaded portions of each of the specific factors represent areas of uniqueness and unrelatedness.

In this instance the unshaded S factors bear no relationship to the G or general factor. Bischof deliberately varied the size of the shaded area for each of the specific intelligences (S^1, S^2, S^3). This is done to indicate the varying influence of G. In accord with the principle of individual differences, discussed earlier in this book, it is well to remember that the size and kind of G and S factors differs from person to person.

It is readily seen that Spearman's G factor theory of intelligence is not an easy one to comprehend. His theory is primarily a mathematical one, and is difficult to consider in other than mathematical terms. Because of the nature of his theory Spearman's definition of terms (such as G and S) tends to be rather vague.

Multifactor theories

Thorndike's (128) multifactor theory of intelligence is somewhat opposed to the view expressed above. Exponents of the multifactor theory maintain that Spearman's G factor is analyzable into a number of specific factors. In essence, then, it is possible to refine this factor G into a number of separate and distinct abilities, all of which put together comprise intelligence. The G or general factor does not exist. Intelligence, then, is comprised of a number of isolated factors. These factors are totally unrelated to one another. Any given skill is made up of a combination of such factors, with the numbers and combination of factors varying from skill to skill.

Although Thorndike was one of the first American psychologists to propose a many-factor theory of intelligence, the later theoretical proposals of Thurstone (131) appear to be the more widely accepted ones. While Thurstone's theory is not unlike the multifactor of Thorndike, there are some significant differences. Thurstone's theory might more accurately be described as the multiple-factor theory of intelligence. His theory appears to have incorporated many of the positive aspects of both Spearman's G or two-factor theory and Thorndike's multifactor theory.

Thurstone's multiple-factor theory maintains that intelligence is comprised of *primary mental abilities*. Each primary ability is composed of a number of specific but interrelated factors. Hence, rather than dealing with intelligence as a number of discrete and specific factors, Thurstone offers a group-factor theory. These clusters of specific factors constitute a group factor. In turn, these group factors are referred to as the primary mental abilities. Thurstone found by statistical means that there are seven such basic factors comprising intelligence:

The *V factor* is one of *verbal comprehension* and plays an important role in tests of vocabulary, reading comprehension, verbal reasoning, and disarranged sentences.

The *W* or *word-fluency* factor reflects the extent of one's verbal versatility or readily available vocabulary.

The *N* or *number factor* deals primarily with simple arithmetical computations, in which the emphasis is placed on speed and accuracy rather than complexity.

The *S* or *spatial-relations factor* is one in which the individual is required to manipulate, symbolically, various objects into a variety of positions.

The *M* or *associated-memory factor* may perhaps best be equated with rote learning and memory.

The *P* or *perceptual-ability factor* is identified with the quick and accurate grouping of visual details.

The *R* or *reasoning factor* is measured by tests of arithmetical reasoning and series completion.

Recent investigations have shown that it is possible to refine these seven basic factors still further. One statistical analysis has indicated that there are twenty-nine basic intelligence factors rather than seven. (41)

Regardless of the number of primary abilities, the factors within any single group are highly interrelated. The relationship among these group or primary factors is comparatively small, however. The fact that relationships within and between abilities exists suggests the presence of a factor that is common to all of them. This presence of a common factor sounds very much like Spearman's G or general factor. It would appear, then, that the differences discussed in the foregoing theories may be primarily ones of emphasis.

While some evidence appears to support both positions, more conclusive data will come only with the constant refinement and improvement of the statistical and measuring instruments used in research. Within the framework of self-analysis Thurstone's group-factor approach would seem to hold greater promise as a diagnostic and predictive device. Assuming that it is possible to analyze a student's abilities in terms of a number of fundamental factors, a greater understanding of the nature of this potential would appear possible.

A group-factor analysis, then, would supply the student with information relative to the extent and location of his intellectual strengths and limitations. This type of mental appraisal enables the student to formulate plans that are in accord with his intellectual profile. He might well be encouraged to explore various educational and vocational areas, and made aware of his limitations in others.

MEASURING INTELLIGENCE

In 1905, Alfred Binet was commissioned by the French government to devise methods for differentiating between normal and feebleminded pupils in the Paris school systems for purposes of providing a more adequate curriculum for each group.

After much experimentation, Binet conceived of the idea of age norms (discussed in an earlier chapter). He found that normal students of a particular age level were capable of completing certain tasks. Normal students of a younger age level were not able to complete these same tasks. A task completed by the average five-year-old, but not by the average four-year-old, was then considered a valid criterion for differentiating intellectually between four-year and five-year-olds. A pupil who was capable of doing tasks completed by the average eight-year-old was said to have a mental age of eight years. Hence, if this pupil was but six years old, he would be accelerated intellectually by two years. If, on the other hand, this pupil had a chronological age of ten years, he would be mentally retarded by two years. By comparing the pupil's performance on a series of tasks with the performance of other youngsters of his age, it was possible to determine the amount of pupil retardation and acceleration. It was on the basis of this comparison that the popular concept of "I.Q." originated.

Concept of I.Q.

It is seen that the I.Q. formula is based on the ratio of mental age to chronological age, with the introduction of the constant 100 in order to eliminate decimals and the need for fractions.

By making the proper substitution in the formula, $\text{I.Q.} = \dfrac{\text{MA}}{\text{CA}} \times 100$,

a ten-year-old pupil who obtains a mental age of eight is found to have an I.Q. of 80. Another pupil, ten years of age, having a mental age of twelve, would have an I.Q. score of 120. Obviously an eight-year-old pupil with a mental age of eight would have an I.Q. of 100. The I.Q. score of 100 is usually taken as the average score, and evaluations are made on the basis of this average. The intelligence quotient has the advantage of allowing for a uniform interpretation of test performance regardless of the individual's age, as long as the individual is not too old.

Although the rate of growth or decline of adult intelligence is experimentally debatable, the fact remains that it is significantly different from the rate of child and adolescent growth. During the preadult years, the growth curve of intelligence suggests rapid acceleration. The peak appears to be reached somewhere between the fifteenth and twenty-fifth year. The concept of I.Q. becomes meaningless once the individual reaches or passes this "tapering-off" period, since the intelligence quotient assumes that a change in chronological age is accompanied by a similar change in mental age. Thus, while a forty-year-old person may be intellectually normal, his mental-age score can never exceed his peak performance. Computing adult I.Q.'s under these circumstances would lead to false results. Hence, distorted I.Q.'s or more meaningful scores such as percentiles must be employed.

Another serious limitation of the I.Q. concept is the difference in the meaning of I.Q. scores from test to test—that is, their lack of comparability. An I.Q. score of 110 on one test may be comparable to an I.Q. score of 125 on another test. Not all intelligence tests are made the same way, nor are they all measuring the same thing. In addition, the I.Q. as a single score assumes a unitary nature of intelligence that is highly debatable and uninformative. Although a single score establishes the general level of intellectual functioning, it appears to conceal a multitude of valuable information in regard to specific strengths and weaknesses.

These limitations may serve to explain the widespread emphasis placed on other methods of interpreting test scores. An I.Q. score of 125 may be more than one of 120, but how much more? Both scores are higher than the average I.Q. of 100, but how much above "average" are they? Even here, the question is meaningless since the concept of "average" is a relative one. Interpreting test scores in terms of percentiles and norms appears to overcome many of the difficulties inherent in the traditional concept of the I.Q.

Until recently, it was commonly believed that the "constancy" of the I.Q. was a well established principle. In fact, one early study (31) found that after the fifth or sixth year, there was a fluctuation, on the average, of less than five points plus or minus from the obtained I.Q.

The constancy of the I.Q. appears to be an oversimplified version of a complex process. On the basis of some twenty-five years of research, Bayley (9:807) has sharply criticized this oversimplified view of the constancy of the I.Q. "I see no reason why we should continue to think of intelligence as an integrated (or single) entity or capacity which grows throughout childhood by steady accretions." Her findings suggest that little if any relationship exists between the intelligence-test performance of infants during their first two years of life and test performance later in life. In fact, it is not until their fifth or sixth year that "children can be reliably classified into broad categories of normal, defective and bright."

The fact that Bayley's findings conflict with the findings of earlier studies may be explained in terms of methodology. Earlier investigators tested and retested the individual's I.Q. within relatively brief intervals and as a result little change was recorded. Apparently, little change occurs in intelligence-test performance during the space of a week, a month or a year or two. Bayley's twenty-five-year study took a longer "look" at the growth of intelligence and found differences that the briefer studies were not able to find.

The I.Q. as a dynamic concept is suggested in Bayley's findings in that intelligence appears to be a "complex of separately timed developing functions." Hence, a given intellectual function will vary in importance and development for each individual according to his age, potential for growth, emotional climate, and general environmental circumstances. The development of motor rather than verbal functions during the early life of the infant suggests the relative importance of one kind of intellectual function at one stage of development rather than another.

Is the I.Q. a consistent phenomenon? In light of Bayley's findings, this is a difficult question to answer. Certainly, intellectual predictions in terms of infant behavior are highly inaccurate. These findings do not suggest, however, that intelligence shifts dramatically or erratically from day to day, but rather that genuine changes in intelligence do occur over relatively long periods of time. Even here, however, individuals appear to fluctuate only within broadly defined limits. An individual classifiable as bright during his fifth or sixth year generally tends to remain in that category later in life. Although the forces acting on and within an individual during a given moment, such as emotional and health factors, may serve seriously to affect his performance on a test of intelligence, this is generally the exception rather than the rule. Such temporary fluctuations do not, of course, represent the individual's true intellectual level, and a period of retesting at a later date would appear to be in order.

Intelligence, then, is conceived of as a series of interrelated mental functions, developing at varying rates and at different times in the life of a given individual. The constancy of the I.Q. (rigidly defined) appears to be a concept that has outlived its usefulness, since it fails adequately to describe the dynamic nature of intelligence.

Intelligence as a process of continued change might be considered analogous to a musical selection described as a "variation on a theme." Within the framework of a dominant theme, changes or elaboration in harmony, rhythm, and melody occur. Thus, one obtains change and diversity within a uniform structure. Intelligence can be conceived to be a similar uniform structure, within which relative changes occur. For each individual there appears to be a consistency rather than a constancy of intellectual development, although Bayley (9:814) uses both terms interchangeably:

> Although each child has his own individual pattern of progress, the patterns are not completely random. After the period of infancy there is a strong underlying consistency. Some children forge ahead and maintain relatively advanced positions after 5 or 6 years of age. Others grow slowly and lag behind. There is some shifting of position, but the changes are gradual over rather long intervals of time. Within such intervals we can expect to obtain fairly constant I.Q.'s.

Tests of intelligence

There is a wide variety of intelligence tests. These tests are generally one of two major types: either group intelligence tests or individual intelligence tests.

Individual intelligence tests. Individual intelligence tests are administered on a person-to-tester basis, and hence only one subject can be tested at a time. The test administrator is usually a highly trained and well qualified person. Administering tests on an individual basis usually ensures the co-operation of the person taking the test, and allows the test administrator the advantages of observing his subject at close range.

A qualitative as well as quantitative analysis is thereby made possible, and a more comprehensive evaluation results. Individual tests may be placed into two categories: *language* and *performance* tests. In language tests the use and understanding of language is required in the solution of a given problem. The testee may be asked to define several words, rearrange words logically in a scrambled sentence, answer questions about a certain paragraph, solve arithmetical problems, furnish information, or memorize increasing lists of digits.

Performance tests can be administered and taken without the use of oral or written language. This type of test usually involves the manipulation of blocks or picture puzzles in certain arrangements and sequences. Other tasks include solving a maze, drawing the human figure, and symbol memorization. Performance tests are found to be especially useful with individuals who present some type of language problem, such as illiteracy or deafness.

Group intelligence tests. Individual tests are usually laborious and time-consuming to administer. When estimates of large numbers are warranted, group intelligence tests are found to be quite practical. The test administrator does not have to be a highly trained specialist, and the scoring of such tests can usually be done by machines. Group tests are either of the language or nonlanguage variety, or a combination of both. The group language test is similar to the individual language test described above, with the distinction resting primarily on the fact that individual language tests are basically oral, whereas the group tests are of the paper-and-pencil variety. Group nonlanguage tests are similar to performance tests except that nonlanguage tests involve the use of paper and pencil rather than the actual manipulation of objects. The individual taking the test uses a pencil to underline, cancel or connect items, or to sketch other nonlinguistic marks.

Dimensions of intelligence tests. Intelligence tests, as well as tests of other mental characteristics (such as aptitude and reading) are usually designed to measure three major dimensions: power, speed, and range. The dimension of power is ascertained by gradually increasing the difficulty of the test items. Most tests, especially intelligence tests, measure the dimension of power since tests have been designed to locate the maximum level or limits of the characteristic being tested. The dimension of speed is measured by means of a time limit so that it is possible to determine the number of problems solved in a given time. Speed is an especially important dimension in tests involving mathematics, quantitative thinking, and, occasionally, vocabulary. Range is measured by the number of problems solved at a given level of difficulty. Once the level has been established, the limits within a particular level are measured. Language or mathematical placement tests represent attempts to measure range as well as level. An individual found capable of doing calculus will be placed in an introductory, advanced, or highly specialized theoretical math course depending upon his versatility at a given level of difficulty. Psychological tests will frequently measure a combination of these dimensions simultaneously. For a detailed description of various intelligence tests the reader is referred to Appendix B.

MEASURING SCHOLASTIC APTITUDE

The research studies regarding the relationship of intelligence to college success are filled with evidence indicating that the more intelligent individuals tend to make better students. The relationship between intelligence and scholastic aptitude is seen as a very significant one.

Most definitions of intelligence stress the capacity of the individual to adapt to his environment. If the school is considered as one kind of environment, scholastic aptitude is then seen as the capacity of the individual to adapt to an academic environment. Scholastic aptitude is thus considered one particular aspect of intelligence. The two terms cannot be equated, however, since intelligence is a more all-inclusive term—that is, it deals with environments of all types, in addition to the highly structured one of the school. It might be well at this point to consider some of the factors that make the school environment a unique one.

In an academic environment, students are confronted with the necessity of reading and understanding, making appropriate associations among facts, reasoning with ideas and concepts, or using mathematical formulas. The student is successful in these activities in direct proportion to his capacity or potential ability to use symbolic processes and to think in abstract terms (with words, concepts, and formulas).

Educators have devised tests for measuring this capacity to learn. An examination of some of these measuring devices may serve still further to clarify the relationship of scholastic aptitude to intelligence.

Scholastic aptitude tests

If scholastic aptitude is defined as the ability to learn in an academic situation, then the test items used should be a sample of the kind of thing that happens in school.

At the college level, the capacity to use symbolic processes and to think in abstract terms becomes extremely important. Scholastic aptitude tests are permeated with items that are designed to test these processes. Since the college curriculum puts a premium on language, scholastic aptitude tests are essentially nothing more than language tests of vocabulary, verbal analogies, reading comprehension, and mathematical manipulation and reasoning. Tests of scholastic aptitude define college success in vary narrow terms— the acquisition of "good" grades. The student's definition of college success, on the other hand, may be much more all-inclusive. Such factors as "making the basketball team," invitation into a fraternity or sorority, election to student council, dating, and acceptance by one's roommates or classmates may well constitute additional and important aspects of a satisfying and successful college experience. Since the discussion that follows is primarily concerned with success as measured by school grades alone, the term "scholastic success," rather than college success, is perhaps a more appropriate term.

Other measures

Among other valid measures of scholastic aptitude are reading tests, high-school records, and interest inventories.

Reading tests. The relevance of tests of reading comprehension as scholastic aptitude measures becomes apparent when one stops to consider the method of study and content of school assignments. The majority of college assignments involve reading. It stands to reason, then, that the poor reader is laboring under a distinct handicap. The carpenter who does all his work with poor or inferior tools will probably do poor or inferior work. So it is with the poor reader. Reading is an indispensable tool in the student's kit of instruments needed for scholastic success.

The variety and types of reading tests currently available are a strong indication of the importance of reading as a fundamental skill in the long and complex process of learning. In fact, it is difficult to separate reading tests from other tests of learning, such as intelligence, scholastic aptitude, and achievement tests. Most group paper-and-pencil tests involve reading activity of one sort or another. It becomes evident, then, that the general test performance of the retarded reader may suffer unfairly. Since intellectual and reading levels appear to be related, however, poor performance on either tests of reading or intelligence might indicate a genuine lack of reading skills, low intellectual functioning or, as suggested earlier, impairment due to emotional factors. Clearly, the interpretation of the significance of test results in general, and reading tests in particular, should not be a matter of concern for the psychologically naïve or the enthusiastic amateur.

High-school records. High-school records also provide valuable data that can be used for prediction. This relationship is not surprising in light of the known fact that past achievement is often an excellent index of future accomplishment. A student who has been getting C grades all his life will probably not do much better if he should go on to college. The perennial honor-roll student stands a good chance of making the "Dean's List" in college. This relationship is not a perfect one, however. It is not unusual to find wide discrepancies between one's high-school record and college achievement. The disinterested high-school student who finds college life stimulating and satisfying may develop a thirst for knowledge, and a drive to succeed, and thus achieve higher grades.

This sudden shift toward improved scholastic performance could be a reflection of a multitude of factors, such as increased physical and mental maturity, occupational-choice development, marital plans, feelings of obligation to the financial sponsor(s) of one's education, or changes in relationships at home. The promising high-school student may fail in college, on the other hand, because of poorly defined goals, continued immaturity, lack of time for study because of part-time work, or lack of money to finance studies. Although it is apparent that the high-school record is not an infallible predictor of scholastic success, its utility as an indicator of future accomplishment cannot be disregarded.

Interest inventories. The correlation between school grades and interest inventory scores is positive, but very low. This is explained in part by the fact that high interest is not always tantamount to success. Cer-

ROBERT HAYES

Meaningful personal planning demands the analysis of many factors and high self-involvement

tain minimal levels of ability or scholastic aptitude are necessary before interest can begin to serve as an effective motivating force. Interest inventory scores can serve as a valuable guidance instrument, however, by assisting the student to choose wisely in selecting courses and curricula. Although the sensitivity of interest inventories as general predictors of scholastic success is minimal, the accuracy of such predictions appears to increase for specific courses and specialized programs of studies.

PREDICTING SCHOLASTIC SUCCESS

Until recently, investigators concerned with the problem of "what makes Johnny tick scholastically" have confined their observations almost exclusively to the importance of intellectual factors. As the preceding discussion would indicate, tests of reading, intelligence, scholastic aptitude, and, to a lesser extent, interest inventories have played a major role in the prediction of scholastic success.

The test interpreter or college admissions officer examines test scores, high-school records and principals' recommendations, makes certain inferences, and draws conclusions. He is in essence making an "educated guess" based on his previous training and present knowledge and experience. As a result, he is able to make reasonably accurate predictions on the basis of mass data concerning the performance of a given group. Predictions governing the individual case, however, have been found to be highly inaccurate. This appears to be the result of a number of factors.

The existence of nonintellectual factors affecting scholastic achievement assumes significant proportions in the predictions of individual behavior. On the basis of test scores Johnny may have high scholastic potential, but whether he uses this potential or not appears to be an entirely different matter.

Although there appears to be safety in numbers regarding scholastic predictions the test interpreter's analysis of individual behavior is based on his own interpretation of the data. What the test interpreter sees and what Johnny feels may not be one and the same thing. Unobservable and unmeasured factors begin to assume real importance in terms of how much or how little the individual can and will produce in a scholastic sense.

The theoretical orientation of earlier chapters suggests a second way of examining and understanding behavior. Rather than attempting to view behavior externally from the test interpreter's point of view, why not examine behavior from the behaver's point of view and attempt to see things the way Johnny sees them? (116)

The way in which the individual himself interprets his environment has important implications for an understanding of individual behavior. If Johnny perceives school as a pleasant, stimulating, and desirable experience, his behavior in school will be quite different than it will be if he views the same experience as distasteful, threatening, and meaningless.

Whether the student has one type of perception or another, the perception appears to be a function of a number of factors. The following discussion draws upon ideas originally expressed by Combs. (35)

Physical factors

Congenital disorders, disease, injuries, malnutrition, and fatigue may all exact a toll in terms of how well Johnny does in school. Combs (35:664) warns, however, that "These people experience different, but not necessarily fewer or poorer perceptions of events than so called 'normals.' " This is illustrated by Calia (25) and Gamble (53) who describe an educational experiment in which two severely physically handicapped and therefore home-bound students were permitted to enroll in college. By means of a two-way telephone device, these students were able to "attend" classes. Both students graduated with high honors.

Socio-economic factors

Some individuals, because of the nature of their environment, move about in an atmosphere conducive to academic learning and motivation. Perhaps one's parents attended college, or the language spoken in the home is grammatically flawless. Some children are awarded a personal library or are provided with private tutoring. In such homes, college life is considered part of one's cultural heritage; one simply accepts the fact that one goes to college.

Students from low socioeconomic areas are, on the other hand, sometimes raised in an environment hardly considered conducive to their prospects as scholars. The language spoken in the home is extremely poor, or a foreign language is the only or the dominant language spoken. Youngsters are rarely encouraged to continue their schooling beyond high school. On the other hand, some college students with this kind of background become "overachievers." The reason may well be that the student wishes to "rise above all this." He is, in effect, compensating for a background that he wishes to overcome, and achieving recognition and status by his high scholastic achievements. Although it is difficult to predict how these factors will affect the individual case, students reared in an educationally oriented climate would appear to be at an advantage, both in terms of requisite educational skills and perceptual predispositions.

Careful thought must be given to planning the future

Motivation

Many students are familiar with the "bright" classmate who is content with "just getting by." He never "cracks a book," but he manages to pass. Students are also familiar with the "plugger," the classmate who is far from outstanding in terms of scholastic aptitude, but who still manages to get more than an expected number of A's and B's.

How does one explain this contrast in achievement, a bright boy with just passing grades, an average pupil with above-average marks? It becomes apparent that motivations, values, drives, and determination are unmeasured but important factors in educational success and may make a student who is mediocre according to test evidence actually a high performer and a success in school. As mentioned in an earlier chapter, motivation is seen as a function of goals and values. It is this existence of goals and the importance one attaches to the attainment of such goals that supplies motivation or driving power.

The role of motivation and values in college success appears to be supported by a number of related research projects. Studies have shown that students who entered college with definite aims in mind, and maintained them, made significantly superior scholarship records compared with those who did not. (38) It is similarly reported that students who made vocational choices prior to entering college and were comparable in ability with the "no choice" group had superior records of scholastic attainment. (130)

Another study found that students having definite vocational choices had superior scholastic records, but relatively mediocre aptitude, those with tentative choices ranked high in both achievement and aptitude, whereas the "undecideds" ranked low on both these factors. (83)

The college student who perceives scholastic success as a means of satisfying his basic needs or achieving a preordained goal will behave quite differently from the student whose perceptions are primarily socially oriented. The former student will probably be concerned with "making the Dean's List," scholarship awards, and graduate study, whereas the latter student will associate college life with "joining the fraternity," "running for student council," attending football games, and organizing school socials. A common experience then, such as "going to college," may be perceived in dissimilar ways, depending upon the individual's goals and values.

Self-concept

The way in which an individual perceives himself has tremendous implications for the kind of behavior he will produce. If he "sees himself" as a basically stupid person, then he will perhaps behave in those terms, whether he is genuinely "stupid" or not! Similarly, the person who visualizes himself as intellectually superior will attempt to manifest behavior in keeping with this picture of himself. He may be a "high achiever" in school, assuming he has the necessary potential, or he may devise other techniques for defending and enhancing this self-picture.

Examples have been reported (76) in which children improved their ability to spell following changes in their self-picture. Other reports indicate changes in intelligence-test performance accompanying attempts to influence self-conceptualization. (11)

The way in which the individual perceives himself in relation to his scholastic environment will have a good deal to do with his subsequent success or failure as a student. If Johnny sees himself as a person having strong mechanical inclinations and is pressured into a program of fine arts, the chances for his success in his misguided environment would appear to be slim indeed, unless his picture or concept of himself should change and the requisite abilities and aptitudes were found to be present.

Emotional influences

Students achieving far beyond their expected level are called "overachievers." These students will work painfully hard and study for long hours, many times at the expense of their health, social life, and occasional recre-

ation. Excessive emphasis on scholastic achievement can also be an undesirable thing. The two extremes of underachieving and overachieving can
both be very negative kinds of traits and are usually associated with emotional
difficulties of some sort. The "underachiever" may find that getting low
grades upsets his parents. He soon learns that this is one way of "getting
even" with his parents. The "overachiever," on the other hand, may be out
to prove that his parents are wrong and that he is capable of much more
than his parents believe.

A happy home appears to play a significant role in the achievement of
scholastic success. Family relationships "set" the emotional climate in
which the student finds himself. As such, they may enhance his feelings of
security and confidence or be quite disturbing in their influence.

Cultures have unique value systems. As a member of a particular culture,
each individual is affected by the customs and habits of his group. Some
cultures encourage intellectual achievement whereas others seek to inhibit
or control it. Frequently, individuals find themselves in conflict with the dictates of their cultural group. When this occurs it is usually accompanied by
emotional distress and a corresponding impairment of intellectual functioning.

The student who feels emotionally threatened must spend considerable
time devising ways of defending himself. Frequently, such students become
so engrossed in their defenses that their performance in school suffers accordingly. In addition, the student's intellectual and rational processes are
disturbed. He cannot seem to "think straight anymore." His perceptions
become narrow or distorted. Dollard and Miller (46:125) refer to this
phenomenon as "a stupid area in the mind." Such a person may be intellectually normal in other respects. It is possible, however, that the student
who is emotionally disturbed may suffer impairment in all aspects of his
behavior, including achievement in school.

There are, therefore, many variables involved in achieving scholastic
success. The influence of such unmeasured factors as physical health, socioeconomic circumstances, motivation, concept of self, and emotional state
cannot be minimized. The poor or underachieving student may be having
scholastic difficulties, not because of his intellectual limitations, but because
of poor health, money problems, poor learning experiences in the past, lack
of well defined goals, conflicting values, inadequate or inferior perceptions of
self, or emotional difficulties. Such factors must be considered in light of
their effect on the perception of the individual.

Scholastic success is seen often as the function of two fundamental factors: intellectual potential and perception. Whereas the former is measurable, the perceptual factors are not so easily tested. Biological or structural
factors may set the intellectual ceiling, but perceptual influences determine
how "close to the ceiling one gets." If the logic of this discussion is valid,

then as Combs (35) suggests, medicinal care, scholarship grants, private or tutorial instruction, encouraging educational experiences, crystallization of goals, reorganizing one's perceptions about one's self, or other forms of psychotherapy, should free the student to function more adequately in his educational environment.

OLD WIVES' TALES

There are probably more common misunderstandings and fanciful tales of dubious origin concerning the nature of intelligence than perhaps any other aspect of human behavior. An attempt shall be made to examine a few of the more prominent ones in order to show their inherent fallacies.

Cultural emphasis on intelligence

A high price is placed on the possession of intelligence in our culture so that a high level of intelligence is generally identified with individuals having high social status or prestige. As Lindgren (80:325) suggests, this overemphasis of intellectual factors appears to be a reflection of somewhat distorted middle-class values. "We tend to accept as worthy members of society those persons who demonstrate the capacity to act intelligently: and we reject, with a mixture of scorn, derision and pity, those persons who do not appear to possess intellectual abilities that are at least as high as those of the 'average person.' " This overemphasis on intelligence is accompanied by a disregard for the importance of emotional factors. As Lindgren warns, to be called "stupid" or "dumb" is a major social catastrophe, whereas the labels "nervous," "quick tempered," and "cynical" are hardly as offensive and threatening. Perhaps the old adage "money isn't everything" might well apply to this concept of placing a cultural premium on intelligence. The possession of intelligence is not a prerequisite to emotional contentment and well-being. In the final analysis, emotional security, "happiness," and "being at peace with oneself" would appear to be more appropriate descriptions of desirable behavioral characteristics and accordingly should receive priority in the cultural hierarchy of values.

The American success story is perhaps as responsible as anything else for the notion that "if you want something hard enough, you can get it if you try." Similarly, the student with severe intellectual limitations and aspirations of medical school feels that if he tries hard enough he will succeed. As mentioned in an earlier chapter, Topps' warning, "you cannot always do it if you try," and Lindgren's label, "the anyone-can-be-intelligent myth," serve to illustrate the implications of the principle of individual differences. There are some intellectual aspirations that are simply beyond the realm of reality for individuals whose intellectual capacity is on the left-hand side of the normal distribution curve. Although the importance of determination and drive cannot be denied, there appear to be limits beyond which motivational forces cease to be effective.

Intelligence level and personality difficulties

People seem to have a number of misconceptions regarding the relationship of personality adjustment and intelligence level. The intellectually gifted child is frequently tabbed as the "crazy genius." Being intellectually superior appears to be tantamount to being "queer" or "one shade removed from insanity." Contrary to popular belief, Anastasi (5:597), on the basis of a number of studies, concludes that:

> Exceptional talents in childhood are not incompatible with good health, physical vigor, longevity, or a well-rounded personality. To be sure, puny, timid, and sickly children can be found among the gifted, as among the intellectually normal or dull. But such cases are very few and cannot be regarded as representative of the group as a whole.

On the opposite end of the intellectual continuum, the seriously mentally retarded are not, *ipso facto,* emotionally disturbed. There is the danger, however, unless their limitations are recognized and dealt with accordingly, that they may not be able to cope with the excessive demands of their environment. This continual inability to fulfill the unrealistic expectations of those about them may eventually serve to precipitate serious emotional disturbances.

Although there appears to be evidence of a relationship between the kind of emotional symptom or disorder and intellectual level, the relationship is less clear with regard to the probability of developing behavioral difficulties. Contrary to public opinion, however, when compared with their intellectually "normal" kinsmen, the intellectually "brighter" individuals seem to have no more than their share of personality problems.

Racial differences

Hitler's doctrine concerning the physical and intellectual superiority of the Aryan race is an example of the thoroughly false notion of genuine racial differences.

To begin with, it is extremely difficult, if not impossible, to isolate such variables as ancestral interracial marriages, socio-economic effects, language barriers, and cultural influences, and then to attribute the results to racial differences. Many quasi-racial groups constitute minority groups and, as such, are subjected to the influence of the ruling majority. As a minority group, they do not have comparable educational and vocational opportunities, and environmental conditions are usually not conducive to the encouragement of intellectual growth. In addition, since intelligence tests are comprised primarily of verbal tasks, the test performance of individuals hampered by problems of language will be seriously affected.

Finally, the importance of cultural differences cannot be underestimated. Many of the intelligence-test items are heavily laden with material having profound cultural connotations. This is aptly illustrated by Anastasi (5:505): "In a sentence completion test of the National Intelligence Scale is found the statement: '———should prevail in churches and libraries.' The word to be inserted in this case is 'silence.' Among Negro children, however, this problem would be complicated by the fact that their own churches are seldom silent. Noise is not only common in their house of worship, but is frequently an integral and essential part of the ritual." An attempt is being made to "control" such factors by devising a culture-free test of intelligence. The task of building such a test is not an easy one, however, and the process of development and improvement is a continuing one.

In light of the above discussion, to attribute differences in intellect to differences in race would be highly irrational and seemingly prejudicial.

SUMMARY

Intelligence is a concept that is not easily defined. Most definitions, however, emphasize versatility or flexibility of response and the ability to think and reason in abstract terms. Contemporary concepts emphasize the dynamic aspects of intelligence, multiplicity of functions, and varying rates of development. This definition of intelligence would imply that it is not only the "bright" student who deals with the "abstract" who is considered intelligent, but also the person who is capable of varying his responses to meet the demands of his total environment. The person who is able to fix the car when it breaks down, who is able to assume responsibility in a leaderless group, and who is able to make the right decisions "when the chips are down" is exhibiting characteristics of intelligence.

Scholastic aptitude is seen as a specific aspect of intelligence. It may be described as the successful adjustment of the individual to one particular kind of environment. Language and linguistic factors are important in the measurement of scholastic aptitude. On the other hand, the significance of such factors as motivation, drive, determination, and other personality variables cannot be ignored. In making predictions about human behavior relevant to any situation, academic or otherwise, the individual in his entirety must always be considered.

In summary, then, no single test or variable is particularly effective as a predictor of scholastic success. When, however, all of the aforementioned variables (test scores, health, motivation, and the like) are combined, one is able to make fairly accurate predictions concerning the individual case. The single test or variable when used alone is limited and varies widely in its prognostic value. Multiple factors, then, make for the most valid predictions.

SUPPLEMENTARY SOURCES

Anastasi, Anne, and John P. Foley, Jr. *Differential Psychology, Individual and Group Differences in Behavior.* New York: The Macmillan Company, 1949.

————, *Psychological Testing.* New York: The Macmillan Company, 1954.

Bischof, L. J., *Intelligence, Statistical Concepts of Its Nature.* New York: Doubleday & Company, Inc., 1954.

Deese, James, *The Psychology of Learning.* New York: McGraw-Hill Book Company, Inc., 1952.

Miner, John B., *Intelligence in the United States. A Survey of Man-Power Utilization.* New York: Springer Publishing Co., Inc., 1957.

Mursell, James L., *Psychological Testing.* New York: Longmans, Green & Company, 1947.

Thorndike, Robert L., and Elizabeth Hagen, *Measurement and Evaluation in Psychology and Education.* New York: John Wiley & Sons, Inc., 1955.

Weitz, H., M. Clarke, and O. Jones, "The Relationships between Choice of a Major Field of Study and Academic Preparation and Performance," *Educational and Psychological Measurement,* 15 (1955), pp. 28-38.

Wolfle, Dael L., *America's Resources of Specialized Talent.* New York: Harper & Brothers, 1954.

Woodrow, H., "The Ability to Learn," *Psychological Review,* 33 (1946), pp. 147-158.

elf-analysis has now progressed through the many areas of personality included in Part III. There are many other areas of personality that might have been made a part of this process but a balanced approach to the analysis of the "student in college" dictated the present choice. It is necessary, however, to include several miscellaneous areas of self-appraisal that are not appropriate elsewhere in this section.

Time, money, health, study habits, the family, the girl or boy friend, even the Armed Forces may be primarily environ-

Chapter 12

THE OTHER FACTORS

mental forces (excepting health) but they can be decisive in a student's adjustment to college. Personality handicaps of a more serious psychological nature may also exist.

Many students have developed precise plans for their futures, but are sometimes unable to recognize that minor factors might become major problems in their accomplishment. Expectation of such happenings is beyond the perspective of any student. Realistic appraisal of all other factors in a particular situation can, however, often reveal predictable and, within limits, controllable problems.

An example may aid in establishing the need for examining all "other factors." John is planning to attend college for four years and then enter the state university medical school. He is the son of a Polish immigrant who settled in this country thirty years ago. He is dating a Greek girl who wants to get married in the near future. John works three nights a week as a night watchman. He has no service experience since he was classified "4-F" because of a potentially serious heart condition. There are certainly predictable and somewhat controllable factors in this situation with which John must concern himself.

193

ETERNAL FACTORS

Time, money, and health need to be considered as related problems. Difficulties in one of these areas may exert a related effect upon the other two.

Time

Philosophers have long been attracted to time as one of the most precious commodities of life. College students may arrive at a similar conclusion, although through more unusual means. The commuting student, the working student, the athlete, the married student, each must budget his time carefully.

An average college week calls for between fifteen and twenty classroom hours. In addition, most schools expect two study hours to be used in preparation for each classroom hour. Beyond these subtotals, time will be used in other school events, such as student activities, library reports, interviews with teachers, and field trips. A student living at home uses time in commuting and in routine family and home duties whereas the dormitory student is in the inevitable bull sessions or in working at a dormitory job.

A student's week may look like this:

        17 hr. of classes, lectures, labs
        34 hr. of homework from these classes
         5 hr. additional connected with classroom and library trips, consulting
            instructors, and the like
        10 hr. school events and activities
        15 hr. commuting, routine duties, dorm discussions
        15 hr. at meals
        10 hr. recreation, instrument practicing, and so forth
        56 hr. sleep, at 8 hr. each day
        ‾‾‾
       162 hours of the 168 in a week

The time schedule listed cannot cover every student. Certainly, many professors would be pleased to see every student spend so many hours in study, but they realize that by no means will every student be so conscientious. Students, however, may do well to assume that the listed schedule of hours is a recommended pattern and that variations should be made only after thorough and thoughtful analysis. Each student will need to pattern his own time to meet what he feels are his obligations and personal desires, but the basic fact is clear that college must be considered to be a *full-time* job. Variations in an ideal time schedule for work or any unusual activity will require a rearrangement of hours devoted to other normal activities.

The working student is particularly sensitive to a time schedule. College histories are replete with stories of working students whose achievements have been outstanding. A lack of funds and a heavy part-time or full-time work load sometimes bring out in a person an exceptional organizational ability to manage time. Other students, however, who attempt to combine college and work because of financial need may find that study habits disintegrate, achievement deteriorates, and perhaps even health may begin to fail.

All students who divert their normal full-time attention from college studies and efforts need to be fully aware of the risks which are involved. Students may perhaps be attempting an impossible task. A compromise or unusual solution may be required if a student wishes to complete college.

The co-operative plan of college attendance is such a compromise or unusual solution. A full freshman-year program is followed by alternating periods of work and school until graduation. The jobs are in areas of the student's vocational choice, becoming more advanced in responsibility and pay as he is better prepared for them by the classroom portions of his school year. After the first year the income during work periods will usually cover all school bills, making the student almost self-supporting. This program is continuous for five or six years. Upon completion each student has had several periods of job experience in the field of his goal, and has achieved both durable contacts with several employers and a good "on-the-job" introduction to his future career.

Other programs are possible with full-time work. Complete diploma and degree curricula are available in university night schools, with supplements through extension services. Separate topical training is available in adult education services of most public-school systems. In summary, varied training programs exist, and many real time problems can be accommodated.

Money

If it may be said that philosophers are concerned with time, it most certainly can also be said that almost everyone else appears to be most concerned with money. College students in many cases reach this conclusion early in their educational careers. Tuition, room and board, transportation, clothing, and miscellaneous expenses reach an impressive total during four years. Lost earnings add to this total.

Parents most often must bear the expense entailed in college. Recent years have added "Uncle Sam" as an additional rich relative. Many students finance their entire education, and this group of "self-financed" students often can serve to illustrate principles of motivation and values treated in Chapter 2. When an individual "foots the bill" an unusual attitudinal change may take place. He begins to question whether or not full dollar value is being received. Many "nonpaying" students could do well to investigate the attitudes of the "value-conscious" students.

Scholarship aid, part-time work, summer work, or even loans can often only partially solve a serious financial problem. Time, as previously discussed, can become a precious commodity. Students need to develop careful budgetary habits in both money and time.

Health

Health becomes the third side of the triangle of which time and money are the other two sides. Personal adjustment, success, and even failure are often associated with a person's possession or lack of a physical state of well-being. Health is a commodity, like time, that cannot be purchased but without which all of life may be meaningless. College students are seldom concerned with the extremes of health but rather are most often closely involved in repeated minor health problems.

Good health is brought about and maintained more through routine and habit than through "one-shot" cures. The effects of "goof-balls" for exam study cannot be overcome by an extra afternoon of sleep. Better planning will give time for both study and regular sleep. After awakening, a full breakfast is necessary for top all-day efficiency. Lunch at the "Greasy Spoon" may have atmosphere, but little nutritional balance. Long hours of exertion in athletics must be compensated for in the diet. Some relaxation from the academic side of college in the form of activities, dates, and trips will be refreshing, but must not be used, however, as an "out"—an imbalance between dating and curriculum has caused many dropouts. Balance in work and relaxation, between sleep and work, and in diet is within the control of most students and thus can be organized toward a high level of college performance. Students occasionally use an all-night study session as a conversational gambit rather than as preparation for an examination. Health is a precious item that will stand much abuse and punishment in certain individuals but in others the stakes may be too high to consider the gamble.

Considering the relationship between health and vocations, why do many dental-supply salesmen have varicose veins and heart conditions? Because many dental offices are on second floors and stairs get hard to climb? Is there a difference in insurance premiums for construction superintendents and teachers? Why is advertising called the "ulcer business?" Why are many firms requiring semiannual checkups and long vacations for their executives? Even though life expectancy for our population as a whole is climbing, a look at the tables of working life for vocational fields can be illuminating.

Maintaining active mental and physical health requires planned and moderate amounts of change of pace for both the mind and the body. The same planning should consider how the student's health status fits his current plans and future goals.

STUDY HABITS AND COMMUNICATIONS SKILLS

Colleges generally assume that students have learned in high school how to study, and how to read, listen, write, and speak. Few colleges give attention to the planting of these skills, but some do give further training in them. The words *habit* and *skill* imply that these are factors that can be sharpened through additional training and practice. This is fortunately correct, but even with developmental study and communications-skills programs, colleges put their main emphasis on the *use* of these tools.

These tools are the primary skills that are necessary for college success. A poor set puts its owner at a great competitive disadvantage. At the present time, between a fourth and a third of all high-school graduates continue into further training. These students who were formerly competing against the middle and bottom of their high-school classes are now working with other students who are just as able as themselves, if not of higher ability. Study methods that earned them B grades in high school may now gain college C's or D's. This change in competitive level is one of the first shocks college students feel.

A second shock is often present in recognizing that "English" is more than just the content of English class. Through all schooling and later in the world of work, human beings are constantly required to receive, evaluate, and transmit ideas. We receive impressions mainly through reading and listening skills, interpret them through critical thinking, and express them to others through our writing and speaking abilities. These study and communications skills are so interrelated in all of life that they cannot be separated. An individual's successful organization of study skills is a compilation of many good habits, drawn from these several areas. This becomes a discipline—a routine that results in the most efficient life as a student and the most efficient life as a person. To reach these goals, every student must evaluate his current level of ability with these tools and assess his chance of getting through college with these skills in their current state of development.

It is beyond the province of this book to analyze the many problems inherent in communications. Each student will need to complete a thorough stocktaking in this field. Assistance in reading or writing laboratories can often make a significant contribution to the level of achievement of a student.

THE FAMILY

The family is the social institution that nurtures and protects the developing child. Even as the family is continuing to build that protective shell, its most difficult function is to wean the child away from the shell's security toward the security of independence and self-reliance. In addition to receiving basic social and philosophical attitudes from the family, the success of each person in the psychological weaning process of childhood and adolescence determines the degree of self-sufficiency and maturity of later life. Of course, even though the child has matured psychologically and physically, he cannot separate his family from all consideration.

A series of questions can aid in highlighting certain of the problems in family adjustment:

1. To what extent have your goals been chosen by yourself, or by your family?
2. Are your aims based on realistic self-evaluation, or a belief in "like father, like son"?
3. If the family is sympathetic to your goals, is this "goal agreement" active or passive?
4. How much have you tried to acquaint your family with your aims and your plans for achieving them?
5. What are the consequences of these plans for your family?
6. Is the family likely to be your main source of support during a training period?
7. Is their support likely to be stable?
8. Are your socioeconomic goals compatible with those of your family? Why?
9. Is such agreement necessary?
10. What problems may arise if these goals disagree?
11. How will your parents feel if you change objectives, flunk out, want to transfer to another college, enter the service, or get married before finishing?

These questions are not intended to provoke problems where problems do not exist. Instead, they are intended to stimulate family thinking and discussion in this area. The family group from which a student comes is just as important a consideration as is the family that later will be formed by the student.

BOY AND GIRL FRIENDS

No student has had a choice in the selection of his parents, but in the choice of his future mate, everyone has a chance of his own. Colleges are wonderful places to date and find a mate. Dating is one part of the process of selection involved in choosing a life partner, and thus dating is part of the preparation for marriage.

College, regardless of whether the students are residents or commuters, males or females, bring together young people from widely separated geographical areas, socioeconomic regions, and philosophical approaches to life. This grouping is often more heterogeneous than the home neighborhood or community. Social experience with diverse personalities thus assembled can contribute immensely to successful marriage. The individual may learn that his own values and interests are shallow or immature, or of much less importance to others than he thought them to be. The adaptiveness acquired in dating serves as a valuable preface to the mutual changes required in marriage. The couple that seeks understanding and the deeper meanings of life can develop mutual trust, concern for each other, and bonds that are more durable than those in many other marriages.

Not every student, however (although it may sometimes appear to be so), is seeking a mate while in college. Students need to learn to utilize dating as a normal portion of college life rather than as a frenzied freedom to ignore the basic tasks of college. Maturity or immaturity is often clearly delineated in courtship behavior. Men and women need to judge carefully, not only the beauty and dress or suaveness and athletic talents in a "date," but the inherent poise, maturity, and responsibility displayed.

Fraternity, sorority, or dormitory life can offer many valuable learning experiences in college. Perhaps a separate section could be devoted to such an area, but the principles listed above with regard to dating can actually apply in all of social life. Each student needs to achieve maturity, responsibility, and balance.

THE ARMED FORCES

Most men will be directly affected by national service needs. Whether the service period comes before, during, or following one's personal educational training period depends on health, academic plans, achievement, and potential. Time in service can produce results that will be whatever the individual wants them to be; his time can be invested for great reward or merely "put in." In general terms, the services feel that America's population resources are small when compared to those of possible adversaries. As a consequence, we must rely on quality rather than quantity, and brainpower but not manpower. Thus, all services are concerned with attracting, training, and utilizing men and women who have completed all possible education before entering the Armed Forces.

Once in uniform, many training possibilities are available to qualified men. The services operate some schools that are the only ones of their kind in the country. Since civilian schools do not supply this training, graduates of such military programs are in great demand in civilian counterpart fields.

Most men gain new experience and wider horizons, mentally as well as geographically. Among other values is the time-off-from-college aspect. Many students have used the service as a breather in which to grow and think and plan. The experience of employers and colleges with World War II and Korean veterans indicates that these men generally were more mature, had greater motivation, performed better, and in general seemed to recognize a greater "value" in life and the operation in which they were involved.

PERSONALITY HANDICAPS

All of the previously discussed "other factors" are relatively uncomplicated psychologically in their basic impingement on or involvement in a person's life. This is, of course, not to say that they cannot *become* overwhelming. A difference, however, needs to be pointed out as these uncomplicated factors are compared with the factors of neurotic, psychotic, or other types of abnormal behavior.

Neurotic and *psychotic* are terms used to identify the more seriously maladjusted patterns of personality or behavior. As earlier indicated, the personality is seriously involved in persons who are mentally ill or disturbed. The problems of personality affect only a small portion of the population, but when present they constitute a most serious complication. Neurotic and psychotic patterns of behavior require professional treatment. Just as with any type of physical illness, it may be necessary to postpone education, training, marriage, or other plans while treatment is in progress and perhaps until it is completed. In other situations treatment can be obtained and other activities can be carried on in a nearly normal fashion.

Individuals need to recognize when professional assistance is needed. This is, however, by no means always possible. An interested teacher, a skilled counselor, a friend, the family physician, or many other resources can be used when there is a concern about patterns of maladjusted behavior. A university or college psychology department, counseling bureau, or a public Red Feather Agency can also many times be a valuable resource or referral source or both in time of need.

Students sometimes assume that neurotic and psychotic, or related, patterns of behavior will destroy any hope of further education. Such concern may be unfounded. Early diagnosis and treatment can provide for a more favorable prognosis and therefore an earlier return to an educational program.

SUMMARY

Preceding this chapter were units on social maturity, individual differences, interest, aptitude, and intelligence. These are factors whose importance in life planning is clearly seen. This chapter has been a presentation concerning the problems of the family, the girl or boy friend, and military service. To some students none of these areas will produce problems, but to other students, one or more will be roadblocks in a career.

Can you spare time now for further training? College is full-time employment in itself for the student motivated to make the most of the opportunity. Other demands on time—a job, need to support a family, commuting distance—are each likely to cut into the time available for a college program.

Can you pay for further training now? Do you have more brains than money? Even the bargain rate of $4.00 per classroom hour makes college expensive. Money alone does not ensure success in college, but it is one obstacle that has kept many students out of college.

What has health to do with college success? Health is one aspect of physical aptitude and physical ability. Physical requirements for good college work are based on a balanced diet of sleep, food, work, play, and thought. In college planning there is a blending of these ingredients; equally necessary is such a blend in one's career planning.

Do you have the basic skills and abilities necessary for college? You have to provide these study and communication "tools" for yourself, in most instances. College grades reflect not only what is being communicated (the subject) but also how well the student (and faculty) communicating has been done. The change in the competitive group from high school to college requires a more precise use of language and study skills. If you call yourself a "slow reader," or if you "know it but can't express it" you may have serious problems.

How have your family attitudes on education affected your planning? From the nurture of the family we all must achieve independence; we all must learn to become self-sufficient persons, making decisions on the basis of reality.

Is dating in opposition to the curriculum? Dating is normal behavior and can increase attention given to academics. Dating provides an opportunity for the student to enlarge his friendships into a cross-sectional group, representing diverse viewpoints and backgrounds. This stimulation of dating can help the student toward maturity or can divert attention and cause loss of time through overindulgence.

Is service in the Armed Forces worthwhile or in the way? Whether it is a help or a hindrance depends partly on factors that are unpredictable, but we can be sure that service is a factor for almost all men to consider in their planning. The broad, new experience provided, and the "time out to think" have benefited many. What results accrue depend mainly on the attitudes with which service is approached and what happens during that period.

Personality handicaps of a more serious nature may be a serious complication. Neurotic or psychotic patterns of behavior require professional treatment. Referral and attention to these problems can provide the means for continuing or returning to the basic plans and goals of life.

SUPPLEMENTARY SOURCES

Bennett, M. E., *College and Life* (4th ed.). New York: McGraw-Hill Book Company, Inc., 1952.

Bernard, Harold W., *Toward Better Personal Adjustment* (2nd ed.). New York: McGraw-Hill Book Company, Inc., 1957.

Heyns, Roger W., *The Psychology of Personal Adjustment.* New York: The Dryden Press, Inc., 1958.

Landis, Paul H., *So This Is College.* New York: McGraw-Hill Book Company, Inc., 1954.

McKinley, Fred, *Psychology of Personal Adjustment* (2nd ed.). New York: John Wiley & Sons, Inc., 1949.

Pressey, Sidney L., and Raymond G. Kuhlen, *Psychological Development through the Life Span.* New York: Harper & Brothers, 1957.

Young, Kimball, *Personality and Problems of Adjustment* (2nd ed.). New York: Appleton-Century-Crofts, Inc., 1952.

Part III of this book was an exploration into the process of self-analysis and self-appraisal. The various areas of personality significant for success as a student in college were presented in both theoretical and practical fashion. The chapters in Part III presented concepts concerning individual differences, vocational interest, aptitudes, and intelligence. Exercises in the appendix and discussions in the classroom, group meetings, and individual interviews will have added and, hopefully, aided in this process. The task at hand is to

Chapter 13

*PROCESS OF
SELF-ANALYSIS*

consolidate and integrate the many aspects of self-analysis and self-appraisal into a meaningful total picture.

Students will find that the "Self-Analysis Student Workbook," Appendix C, will be useful as they read this chapter. It is assumed that students after reading this chapter will turn to the workbook and complete the questions included there. After the workbook is complete, or nearly complete, it may be necessary to re-read this chapter before attempting to write the "self-analysis essay" based on the workbook.

The teacher-counselor is an unseen partner in the process of self-analysis. Discussion with a teacher-counselor in small groups and in personal counseling interviews can help students to clarify issues or facts which may be confusing to them. The major problem in the completion of a "self-analysis essay" is to relate and correlate factual data on a higher level of abstraction or thinking. It is not enough simply to list facts or relate items requested. The process of thinking must involve the establishment of relationships and application. In this process of self-analysis, the student must constantly ask the question of, "—so?"

203

DATA FOR SELF-ANALYSIS

Through self-understanding each student can think more critically and make decisions more effectively, and thus plan for the future with greater confidence and assurance. Students have been able to collect and order data and must now seek an insightful view of all known data. It is not assumed or hoped that individuals in this process are to alter radically or even change significantly their total personality. Selected patterns of behavior may be modified, but the goal of the process of self-analysis is to provide meaningful understandings concerning the on-going functioning of personality. Such understandings can then be translated into conclusions and generalizations that can be utilized in future actions.

Orientation to self-analysis

College students find themselves in a unique environment as they enter upon the growth experience of study and learning in an institution of higher learning. In order to understand the uniqueness of such an experience, students need to look at their motivational and value patterns as well as the process of learning in college. Chapters 2 and 3 were concerned with these areas. Questions such as the following need to be answered in order to begin the process of self-analysis:

1. Why am I in college?
2. What do I expect from college?
3. What does education mean to me?
4. How can I learn?
5. What do I bring to the learning process?

Students may be able to organize partial answers to these questions, but full and complete answers are seldom if ever possible. Chapters 2 and 3 in review may aid in the answering of these questions, but students will need to retain these issues and questions clearly in their minds as they progress through the collection and interpretation of data for the "self-analysis essay." After the completion of the essay a return to these questions with further learnings and answers may aid students in securing an adequate perspective of their "selves" in action.

Foundations of self-analysis

Chapters 4, 5, 6, and 7, "Causes of Human Behavior," "Theories of Learning," "Personality," and "Psychological and Social Maturity," were presented as a foundation for students involved in a study of personal adjustment, personality, and psychology. The facts, principles, and implications of these chapters are the substance out of which man's behavior and man can be at least partially understood. Meaningful and substantial answers to the following questions should now be available to students:

1. What are the major causes or forces underlying man's behavior?
2. How does learning take place?
3. What is personality? How is it formed? How does it function?
4. What is maturity?

Collection of data

Chapters 8 through 12 have been written to assist students in collecting and establishing facts and information about themselves. Students have examined these concepts and ideas because they are central to success in college and life.

A review of concepts presented in Part III will allow each student to determine whether all areas of self-analysis have been understood before attempting to synthesize these many factors into a self-analysis essay and a clearly seen "self-picture." The review that follows is presented in the same order as were the topics in the chapters.

Individual differences. Chapter 8, "Individual Differences," was an approach to the ways in which persons differ from one another and a presentation of the major methods of determining the approximate degree of these differences. A *quantitative* and *comparative* approach was offered through the study of the principles of measurement. Each student needs to review these concepts by adequately answering these questions:

1. What is the meaning of the concept of "individual differences"?
2. What are the implications for me in such a concept?
3. What are the major principles of measurement needed for a quantitative and comparative study of the self?
   a. What are "central tendencies"?
   b. What are "percentiles"?
   c. What are "norm groups"?
   d. What are "derived scores"?

At this stage in the process of self-analysis and self-appraisal these questions must be fully answered or subsequent areas of study dependent upon these concepts will be meaningless.

Vocational interest. Vocational interest becomes the first area of study of the self in quantitative *comparison with others*. The adequacy of each student's knowledge concerning the meaning of vocational interest is, of necessity, primary. As this term is understood the following questions must be answered:

1. What is my *pattern* of interests?
    a. What inventories were used to measure my interests?
    b. What are my highest areas of interest?
    c. What are my lowest areas of interest?
2. What are my likes and dislikes?
3. What are my hobbies?
4. What jobs and work experience have I liked?
5. What else do I need to know in addition to my interests?

Question 5 serves as the transition to the other areas of self-analysis and critical thinking. Interest is only an *introductory factor*. What the other factors of self-analysis reveal must be seen in conjunction with vocational interest.

The actual plotting of interest on the psychological test data sheet (see Appendix A) should be done now if it has not been done before.

Concepts and types of aptitudes. "Aptitude" is an important word. Does it mean the same as interest or is it something different? Actually, the two words connote something unique, but are often confused in meaning. Aptitude is the second area of a *comparative, quantitative* study of the self. An aptitude must first be defined and then understood. As this is done the following questions must be answered:

1. What aptitudes do I have?
2. In what areas are my aptitudes high or low?
3. Are my interests and aptitudes in similar areas?
    a. What interests on the psychological test data sheet coincide or relate to aptitudes?
    b. What interests on the psychological test data sheet are opposite from aptitudes?
4. Is my aptitude high enough when compared with appropriate norm groups to hope for any success in my chosen field?

The above-listed questions should have been answered during the initial study of aptitude and are now merely reviewed. Any results of aptitude tests should be entered on the psychological test data sheet, Appendix A, so that a comparative study may be made. The exact function of each aptitude test needs to be clearly seen and understood. (See the student's psychological test glossary, Appendix B.)

Intelligence and scholastic aptitude. Intelligence is a concept that is little understood by students, or by the general public. If questions are still present with regard to the meaning of intelligence, reference should be made back to Chapter 11. Scholastic aptitude is directly related to intelligence, but not identical with intelligence.

If intelligence and scholastic aptitude are understood the following questions should aid in analyzing these factors:

1. What is my intelligence level?
    a. What is my intelligence when compared to most people?
    b. What is my intelligence when compared to college freshmen?
    c. What tests measure intelligence?
2. What is my scholastic aptitude level?
    a. What are the major factors involved in scholastic aptitude?
    b. What tests measure scholastic aptitude?
3. What part does reading play in scholastic aptitude?
    a. What is my reading ability level and speed?
    b. Can I raise my reading speed and comprehension?
    c. Can I raise my scholastic aptitude?
4. Can I raise my intelligence?
5. What relationship exists between intelligence and "college success" and "success"?

The interrelationships of intelligence, scholastic aptitude, and reading speed and comprehension are delicate and complicated. Yet in this area lie some of the most vital types of information for self-analysis and self-understanding. The results of all appropriate psychological tests should be entered on the psychological test data sheet, Appendix A.

Other factors. The major elements of self-understanding have been listed and summarized. There are other factors, however, that may or may not loom large in an individual case. The relatively simple problems of time, money, family, girl friends or boy friends, and the Armed Forces, as well as the more serious problems of personality handicaps, can sometimes be a deciding force in an individual's existence. A view of these many factors can be summarized by reviewing such questions as:

1. What are the other factors that are important for me?
2. How significant are these factors and how do they affect me?
3. What control can be exacted by me in these areas?
4. What are the interrelationships of these factors with other data I know about myself?

This chapter discusses additional features that aid in distinguishing each person from every other person. Although many facts may be the same for two people, the many other factors individualize each problem and each person.

Integration of facts

The interrelationships of the many areas and facts involved in self-analysis are particularly difficult to see clearly. They cannot be seen as a series of factors to be added or to be mixed, or as simply unrelated aspects of personality. They must be seen as factors, facts, forces, and areas that have many overlapping and integrative elements.

As an example, vocational interest can be seen as a key factor in self-analysis. Many students are inclined to utilize interest as a sole determining force while planning for the future. Interest alone is meaningless in terms of a total understanding of personality. The same strong statement can be made concerning any *single* factor previously studied. All areas need to be seen in relation to other factors and the total picture.

Although no one factor or area can be said to be most important it is necessary to say that each pattern is composed of varying elements and varying emphases of elements. Self-analysis depends upon the student's ability to relate each fact or factor to every other fact or factor. Each area needs to be examined in light of all other areas. When such an examination has been completed, an integrated picture can result as generalizations are drawn and implications seen.

PROCEDURE FOR SELF-ANALYSIS

After the student has collected the facts and attempted to integrate them, the process of self-analysis may begin. A written essay will provide an opportunity for each person to express his ideas and knowledge of facts in a unified and clear manner.

A suggested outline of topics is to be offered to aid the student in organizing a "self-analysis essay." An over-all view of the problems inherent in each area will aid the student in composing the "self-analysis essay."

Suggested outline

    I. My strengths and weaknesses as a student and person
    II. My goals in life
    III. My motivation for college
    IV. My social maturity
    V. My vocational interest pattern
    VI. My aptitudes
    VII. My intelligence and scholastic aptitude
    VIII. Other significant factors
    IX. My personality
    X. A look ahead
    XI. Summary and conclusions

Each student should feel free to adapt or adopt the outline suggested above in accord with individual needs or approaches. The areas may be presented in a different fashion or order if so desired. All topics ought to be included but freedom of style is necessary for all students.

Students should note carefully that the outline does not request or indicate that all facts are simply to be restated. The problem throughout the writing of the paper is to use facts, information, and data in a *creative, meaningful* fashion. To move ideationally and rationally from a series of facts to an integrated statement of self-understanding will require that students utilize a higher level of abstract thinking than is demanded in the collection of facts.

> *Facts need to be integrated into patterns and implications that are clearly stated. Students should not simply attempt to offer a series of facts as an unrelated summary of isolated details.*

Interpretation of facts

In accord with the outline offered students can profit from a discussion of selected problems that may occur as each area is investigated. Not every problem can possibly, however, be foreseen. The student will need to discuss with a teacher-counselor certain problems that will seldom be solved by solitary thought. A counselor is the unseen partner in the composition of a "self-analysis essay."

Strengths and weaknesses. The college student, in order to launch the process of self-analysis, can utilize a "stocktaking" procedure. Strong points, weak areas, effective habits, and unrewarding tendencies are surface views of personality in action and commonplace views of adjustment processes that can lead the student gradually into the more complex and delicate issues that will be discussed in succeeding sections of this essay.

Goals of life. Goals in life give meaning to behavior. The objectives or even dimly seen hopes for the future serve to direct efforts and strivings. No student will be able clearly to formulate a hierarchy of goals and values but an attempt to isolate major goals can aid in determining pathways of and for the future.

Each student needs to attempt to set down a series of goals that have personally been determined to be important. Vocational goals, marriage goals, financial objectives, social strivings, social-service hopes, and even the quiet lonely hopes of life are important for each student. Every person will need to order and qualify each area in relation to self-hopes, self-fears, and self-dreams.

College and motivation. Each student has selected and entered a college for a particular series of reasons. When past behavior can thus be seen and understood, a student can begin to isolate present and future motivational elements of behavior. College can serve as a means for fulfilling life's goals or objectives. College is more, however, than a means to an end. College is a period of life that is only experienced once.

Each person will undergo a personal series of four years of college. Critical analysis of plans, courses, time, friends, and experiences can reward the thoughtful student. Analysis of motives and motivational patterns can allow the person to assume a degree of control over and responsibility for the future.

Vocational interest patterns. The word *pattern* becomes significant in an essay on the self. Many isolated and seemingly insignificant facts and experiences here need to be drawn together in order to form a pattern of vocational interest. Meaningful part-time or full-time work experiences, rewarding hobbies and leisure-time reading, remembered (fondly or otherwise) school courses, influential teachers, thoughtful and interested friends and their advice, these are the parts of the puzzle that, when properly patterned, can reveal a thread or threads of one's vocational interest pattern.

Students may wish to use their vocational interest inventory scores as either a starting point or an evaluative summary of interest areas. Critical analysis and reflective thought can reward the painstaking student. A vocational interest *pattern* can help to guide the remaining self-analysis processes.

Aptitudes. Aptitudes are promises of future ability. High, medium, and low aptitudes need to be seen independently and in light of previously stated interests. Aptitudes need to be related to goals, objectives, and motivations that are operative in a life pattern. Psychological test scores will of course be useful in assessing the presence or lack of particular aptitudes and aptitude patterns. Other experiences may also reveal aptitudes not capable of measurement through test procedures. School activities such as drama clubs, newspapers, yearbooks, bands, orchestras, literary writing, and debating, and a host of other experiences can be profitably examined to determine whether or not talent, a "flair," or, perhaps, aptitude is present.

Intelligence and scholastic aptitude. Intelligence and scholastic aptitude are controlling forces in much of college life. Ability to understand and manipulate academic concepts is a hallmark of most successful college students. Each student will need to consider carefully his or her own level of ability and scholastic aptitude in order to plan for a future that contains college training. Intelligence may be inferred from test scores (such as mental-ability tests), particular aptitude measures (verbal, reasoning, and numerical ability) or even scholastic achievement. Test scores are easily seen as measures of intelligence. School or college grades are not as clear-cut in their ability to measure intelligence or scholastic aptitude. High grades (A or superior) earned with little or very little study may sometimes reveal scholastic ability. The reverse, low grades earned with long hours of study, may also reveal a low level of scholastic ability or aptitude. Exceptions and confusing reversals, however, are common in any process that attempts clearly to infer ability from grades. Patterns of achievement supported by independent measures of ability are better examples of consistent intelligence and scholastic aptitude.

Other significant factors. Students who must work part time or full time in order to finance the cost of college are likely to look upon money as basic in their problem of achieving success in college. Other students with pressing problems in other areas may feel their problems to be as basic as does the student who seeks financial solvency through work. Students will need to inventory their own situations to determine which particular factors will be important for future success. It will be difficult for students to extract various influential factors in a process of self-analysis; any check list will fall short of offering all possible factors that may be important. Students will need to talk with parents, relatives, friends, and particularly with their teachers and counselors in order to exhaust the many possible "outside influences."

More serious personality handicaps, or problem areas of adjustment, are beyond the province of students in a process of guided self-analysis. A professional specialist in psychology is needed in such areas.

Summary. The summary section permits the students to begin to integrate the important factors in their own self-pictures. Traits, interests, abilities, even dress and speech patterns must be integrated within a *person*. All factors have previously been isolated in order to provide for a manageable process of analysis. The picture must now be redrawn in light of total knowledge.

"Myself as I see myself," "As others see me," "How I affect others," and "I," are all terms and phrases that students have used in describing their personalities. It is more important to describe the "self" freely in everyday words and phrases than to attempt to be scientific and precise in the use of psychological or technical terms that may be only partially understood. Students many times find this to be the most difficult section of the entire "self-analysis essay." Careful reflective thought will reward the students as attempts are made to "objectify" or see one's self as others do.

A look ahead. Most students in college have approximately two thirds of their lifetimes still ahead. Personality will continue to develop and to be modified by experience. Students need to look beyond today in order to influence tomorrow. Students may wish in this section to outline developments that they may desire in the future.

Personality has been described as the total present life pattern of a person derived from the interaction of environmental and hereditary factors. Radical changes in personality are virtually impossible. Directions and effects of personality can, however, be thoroughly understood and partially altered. Students need to grow in self-understanding in order that they may more carefully look ahead to tomorrow and the future.

Conclusions. The entire outline of the self-analysis essay has provided an opportunity for students to draw together their knowledge of themselves. The final section of the essay will allow a more terse and direct summary. Many students have found it profitable to review the effect of the process of self-analysis upon themselves. Students occasionally report that self-analysis is a simple and direct process that was completed with ease. Most students, however, experience self-analysis as a difficult and demanding task. Long hours of self-study, thought, and self-evaluation enter into the process. Appendix D, selected self-analysis essays, may aid students in planning and completing their own self-analysis. Several examples are presented of how previous students have approached and solved the problem of writing a "self-analysis essay."

SUMMARY

Personality ultimately makes every individual unique and unlike any other person in the world. Individuals with identical heredity, interests, aptitudes, intelligence, and scholastic aptitude can still be dissimilar individuals because of personality. Personality becomes the "personal" factor in self-analysis and self-evaluation. After a study of the basic principles of personality the following questions need to be answered from a view of applied study of personality:

1. What is personality?
2. How is personality developed?
3. What is self-concept?
4. How are personality and adjustment related?
5. What is my personality?

Question 5 brings each person face to face with the difficult task of looking at the self and his own personality as others see these factors. The problem of recognizing personality is more vital than attempts to change personality, which is exceedingly difficult to do. A counselor can and must aid in the individual analysis of personality change.

Personality must also operate within an environment. The largest effect of an individual on our society is the effect of personality on life and work. As we mentioned earlier, research has shown that personality is at the root of most of the maladjustment in marriage and work and of other social and emotional problems. The discussion of the im-

pact of personality in the various areas of life and work should help each person to answer such additional questions as:

6. How has my family affected the development of my personality?
7. What cultural forces are important for me?
8. What effect will my personality have on my future job; marriage; personal life?
9. What occupations are appropriate (inappropriate) in view of my personality?

SUPPLEMENTARY SOURCES

Bennett, Margaret E., *College and Life* (4th ed.). New York: McGraw-Hill Book Company, Inc., 1952.

Jersild, Arthur T., *In Search of Self*. New York: Bureau of Publications, Teachers College, Columbia University, 1955.

Lecky, P., *Self-Consistency*. New York: Island Press, 1945.

Lindgren, Henry Clay, *Psychology of Personal and Social Adjustment*. New York: American Book Company, 1953.

Murphy, Gardner, *Personality, A Biosocial Approach to Origins and Structure*. New York: Harper & Brothers, 1947.

Snygg, Donald, and Arthur W. Combs, *Individual Behavior*. New York: Harper & Brothers, 1949.

Correct evaluation of abilities and aptitudes is important

Part IV

OCCUPATIONAL AND
EDUCATIONAL PLANNING

*Part IV offers students the opportunity to test the learn-
ings and knowledge gained in the chapters of the first
three parts of the book. The self-picture that hopefully
emerged from Part III can now be looked upon in light
of future plans for education and work.*

*Chapter 14 describes the process involved in viewing
the self and an occupation. The problems of bringing
each of these personal factors into agreement and accord
are fully described and analyzed in the chapter. Chapter*

15 surveys the entire field of source materials useful to students in planning for the future. Chapter 16 describes the process involved in writing a concrete example of occupational planning.

Part IV, therefore, brings to a close the process of self-analysis, critical thinking, and planning for the future. The chapter on research does not assume a final vocational choice but illustrates the actual process of vocational and educational planning.

very day, year in and year out, millions of men and women all over the world spend at least half of their waking hours engaged in some form of work. Miners, farmers, butchers, salesmen, milkmen, doctors, truckdrivers, teachers, and politicians all contribute in some small way to the social welfare of others in our society. Some of these individuals work with physical strength, others work with mental effort, some grow and succeed in their jobs, and others reap failure. Each one helps to make it possible for

Chapter 14

IMPORTANCE OF PLANNING

others to specialize in a particular occupation in our society. Many are happy as they work, secure in their own minds that theirs is an honored and worthy occupation. They radiate enthusiasm and are an inspiration to some people and a source of bewilderment and annoyance to others. Others are unhappy as they work, confused and frustrated by the effrontery of a world requiring so much work. They exude misery and despair as they put in the necessary hours of labor so that they may indulge in what for them are more pleasant pastimes. Varying degrees of satisfaction and determination regarding school work and educational planning are apparent in any group of students, whether they are in high school or in college. Some attend classes eagerly with a thirst for knowledge. It is obvious that education for them brings satisfaction and pleasure. Others habitually miss classes or sit disgruntled and defiant surrounded by an aura of disdainful detachment when they do attend. For the latter group, education would appear to be a source of frustration and antagonism.

For most individuals the choice of an occupation (and the

217

education and training necessary for success) and the choice of a marriage partner constitute the two most important decisions made during their lives. It is ironic that these two vital decisions should be viewed by so many people as chance or impulsive events, possibly influenced by supernatural powers.

Titles of recent publications, such as *The Psychology of Careers* (123) and *The Psychology of Occupations* (111), reflect the growing concern of professional workers with the whole area of work. The use of such terms as "vocational development" and "vocational maturity" in these books suggests that we are only beginning to grasp the importance of work in the psychological make-up of the individual.

Does the difference in personal satisfaction lie in the type of work or educational program involved, or within the individual? Is it inherent with either, or due to a combination of factors? Is it simply a matter of finding the correct occupational niche for everyone so that all will be happy with their work? How important is the choice of an occupation? How important is a choice of a school? How important is the choice of a program? How can guidance help? How are self-analysis and self-understanding related to educational and vocational planning?

GROWTH AND DEVELOPMENT OF AN OCCUPATIONAL CHOICE

The great American myth of success is perhaps the most pervading influence in the lives of typical middle-class students in the United States today. Every high-school graduate can cite numerous contemporary and historic personages as exemplary proof that America is the land of opportunity. Many young people can point with justifiable pride to successful parents or grandparents who arrived in America with little more than a suitcase full of mementos, heads full of dreams, and hearts full of ambition.

Promulgated earlier through novels of the Horatio Alger (*Bound to Rise, Strive and Succeed*) type, today the great American myth is foisted on young people largely through the mass media of radio, television, and motion pictures. In the eyes of many persons it is tantamount to un-Americanlike activity to challenge the truthfulness of this myth. Is it not stated in the Declaration of Independence that all men are created equal and that all men are guaranteed the right to the pursuit of happiness?

Bearing his rights firmly in mind, the average high-school graduate blithely states his goal in life as "success," turns his back on the past, and through rose-colored glasses (or perhaps through the tinted windshield of a new sportscar) he wishfully contemplates the future. He dreams of a rosy tomorrow, resplendent with the latest in labor-saving gadgets, devoted to the pursuit of leisure-time activities, and devoid of anything as debasing as work. His will be a *career,* not a *job*. This career will ensure many vague opportunities for self-expression and will involve only a modicum of responsibility for mental or physical exertion. Success will be attained by dint of sheer drive and perseverance. Often as not the degree of success attained will be measured largely in terms of financial income.

Success thus defined and measured cannot help but doom the majority of people to a life of frustration, disillusionment, and maladjustment. As was stated earlier, each individual must define success for himself if he is to lead a productive life. Such an individualized definition demands the formulation of a personal philosophy of life. Reality testing must play a prominent role in the development of such a philosophy.

For most people adequate reality testing will inevitably lead to modification of the myth of success. Lindgren (80) points out that work need not be perceived as a barrier to need satisfaction or simply as a means of earning a living. Work can be a means of gaining satisfaction. Adequate self-analysis can lead to a better understanding of individual needs that must be satisfied. Of equal importance, self-analysis will provide for a more realistic definition of success in terms of personal aptitudes, attitudes, values, skills, and standards.

Choice—a right or a responsibility?

Numerous studies attest to the shortage of critical thinking involved in vocational decision-making for a majority of college students. One study by McKinney reports that only eight of sixty-one students in a psychology class had planned for a specific vocation. Twenty-four endorsed the following as typical of the process by which they selected a general area of concentration:

> No, I don't think I would like medicine. I never did care to be near hospitals, or to visit the offices of physicians. Law doesn't interest me, I am not a good speaker, and a lawyer should be able to sway a jury. I am not mechanically inclined, so that eliminates engineering. I know I would never make a good minister, and I would not want to be a teacher all my life. I cannot write, although journalism ought to be interesting. Well, what is left to choose from? Business. Yes, business—I'll enter the business school at the University. (87:302-3)

In all too many instances occupational choices are made from a scarcity rather than from an abundance of information. Note in the statement above the casual approach, the shallowness of thought, the lack of critical thinking, and the limited number of alternatives considered in making a choice.

As in the case of many other rights granted to citizens of the United States today, the right to choose, prepare for, and enter into the occupation of one's choice is often taken for granted. Such freedom of choice is a relatively modern phenomenon. In most primitive societies and in many civilized countries individual freedom of choice is virtually nonexistent. Choice may be prescribed by sex, age, and inheritance, or it may be precluded or severely limited through obvious manipulation of the economic system and manpower.

Such a planned existence obviates many of the problems faced by individuals in a more civilized society, since the individual has few if any decisions to make regarding his own future or occupation. It is generally a case of learning one's prescribed role in a society, and then adjusting to it.

In the United States today, every man is born with certain rights guaranteed to him by our system of government. In granting such rights to the individual, society assumes the responsibility of protecting the individual's rights, but it is to be expected that along with every right granted, the individual must assume certain responsibilities. Most important of these responsibilities is the need to utilize effectively the right that has been granted. This is not to imply that the individual has absolute freedom of choice, even in this country. The individual is free to choose insofar as his choice is constructive and beneficial to society. He is not free to choose an occupation that is illegal without suffering the consequences of the law. Other limitations must obviously be faced in terms of aptitude, ability, skills, and appropriateness.

The right to choose one's occupation is very similar to the right to vote; it is granted with the assumption that each individual will exercise it, thereby ensuring the group welfare of society. One of the basic premises of a democracy is that the individual members of a society are capable of making wise decisions and that a consensus of their decisions will be the best course of action in a given matter. It therefore becomes imperative for each individual to accept his responsibility to society as a whole. It is easy to postpone decision-making, particularly if one attempts to make decisions with a scarcity of information about the various alternative choices. It is also especially easy to avoid making decisions when one cannot see the direct effect of the decision immediately or if one is content to let others make the important decisions. Many intelligent, mature individuals who have been and are relatively successful in life are entirely naïve in regard to understanding how they have arrived at a particular occupational choice. This naïveté exists in spite of the fact that the right to choose one's occupation is one of the outstanding characteristics of our free society.

Individual and societal importance

Of all the decisions made by man during his life, few are as important in far-reaching implications and ramifications as the choice of an occupation. In choosing a particular occupation, one directly or indirectly influences many decisions that may follow. Some occupational-choice effects and causes are apparent even to a casual observer's eyes. Other occupational-choice causes and subsequent influences are less easily discerned and are more subtle in their relationship to the original choice. Consider the following as they are related to occupational choice: a man's education, his friends, his clubs, where he lives, his leisure-time activities, how he lives, the location of his peer group, his way of life, the choice of neighborhood church, the choice of a wife, the number of children and the schools they attend, the dress of the children, the desires of the children for further education, and the choice of a college or university. The foregoing is a suggestive rather than an exhaustive listing. Contemplation on the subject should allow the reader to add to those already listed many factors influencing an individual's choice of an occupation or subsequently affecting later decisions of life.

The fact that society places considerable importance on the matter of choosing an occupation is indicated, not necessarily by overt action or by laws, but many times by the anxiety that certain adults are unable to repress over their concern for the appropriateness of choice on the part of the coming generation.

A father awaiting the birth of his child is sure that it will be a son so that he will grow up to take his place as a chairman of the board. As soon as the child is old enough to answer simple questions, anxious adults begin to hound him with questions such as, "What are you going to do when you grow up?" At the same time, and for years to come, the child is presented with toys, games, and books that are all designed to acquaint him with the adult world of work and most of all to make him aware of the difference between work and play, and to impress him with the fact that adults must work for a living. By the time he leaves junior high school, the teen-ager is usually well aware of the fact that society is anxiously awaiting the occupational decision that must be made. Even at this young age, each individual must choose appropriate courses within a high-school program. Many teen-agers have long since known what they wanted, while others are still uncertain and confused.

It is significantly unfortunate that such vital decisions must be reached while the individual is still an adolescent, developing intellectually, emotionally, and physically. Numerous studies have shown that adolescence in the United States is a period characterized by "storm and stress" not found in certain other types of society. Furthermore, the adolescent is struggling to achieve the identification and independence of an adult while at the same time he is still very much dependent upon parents and adults from an economic point of view.

An event or a process

Eli Ginzberg and associates (57) (to whom should go much of the credit for making explicit the developmental process of an occupational choice) state, as have others, that each individual comes to select a particular occupation not through chance, but through developing patterns of activities that are largely irreversible and take place throughout all the formative years of a child's life.

Early in a child's life, certain fantasy-type decisions are made with regard to occupational planning. Children impressed by the color, the noise, and the sound may wish to become firemen or policemen; impressed with the glamour and action of the cowboys or of the airplane pilot they may select another equally unrealistic vocational choice. Soon, however, these choices must be tested against reality. The child soon begins to discard such choices made on the basis of fantasy. As the child grows older there are other tentative choices that are made throughout his life; these are tested against reality and rejected. Others are tested and found to be desirable; plans are made, interests grow, and aptitudes develop. The entire process of selecting an occupation is largely one of a negative procedure in which it is easier to discard that which is undesirable than it is to select that which is positively to be sought after.

The individual who points to accident or impulse as an explanation for a given occupational choice ignores the fact that man is not a passive agent acted upon by mysterious forces. It is true that various forces influence the life of an individual but the individual exercises a degree of personal option or self-direction in reacting to these forces. As Ginzberg points out, it is a gross oversimplification to attribute choice of an occupation to an accident or to an impulsive act.

Although vocational choice may appear to be an event or a single decision by an individual, such a view ignores all of the years of trial and error with various roles that have made it possible for the final choice to be made. To be understood fully, vocational choice must be seen as the logical culmination of a process wherein the individual is struggling for self-identification. The vocational or occupational choice of the individual is one of the realities against which the emerging concept of self is tested. The testing is an on-going process in which constant change is taking place, both within the self-picture and the individual's view of the occupational world.

SELF-UNDERSTANDING AND VOCATIONAL CHOICE

One of the major facets in an individual's personality is the capacity to perceive himself. This self-understanding or self-awareness is possibly the most important aspect of personality in that it constitutes the very essence of one's individuality. This view of self is built up gradually through the years of life and as time passes it tends to become more stable. This self-picture transcends the tangible aspects of personality. It is much more than the mere combination and integration of such factors as intelligence, aptitude, interest, and social skills. It involves emotion-laden attitudes and value judgments concerning all aspects of personality. The self-picture is dynamic rather than static. The individual selectively modifies this self-picture in terms of various life experiences. Tangible as well as intangible aspects of the physical, physiological and psychological environments are gradually incorporated to form that which the individual refers to as "I."

Varying degrees of sureness or personal, psychological security in many situations lead to the rejection or adoption of significant roles. Each role is modified by the individual to provide for an element of consistency from role to role. Gradually the individual becomes aware that he is or would like to be a certain type of person. This awareness or coming into consciousness of individuality is not a sudden event. Rather, it is a slow process in which maturity and insight provide for increasing self-awareness and understanding.

The importance of this self-picture to the individual is pointed out by Snygg and Combs (116) who see in it the ultimate cause of all behavior. They postulate that the basic human need is the protection and improvement of one's self-picture. Thus it is possible to view occupational decision-making as a further attempt on the part of the individual to enhance or defend his self-picture. Occupational choice as a process, then, is intimately related to the process of maturation. The ultimate decision to prepare for a certain vocation is but one step in a long process of logically related decisions.

It is true that many of the important decisions leading to the vital final decision may have been made by default. The individual with only a vague notion of who he is and what he is like may easily find himself apparently drifting through life subject to the wiles of fate. The individual in this plight has chosen what appears to him the path of least resistance. Such a choice usually involves an uncritical acceptance of the myth of success and reflects inadequate perception of self-picture. The joint problems of self-perceptions and occupational-perception are therefore problems of both an independent and dependent nature. Each must be resolved singly and then integrated.

LITTLE MAN ON CAMPUS   by Dick Bibler

COURTESY BIBLER FEATURE SERVICE

Self-concept needs may dictate the development of unusual occupational and educational plans for the future!

Perception of self

Perception, the process wherein the individual interprets or gives meaning to the various stimuli received by his sensory equipment, allows a certain amount of distortion or elaboration of objective reality. Thus, a certain note or tone that may be identified as a bell is almost at the same instant perceived as the telephone, the doorbell, the alarm clock, or possibly as a fire alarm depending upon the meaning attached to the sound. Certain vegetables, meats, or even insects are perceived by some persons as edible and at the same time by others as inedible. It is through this process of perception that each person comes to know himself.

Much as a person born blind can never really comprehend what the world of visual reality is like from his other senses, a normal individual with all of his senses can never really comprehend himself as others see him. All an individual can ever know is the subjective reality of the world as it is perceived through his own sensory equipment. As the world is seen this way, the individual tends to see himself as he is reflected by other individuals within this world. He judges himself by the reactions of others. These reactions are interpreted and evaluated by the individual, enabling him to build, in many instances, a highly idealized or sometimes distorted concept of self. Unless the individual is willing to test the self-concept in various life situations to verify the individual interpretation of other people's impressions, distorted ideas of self may make for difficult adjustment problems within society and life as a whole. The individual, in attempting to defend and enhance himself, may build up elaborate systems of defense mechanisms, thus distorting other aspects of external reality.

The self-concept therefore needs to be a concept that is relatively in line with reality—reality being the external reality of the world rather than the reality of the individual's view of the world.

Research studies (24, 60, 69) have demonstrated that each person tends to see himself in at least three lights: (a) as he perceives himself, (b) as he thinks others see him, and (c) as he would like to be ideally. It has been clinically verified that there is a relationship between the degree of agreement of these three self-pictures and the adjustment of the individual. The normal individual tends to have some discrepancies but these are within a reasonably predictable range.

Perception of an occupational choice

A recent study (60) reports that individuals have a similar threefold perception of their occupational objectives. Each person in the study appeared to have an idealistic goal, a realistic goal, and a goal for which they would settle. For example, ideally, Johnny Jones would like to become an industrial tycoon; realistically, he is going to college and planning to major in management; in the event of some unforeseen circumstance, however, he will settle for a position as a salesman in his uncle's business.

Just as the description, previously related, of the individual's perception of himself as a person is important, it is vital to see whether the individual views an occupation realistically or from a distorted point of view. Super (124) has pointed out that many times in making an occupational choice an individual is putting the self-concept to a test of reality by saying in essence, "I am, or would like to be this type of person." Since one of the basic tasks of all individuals is to defend and to enhance the self, it is easily seen that this decision is an important one for an individual and also why certain individuals are more likely to postpone, repress, or refuse to make an occupational choice. Inappropriate choices now may become understandable as attempts to defend or enhance the self-concept of the individual. Failure to make a choice may become comprehensible as a means of avoiding a commitment about the individual's self-concept. Calia (24) has suggested that by refusing to make an occupational choice the individual does not have to test the self-concept against reality. Such an individual appears to be afraid, since failure to achieve the desired status would, in effect, destroy or at least injure part of the self-concept. Of course there is another possibility that in refusing to make a choice the individual might be using an indecisive action as an attempt to frustrate adults, often parents, who are anxiously concerned and interested in the occupational choice of their children.

Distortions

The following diagrams depict in a simplified manner the normal situation, along with three basic types of inappropriate vocational-choice decisions.
    Realistic self—realistic occupational choice. In the first diagram there is depicted a young person who is able to perceive himself realistically and who views an occupational choice in a realistic manner. The individual's ideas about the self are reasonably in line with the impressions that others have. The individual has determined his aptitudes, abilities, skills, and limitations as well as his values, basic motivations, and interests. He has selected an occupation after carefully analyzing all aspects of the vocation, and has related all of the data concerning the self to the requirements of the job or the occupation to which the level of aspiration points. This person presents few problems and should become a reasonably well-adjusted and successful worker in his chosen occupation.

Realistic self—unrealistic occupational objective. In the second diagram, an individual is depicted who is similar to the first individual in that he has made a realistic and appropriate appraisal of the self, and has related himself to the requirements of an occupation *as he sees the occupation.* Due to the scarcity of information, however, about the job or because of misinformation, perception of the job is seriously distorted. Possibly the individual has learned everything about the occupation from inaccurate sources, such as glamorized novels or motion pictures. Perhaps the view of the task or of the occupation is a romantic version that has been perceived through various "rose-colored" observations. This individual seems to be destined for maladjustment and dissatisfaction unless he can clear this distorted view of the occupation. The solution to this individual's problem appears relatively simple in that accurate, up-to-date, and realistic occupational information would be helpful in bringing the self-concept and the occupational choice into realistic accord.

Unrealistic self—realistic occupational objective. In the third illustration the individual is depicted as being realistic in the perception and understanding of the occupation, but has not been able to view the self appropriately and realistically. Perhaps the individual is actually a very average person physically, but his concept of self is distorted to the extent that he may think of himself as a potential "Mr. America" possessed of outstanding physical attributes. The occupation of his choice perhaps calls for considerable physical stamina and physical skill. It is easily seen, therefore, that the individual will soon come into conflict, even though his view of the occupation is appropriate; he will be unable to meet the requirements of this occupation. In this instance, the problem is more serious than that of the second illustration because the individual needs to take a more realistic view of his self. One way to accomplish this is through a process of self-study and self-analysis. It is important to realize, however, that outside assistance from a counselor is required if this step is to be taken effectively. The self is a much more difficult object to analyze than is an occupation.

Unrealistic self—unrealistic occupational choice. In the fourth illustration, the individual is in serious difficulty in that he is able to perceive neither the self nor the occupation realistically. The self-concept is far removed from reality; it is distorted so that perception of the world is also distorted in order to preserve and defend this self-picture. This individual would need considerable outside help in order to make any sort of appropriate plans for the future in terms of an occupation. Both the occupation and the self are distorted, and because of the interrelationships between the two it will be difficult to clarify them singly. They must be approached through the joint study of the self and the occupation with counseling assistance.

PLACE OF SELF-ANALYSIS

The foregoing discussion of the process of occupational choice and its relationship to the concept of the self should help the reader to understand the relationships of these two important areas. Self-analysis is the first step in selecting an occupation. Without this first step it is impossible to take the next in a profitable manner. Many young people who profess that they are unable to make a vocational choice are actually revealing their failure to understand themselves. In making a vocational choice, as has been seen, the individual must have a concept of himself, and this concept of the self must be projected into the future so that it may be tested against the reality of the occupational world.

The second step in selecting an occupation is to secure an abundance of realistic, up-to-date information about an occupation. It is necessary to gather this information in a systematic manner, evaluating each factor carefully before adding it to the data already compiled. Thus far, little has been said about occupational information. Perhaps the reader may feel that this is an indication that occupational information is of negligible importance. The fact that this book contains many chapters and that it devotes only three chapters to this topic should not be interpreted as an indication of the unimportance of occupational information. Rather, it should be noted that the three chapters come toward the end of the book after the reader has been able to absorb the information and suggestions made in the earlier chapters. It is usually true that an individual who has completed successfully the first step of self-analysis will be able to undertake the second step of occupational analysis. It will be noted in the following outline of factors to be considered in selecting an occupation that many of the topics have been discussed in earlier chapters. Others will be discussed in the concluding chapters.

Occupational planning

For self-analysis to be effective, it must be undertaken in a systematic manner under the direction of a trained counselor. At its best, self-analysis is difficult, and particular care must be taken in the interpretation and synthesis of data because of the amount of ego involvement in such a project. The assistance of a counselor throughout this experience is actually mandatory.

As in the process of self-analysis it is first necessary to gather data and facts and to organize them before undertaking analysis of an occupation. Essentially, there are four major sources of occupational information:

1. Actual work experience
2. Observations of occupational processes
3. Interviews with workers
4. Occupational literature

Educational planning

Lovejoy (81, 82) has compiled in two volumes descriptions of more than 6500 private and public vocational schools and descriptions of 2049 colleges and universities. There are undoubtedly many schools and colleges not listed in either volume. Every institution is prepared to meet the demands of a particular body of students. Entrance requirements vary as do the curricula offered. In view of such variety it is safe to say that there exists somewhere in the United States a college, vocational, trade, or special school with entrance requirements and curriculum suitable for any normal, literate individual of at least average intelligence who desires education beyond the high-school level.

Attending college today involves a tremendous investment in money and energy. Of more importance, however, is the investment in time. Monetary losses may be recouped but lost time can never be regained. Furthermore, the experience of failure in an inappropriately chosen college can have more lasting bad effects on an individual than if he had never been admitted in the first place. The first two years of college life provide numerous oppor-

BOSTON UNIVERSITY PHOTO SERVICE

Adequate counseling can help the student help himself

tunities for the student to test his self-picture in an academic setting. After completing successfully one or two years of college, it again becomes necessary for every student to re-examine his objectives. Additional evidence is available. The reality of grades and of adjustment to college life must be taken into consideration. Are course grades an accurate reflection of the amount of time and energy put in by the student? Is there a sense of accomplishment and pride in having completed the first years of study?

In general, it is wise to choose or continue study in the best school for which one is qualified in terms of one's individual potentials, aptitudes, skills, interests, intelligence, personality, values, and personal needs.

Everything said above about choice of a school would apply equally well with regard to a curriculum or program. Most colleges today in one manner or another ensure that all students meet certain minimum general education requirements. The junior and senior years of college are usually devoted to specialization in one or two fields of study. In choosing a program for advanced undergraduate or for graduate study the student is narrowing down and focusing his preparation for employment. Many freshman and sophomore students are impatient to begin specializing. A common cry among first-year and second-year students is, "What good is this or that course? I want to be a ————." The broader one's general background the wiser should be the choice of field and the firmer the foundation for specialization.

Having ascertained the appropriateness of a four-year program of study, just as much thought and critical evaluation should go into the choice of the program of concentration. It should go without saying that self-analysis is the first step in making such a choice. Analysis of various opportunities for specialization should be next; both are part of the larger process of choosing an occupation.

SUMMARY

It is important to select the most important factors contributing to happiness, adjustment and satisfaction on the job. It is safe to assume that in certain occupations there are some inherently unattractive features, and that occupations vary with respect to their attractiveness to individuals. For each individual has within himself certain values, attitudes, wishes, wants, and desires that need to be satisfied. Also, and of more importance, each individual is unique. Each has a self-concept and a basic need to defend and enhance this concept. So, we may reason that the man who is happy with his work finds in the occupation an opportunity to preserve and enhance his self-concept. The unhappy worker may find his work extremely threatening or de-

grading to his self-concept. The actual reasons why this is so are probably manifold and complex. However, with the same individuals doing identical tasks, with one being happy and one being unhappy, the assumption must then be that the problem lies within the individual rather than with the work.

The concept of an occupational "niche" is a dangerous fallacy somewhat akin to the romantic myth of the ideal marrtage partner who can be found through diligent search. The fact that myths have grown up around each of these two areas involving choice may suggest the degree of emotional involvement that is associated with each of them. Actually, choosing an occupation and selecting a mate have much in common. Each is selected as a result of deep-rooted emotional needs and desires. Each decision is made for a long period of time and may appear on the surface to be the result of operational chance factors. The fact is, however, that a multitude of physical, psychological, and physiological factors not clearly understood by the individual are involved in both decisions.

Most abilities and aptitudes tend to be general rather than specific. That is to say, a person does not have an aptitude for a particular vocation but instead possesses certain traits, aptitudes, abilities, and interests that can allow for success in certain types of occupations. These same traits, aptitudes, interests, and abilities with appropriate education and training might just as easily allow for success in a number of other similar and sometimes even unrelated occupations. For example, an individual who can successfully complete a medical education, in all probability, can make a successful career of the law or any other profession if his personality and other factors point in this direction. Intelligence and aptitude appear to be of primary importance in determining the level of one's occupational choice. At any given level, however, there is a broad field of alternatives open to the individual. Once the individual has determined the appropriate level in terms of scholastic aptitude he may select from various fields on the basis of interest and personality. Another way to approach the problem is to find a field of endeavor on the basis of interest, personality, and other factors, and then to determine the appropriate level within the field on the basis of intelligence and aptitude. Under no circumstances should a person labor under the misguided impression that there is a special occupational niche for every person, and that the task is only to seek and to find this mythical round or square hole.

The choice of an occupation involves the narrowing down of possible occupational alternatives until one is able to select an occupation with requirements resembling one's own qualifications. In the final analysis, there are very few "tailor-made" occupational opportunities. One must sometimes "squeeze" a little on one aspect of the requirements and plan to "grow" into other aspects of the job. Possibly, one might plan to discard the original job as he finds it too big or if he finds that he has grown too large for the task. Vocational planning and choice must be flexible with alternatives available if they are needed. Inasmuch as the choice of an occupation is directly or indirectly influential in many other choices made during life, it is important for the individual to choose wisely.

Guidance can help an individual to the extent that he is willing to seek and to accept help. If the individual is willing to exert effort in a search for valid information about himself and about an occupation, the counselor is prepared to assist him in his search. Guidance cannot work miracles, nor can a counselor become a prophet. Together, the counselor and the student can examine facts, define problems, delimit alternatives, and narrow down possible choices. In the last analysis, however, the individual student must make his own decisions and live with them. The decision can never be that of a counselor, of a parent, or of a teacher. The individual must take full responsibility for his own decisions.

Choice of an appropriate college or program for specialized training can save not only money but, more important, it will insure against the loss of time. Because of the vast number of schools and colleges in the United States it is possible for every student to find an appropriate college or program of training. Appropriate education is a means toward reaching an occupational goal. Education, however, is for many persons an end in and of itself. A sound education will contribute much toward the enjoyment of life and the appreciation of the many finer things that tend to make life fuller.

SUPPLEMENTARY SOURCES

Beilin, Harry, "The Application of General Developmental Principles to the Vocational Area," *Journal of Counseling Psychology*, 2 (1955), pp. 53-57.

Ginzberg, Eli, and associates, *Occupational Choice*. New York: Columbia University Press, 1951.

Gray, J. Stanley, *Psychology Applied to Human Affairs* (2nd ed.). New York: McGraw-Hill Book Company, Inc., 1954.

Hoppock, Robert, *Occupational Information.* New York: McGraw-Hill Book Company, Inc., 1957.

McKinney, Fred, *Psychology of Personal Adjustment* (2nd ed.). New York: John Wiley & Sons, Inc., 1949.

Meadows, Lloyd, "Toward a Theory of Vocational Choice," *Journal of Counseling Psychology,* 2 (1955), pp. 108-112.

Pressey, Sidney L., and Raymond G. Kuhlen, *Psychological Development through the Life Span.* New York: Harper & Brothers, 1957.

Roe, Anne, *The Psychology of Occupations.* New York: John Wiley & Sons, Inc., 1956.

Super, Donald E., *The Psychology of Careers.* New York: Harper & Brothers, 1957.

————, "Vocational Development, the Process of Compromise or Synthesis?" *Journal of Counseling Psychology,* 3 (1956), pp. 250-255.

*S*ome persons have argued that knowledge in and of itself has value and should be sought for its own sake. There are others who maintain that knowledge has little or no intrinsic value and that it is only in the application of knowledge that there can be any real value. Self-knowledge in and of itself appears to provide for a certain amount of security or insecurity for the individual. It is, however, in the application of self-knowledge and the implementation of self-knowledge (in overt behavior) that one comes to appreciate the fullest reali-

Chapter 15

OCCUPATIONAL AND
EDUCATIONAL INFORMATION

zation of the value of self-knowledge. Having expended the time and energy required in the acquisition of adequate self-knowledge it would be useless extravagance not to utilize this knowledge in the selection of an occupation. Furthermore, it would be folly to spend time and energy in a comprehensive self-analysis without spending a proportionate amount of time in considering the occupation of one's choice.

The problem of securing occupational and educational information has long been a concern for students, teachers, and counselors as well as parents, employers, and placement agencies. Vocational counseling was one of the early guidance services offered to students and clients seeking aid in personal planning. Many techniques and resources have been developed through the years in order to help to provide meaningful data to persons concerned with a vocational choice.

Observation of occupational practices, actual work experience, occupational literature, occupational libraries, government publications, private publishing firms, personal interviews, college catalogs, and guidance services are but a few of the many resources that students may draw upon now.

235

OBSERVATIONS OF OCCUPATIONAL PROCESSES

Benjamin Franklin in his autobiography writes that he was led about the streets of Boston by his father who showed him the "several opportunities" and helped him in the selection of a trade. As they walked through what was then a small city, it was easy to step into the various shops to see the men at work, or to view them from the street at benches and counters—in the eighteenth century.

In the twentieth century, however, vocational guidance, except for the fortunate, is not nearly so easy. A father attempting to show his son the occupational opportunities available in an average-sized city would find it a very frustrating task. He would have to devote a tremendous amount of time and energy to the process and would probably have considerable difficulty gaining access to many firms or occupational processes. Furthermore, were he able to visit and observe every available occupation he would find himself very hard pressed to explain to his son the particular qualities and operations involved in more than a very few of the occupations that they viewed.

Today, many high schools and colleges arrange for field trips to various industries as part of their core program of studies. On these tours the student has some opportunity to watch various workers at their jobs and the tour guide will usually answer questions about the work. The student, however, must remember that industry usually "rolls out the plush carpets and puts up its best front" for such tours. Furthermore, on the usual field trip one sees only part of the activities connected with a given occupation, and these are viewed very rapidly.

Commercial motion pictures as well as commercial radio and television programs often provide opportunities for the observation of occupational processes. The viewer or listener must be careful in making generalizations or reaching conclusions solely on the basis of such observations. Extraordinary aspects of an occupation, as presented in the context of a dramatic plot, can make for highly distorted ideas about a job if not supplemented by further investigation.

Educational films dealing with specific vocations or occupational fields are valuable, providing they are current. These films often are presented on commercial television and motion-picture screens as well as by schools, colleges, and civic organizations. With the advent of educational television many more young people will be able to gain valuable occupational information in their own homes. The evaluation of such material will be a significant problem for all students. Realistic data is useful; information obtained through "rose-colored glasses" is dangerous.

ACTUAL WORK EXPERIENCE

The average college freshman or sophomore may tend to rule out work experience as a source of occupational information without realizing the abundance of work experience that is his. Possibly, his experience is not in the specific area of his present vocational choice. Even then, however, it is valuable in that he has learned first hand what it is to work. Possibly, these early successes or failures at work have helped the student to narrow down the alternatives in his search for a vocational objective. On the other hand, many students have had considerable entry experience (jobs requiring no previous experience) in the actual vocation for which they are now preparing. For example, a future teacher or social worker may have worked summers and part time as a junior counselor in a YMCA or other community service project. Possibly a future reporter has earned his tuition by working part time in a newspaper office as a copy boy. For those who have actually had no work experience the college placement office usually has a variety of interesting part-time jobs available for anyone with the time and the inclination to gain valuable work experience and knowledge.

Care should be taken in evaluating work experience as it is very easy for a young person to overlook many unsatisfactory aspects of a job in favor of the more satisfactory and possibly more glamorous factors.

OCCUPATIONAL LITERATURE

In planning the analysis of a given occupation a logical first step is to survey the available literature. This provides the researcher with valuable background material as well as a rapid survey of the field. There are books available dealing with general fields or broad occupational areas. A person seriously in doubt might start with such a source. Other books deal with specific vocations. Books, more so than pamphlets, have a tendency to become outdated. Care should be used in choosing books to see that they have a recent date of publication, or it is possible at times to find that a particularly interesting occupation described in glowing terms may not even exist today.

Any competent librarian can provide the student with a bibliography of suggested readings concerning a particular vocation. Many fiction as well as nonfiction books deal with specific vocational careers. Thousands of books contain informative background information about industries and professions.

Pamphlets, periodicals, and trade journals are available in abundance. No search of the literature should overlook such sources. Again, these materials should all be read critically and the date of publication noted. Students need to beware of glittering generalities unsupported by facts; overglamorous and romantic appeals can be misleading. Students should keep in mind the following suggestions:

1. View with suspicion any occupational materials in which statements are not supported by facts. If an occupational description says that opportunities are "very good," look for supporting evidence. If you do not find it, the author may be merely expressing his opinion.

2. Beware of occupational materials that tend to glamorize the occupation. It is very likely that such material will contain misleading information.

3. Look at the date when the material was published. Out-of-date materials are likely to be inaccurate about the types of opportunities, salaries, and trends. The duties, qualifications, advantages, and disadvantages, however, are not likely to change. It is possible that they may be better described in older publications than in more recent pamphlets.

4. The best occupational materials are those prepared from original sources. Check closely on the professional status of the author or the organization sponsoring the study. Professional organizations, with a professional code of ethics, furnish the most reliable material.

5. Recruiting bulletins of schools, colleges, and certain industrial establishments supply occupational information that must be viewed critically. Check carefully such material and note whether or not care is taken in presenting the advantages and disadvantages of the occupation under consideration.

Source books

There are currently available many excellent books written primarily for teachers, counselors and librarians on the topic of occupational information. These source books can be of invaluable assistance to the student attempting to locate reliable occupational information not available to him from local sources.

Occupational Information; Its Development and Application (114) is a classic in the field, written by Carroll L. Shartle. It contains a detailed examination into the many techniques for gathering occupational information first hand. It also provides a thorough discussion of the *Dictionary of Occupational Titles* (43) with instructions for using it to advantage.

A Basic Text for Guidance Workers (49), edited by Clifford Erickson, contains a chapter on "Sources of Information and Assistance" that includes several listings and a discussion of sources of reliable information on occupations.

Occupational Information; Its Nature and Use (8), written by Max F. Baer and Edward C. Roeber, contains a detailed listing of occupational information sources.

Perhaps the most exhaustive, organized listing of occupational information sources is to be found in *Occupational Literature; An Annotated Bibliography* (51), by Gertrude Forrester. This excellent index lists approximately 3200 selected references in an annotated bibliographic form. Prices are indicated and many pamphlets are available for a few cents, or free upon request to the source indicated. The student can acquire at very little expense valuable, up-to-date, authenticated information about a particular occupation.

The four sources mentioned above are representative of the many that are available. A counselor or a librarian will be able to suggest others that would be of equal assistance to the student. The counselor and librarian will also have access to one or more indexes of occupational information such as *Career Index, Counselors Information Service,* or *Guidance Index.* These indexes list in annotated form, and give the cost of, currently available occupational information. Students may also wish to utilize the bibliography at the end of this chapter as an additional source of occupational and educational literature. All sources mentioned in this chapter, as well as other selected materials, are included in the bibliography. However, the bibliography at the end of this chapter is not meant to be exhaustive. Occupational and educational literature sources are virtually limitless.

Government agencies

Many of the bureaus and agencies of the federal government prepare bulletins and pamphlets on occupations and occupational trends that are published by the Government Printing Office, Washington, D. C.

The Department of Labor includes many bureaus, such as the United States Employment Service, which is responsible for the *Dictionary of Occupational Titles.* This valuable source, often referred to as the "D.O.T.," consists of three separate volumes and a supplement.

Volume I, *Definitions of Titles,* contains the definitions of the occupational titles listed alphabetically. These definitions are brief descriptions of the work performed, including statements of "what the worker does," "how he does it," "why he does it," and usually an indication of the skill involved in carrying out these activities. In looking for a definition of an occupation the student should always use Volume I.

Volume II, *Titles and Codes,* consists of five sections:

Section I "The Occupation Classification Structure": Individual jobs are arranged according to their code numbers.

Section II "Index of Commodities": An index of goods frequently sold in the retail and wholesale trade. It is designed to assist in classifying persons engaged in the various sales jobs.

Section III "Glossary": Serves to clarify the various technical terms used in the job definitions.

Section IV "Occupational Titles Arranged by Industry": Classifies the jobs defined in Volume I according to where these jobs are found in industry, and defines each major industrial classification.

Section V "Industry Index": An alphabetical index of various industrial designations. In discovering the occupations that have a given code number or in finding related occupations, the student should use Volume II.

The "Supplement" contains additions to, and revisions of, Volumes I and II of the *Dictionary*.

Volume IV, *Entry—Occupational Classification,* classifies fields of work for entry job seekers. Entry occupations are those in which a person without previous work experience may obtain employment. Entry jobs usually are less demanding in terms of education required, length of training time on the job, and other factors that tend to make the job somewhat complex.

The following breakdown of the *Dictionary of Occupational Titles* (D.O.T.) will aid the student in his search for occupational information. The seven major occupational divisions are indicated by the first left-hand digit in the series.

0.	Professional and managerial occupations
1.	Clerical and sales occupations
2.	Service occupations
3.	Agriculture, fishery, forestry, and related occupations
4. & 5.	Skilled occupations
6. & 7.	Semi-skilled occupations
8. & 9.	Unskilled occupations

The major groupings are further divided into subgroupings indicated by the middle two digits in the series.

Professional — Managerial

0.01 – 39	Professional
0.41 – 69	Semi-professional
0.71 – 99	Managerial and official

Clerical — Sales

1.01 – 49	Clerical and kindred
1.01 – 97	Sales and kindred

Service

2.01 – 09	Domestic
2.21 – 50	Personal service
2.61 – 95	Protective

Agriculture — Fishery — Forestry

3.01 – 49	Agriculture and kindred
3.87 – 89	Fishery
3.91 – 97	Forestry kindred, except logging

4 — 5 Skilled

4:91 – 18	Manufacturing
4:20 – 61	Non-manufacturing
4:63 – 89	Miscellaneous
5:91 – 5:99	Foremen

6 — 7 Semi-skilled

6:01 – 18	Manufacturing
6:20 – 61	Non-manufacturing
6:63 – 89	Miscellaneous
7:39 – 7:99	Apprentices

8 — 9 Unskilled

8:01 – 18	Manufacturing
8:20 – 61	Non-manufacturing
8:63 – 89	Miscellaneous

The Occupational Outlook Branch of the Department of Labor has released several series, such as the *Occupational Outlook Bulletins, Occupational Outlook Summaries, Special Reports,* and *The Occupational Outlook Handbook* (133). This last-mentioned publication covers more than 400 occupations reporting on trends, training, and qualifications required in each. The bulletins report on nationwide surveys of various occupations and occupational areas. A free catalog, *Occupational Outlook Publications,* is available from the Bureau of Labor Statistics. The Bureau of Apprenticeship has released a number of bulletins on apprenticeship training programs. These are listed in the *National Apprenticeship Program,* available upon request. The Women's Bureau has released a number of bulletins on specific occupations and reports on surveys of opportunities for women. These are listed in the Bureau's publication catalog.

The Department of Commerce is responsible through the Bureau of the Census for the many varieties of census reports. Reports for the entire United States are prepared every ten years. The statistics are available in various breakdowns.

Summaries of the whole United States, by regions and by states, enable one to determine not only the number of workers in different areas, but also length of employment and income along with many other vital statistics. A system similar to the D.O.T. system is used for classification purposes. Copies of these reports may be purchased directly from the Superintendent of Documents, U. S. Government Printing Office, Washington, D. C. Of course, they are available also in most libraries. The Department of Commerce has also published through the Government Printing Office several handbooks on subjects pertaining to small-business ownership and retail management.

The Office of Education, Federal Security Agency, through its Guidance and Counseling branch, has prepared a series of thirteen *Guidance Leaflets,* which, although somewhat outdated, have been supplemented.

The Department of the Interior Fish and Wildlife Service has available two free bulletins: *Employment Possibilities in the Fish and Wildlife Service,* and *Fish Culture as a Livelihood.*

The Armed Forces have bulletins that can be obtained at most recruiting stations from the Air Force, Army, or Navy.

The United States Civil Service Commission publishes announcements of examinations for specific jobs. These are distributed through schools, libraries, and post offices. *Working for the U.S.A.* is a pamphlet giving general information on opportunities and how to apply. It is available free.

The Superintendent of Documents, Washington 25, D. C., also has available a series of fifty-three booklets on various occupations. Priced at five cents each, these booklets are brief and simply written.

Private and commercial sources

It would be impossible in a single chapter to list and discuss the many publishing houses that make available reliable occupational information. Those that are included are presented as representative. The student should refer to Gertrude Forrester's *Occupational Literature—An Annotated Bibliography* (51) for a more detailed listing of publishing houses and of actual publications.

Bellman Publishing Company, Inc., P. O. Box 172, Cambridge, 38, Massachusetts, publishes a series of pamphlets called *Vocational and Professional Monographs* at a cost of one dollar each. These pamphlets include information on the history of the job or profession, personal qualifications, scholastic training required, employment possibilities, salary, advancement, advantages and disadvantages, opportunities for men and women, and professional associations.

Another series of pamphlets called the *American Industries Series,* selling for one to two dollars apiece, describes the history of the industry under consideration, future development, employment opportunities, and geographic distribution of the industry as well as short descriptions of the many jobs making up the industry.

B'nai B'rith Vocational Service Bureau, 1761 R Street, N.W., Washington 9, D. C., publishes several series of pamphlets and a bimonthly bulletin called *Career News.* These pamphlets describe qualifications, preparation and entry, outlook earnings, advancement, conditions of work, and advantages and disadvantages of the career or occupation under consideration.

Glamour, the Magazine for the Girl with a Job, 420 Lexington Avenue, New York City 17, N. Y., includes in its monthly magazine much information on careers for women. Reprints of many articles are available for ten cents each. A series of *Fact Sheets* priced at five cents each includes information on training, qualifications, and entry to various occupations of particular interest to women.

The Institute for Research, 537 South Dearborn Street, Chicago 5, Illinois, publishes an extensive series of two hundred thirty-seven pamphlets called *Careers Research Monographs.* Single copies cost one dollar each. In addition to the usual treatment of an occupation, these pamphlets include information on professional and trade organizations as well as schools offering the required training.

Mademoiselle—the Quality Magazine for Smart Young Women, 575 Madison Avenue, New York 22, N. Y., publishes a series of reprints called the *Jobs and Futures File.* These are priced at ten cents for individual reprints.

The National League for Nursing, Committee on Careers, 2 Park Avenue, New York 16, N. Y., prepares and distributes many valuable low-priced pamphlets and booklets on careers in nursing.

The New York Life Insurance Company, Public Relations Department, 51 Madison Avenue, New York 10, N. Y., will furnish free upon request a series of booklets written by prominent individuals in various professions.

Personnel Services, Inc., Peapack, New Jersey, publishes an extensive series of abstracts at a cost of twenty-five cents apiece. A valuable feature of this series is the appraisal of literature pertaining to the subject occupation.

Science Research Associates, Inc., 57 West Grand Avenue, Chicago 10, Illinois, publishes the *Life Adjustment Booklets* at a cost of forty cents apiece and *The American Job Series of Occupational Monographs.*

Seventeen Magazine, Triangle Publications Inc., 488 Madison Avenue, New York 22, N. Y., has available, at a cost of ten cents apiece, a series of booklets called *Career Reprints.*

Schools, colleges and universities often have available free recruiting bulletins prepared on occupations and professions for which they offer training. The following is a sampling of such publications:

Boston University, School and College Relations, 705 Commonwealth Avenue, Boston 15, Massachusetts, publishes a series called *Career Monographs.*

Endicott Junior College, Beverly, Massachusetts, publishes *Career Brochures.*

Lehigh University, Office of Admissions, Bethlehem, Pennsylvania, publishes *Guidance Brochures.*

Michigan College of Mining and Technology, Department of Public Relations, Houghton, Michigan, publishes *Vocational Guidance Bulletins.*

Rochester Institute of Technology, 65 South Plymouth Avenue, Rochester 8, N. Y., publishes *The Vocational Guidance Series.*

Simmons College, 300 The Fenway, Boston 15, Massachusetts, publishes *Vocational Guidance Series for Young Women.*

Professional societies

Professional organizations and societies are very often interested in helping young people with their plans for the future. Counselors, librarians, or workers in a particular profession can often supply a list of such organizations and societies. *Occupational Information—Its Nature and Use,* by Max F. Baer and Edward C. Roeber (8) also lists many organizations (pp. 232-250) that may be able to supply occupational information.

INTERVIEWS WITH WORKERS AND EXPERTS

The interview as a source of occupational information is valuable in that a person is given an opportunity to compare what he has read about an occupation with the opinion of someone actually engaged in work in the occupation. Many students have already discussed certain occupations with their parents or relatives. In such discussion, however, it is wise to listen carefully and to verify opinions by consulting a more distinterested party than a relative or friend. Experts and workers can usually give up-to-date information about local trends in their occupations as well as valuable hints and suggestions on necessary preparation and entry jobs not to be found in books or pamphlets.

Personal interview

Students may supplement all other sources of data by arranging to have a personal interview with one or more persons actively engaged in work in an occupation. Specific use of the interview as a method of obtaining occupational information should include plans for carrying out a complete study and for reporting the results of interviews before making an appointment for an interview. Additional suggestions for conducting occupational interviews will be given in order to aid in student use and understanding of this technique.

Reports of interviews may be included as an appendix in a formal report. A more effective use of interview material is to integrate the information thus obtained into the body of a report written on the occupation. If the latter approach is used, footnote references must indicate the source of each referral to an interview source. In either case, the names, positions, and business addresses of all persons interviewed should be reported in the bibliography.

The student should remember that he is a representative of his school or college wherever he goes, and that people will judge not only him but his school by his conduct. As such, it is important that he be courteous and prompt in keeping an appointment with a businessman. Time is very important to the businessman, and the student should be careful to avoid wasting it. To this end the student should have prepared a list of specific topics he wishes to discuss and specific questions he wants to have answered. Possibly, in the literature there has been a scarcity of information about preparation required, or retirement benefits. The interview should be used as a means of gathering specific information on topics that appear vague or contradictory in the literature as well as on topics not covered in the literature.

The student should explain the nature of his interest or project to the businessman in sufficient detail to satisfy his curiosity without boring him with unnecessary trivia. The businessman may be interested to the extent that he would like to see the finished project or report. If so, the student should arrange to have an extra copy typed or else see that the businessman examines the final copy.

The student should be conscious of the time set for concluding the interview. He should realize that, as interesting as the discussion may be to him, time is money to the businessman and other matters are probably waiting while he talks with the student. At the close of the interview the student should be sure to thank the businessman for his courtesy in granting him an interview. A short written note of appreciation should also be sent by the student to the businessman.

Interview by mail

In many pamphlets, or in previously mentioned sources, there will be found references to trade and professional associations. Such associations are becoming more and more important as sources of occupational information. Most trade and professional associations are quite willing to answer specific questions about occupation information. If the material available locally is insufficient for personal planning, students might well write a letter to a trade or professional organization and request answers to specific questions. Following is a list of questions that might be used. Of course, the questions must be modified to meet the unique needs of a particular inquiry, and by no means should students attempt to seek answers, by letter, to every question listed.

1. May I have the names and a description of any jobs in the _____ industry that show promising trends in view of today's economic trends?
2. Where may I obtain the best education or training for a job in the _____ industry?
3. Does your organization recommend any particular school for such training?
4. May I have a list of personal characteristics that you consider of primary importance in a potential employee for _____ position? Please consider physical requirements, personality, education, and interests as they relate to a trainee.
5. May I have information concerning the hiring, training and promoting of workers in the _____ occupation?
6. Will you please indicate the usual salary schedule according to the following outline:
   a. Beginning trainee.
   b. An individual with training in your company.
   c. An individual with training in college.
   d. An individual with 5–10 years' experience.

EDUCATIONAL INFORMATION

It is important that students periodically review their plans. Appropriate long-range plans may need revision in terms of short-range objectives (new curricula or courses). Or, it may be that new information is available or that new growth and maturity on the part of the student may call for the modification of plans that were previously appropriate but now appear inadequate.

A change of school or curriculum introduces new variables to the total picture of student adjustment. Even a normal progression through a single school, from freshman to the graduate level, calls for a continuous process of adjustment by the student if he is to ensure that he eventually reaches his goal.

Educational information is available in several forms, from many sources. Most students are aware of the major sources but not all students make an effort to use them. Not only because of the amount of money and time involved, but because of the tremendous personal import, the individual cannot be too careful in the consideration of a new school or program of studies.

Informal sources

Perhaps the student has talked with a friend about another college or particular program of studies. Usually, one or two colleges, schools, or areas of speculation are discussed from a highly personal and subjective point of view. Parents and relatives often provide similar opportunities for the discussion of particular schools. In all such instances the student seeking reliable information should be aware that what he hears is not always an unbiased presentation of the merits of a school. A winning football team or one new laboratory are not infallible signs of superior educational facilities.

College recruiting

Most colleges today employ professionally trained persons to publicize their services. Such persons, it should be remembered, may not always be the most objective source of educational information since part of their job is to attract qualified candidates for admission or transfer to their particular school. These recruiters can be valuable as long as the student weighs carefully all that is said. For example, the recruiter will usually stress only the attractive and strong features of his institution. The student must determine by discreet questioning the weak or unattractive features of the school. As in making any important decision, it is always wise to gather information from a number of sources before making any type of a formal commitment.

College catalogs and brochures

All schools and colleges supply catalogs and brochures to interested students. A post card is usually sufficient to guarantee a number of such publications from a particular school.

Brochures may be highly slanted, pictorial reviews presenting the school in its most favorable light. On occasion a student may find that most of the interesting photographs, which suggest a sprawling campus and an abundance of facilities, have been taken in, or of, one or two buildings. A personal visit to the campus will often avoid disappointment because of the possibility of this type of presentation.

Traditionally, the college catalogs have been written in such pedantic, obscure, "educational jargonese" that even the most capable, trained educator is often at a loss to understand them. However, application, persistence, and possibly help from a professional counselor will usually enable the student to uncover some valuable information from even the most obscurely written catalog. Entrance requirements, tuition, attendance policy, and facilities such as libraries, laboratories, classrooms, and dormitories are usually presented in an understandable form, but school philosophy, course descriptions, and degree requirements are often very obscure. Again, a personal interview will usually clarify most questionable areas.

Educational information for a transfer of program or college, specialized curricula, or advanced post-graduate education is a significant resource for the student in establishing a plan for the future. Care needs to be taken in the evaluation process.

Professional publications and guidance source books

There are available in most libraries many source books that will assist the student in evaluating and choosing a school or special program of studies. Publications such as the following may be found to assist in the discovery of an appropriate school, college, or program:

*A Guide to Colleges, Universities and Professional Schools
   in the United States* (1)
American Junior Colleges (18)
College Blue Book (34)
Junior Colleges and Specialized Schools and Colleges (71)
Lovejoy's College Guide (81)
Lovejoy's Vocational School Guide (82)
Patterson's American Education (106)
Vocational Training Directory of the United States (32)

Such publications are usually unbiased in their presentations. They do not replace any of the previously mentioned sources but do serve as a good starting point in special planning.

Actually, choice of a special school or curriculum does not, or at least *should not,* begin with a search for a school or curriculum. Self-analysis is the first step in planning for the future; the second step is a tentative occupational decision. In testing one's potentials and capacities against the realistic requirements of an occupation it becomes necessary in most cases to consider one's potential and capacity for further education. To this end, all of the factors mentioned previously as part of self-analysis must be evaluated in relation to the educational preparation as well as in relation to the on-the-job requirements that are a part of the occupation of one's choice.

SUMMARY

It is desirable that the student organize all of the information available that is pertinent to his occupational objective. This will include information about himself (self-analysis), information about his occupation, and information about the educational preparation necessary to reach his objective. However, no amount of organization, outlining or analysis of an occupation will make for realistic, effective planning if the first step of self-analysis is made haphazardly.

Basically, for purposes of classification, there are four sources of occupational information:

1. Actual work experience
2. Observation of occupational processes
3. Occupational literature
4. Interviews with workers or experts

Most students, by the time they reach college, have considerable first-hand information about several occupations in which they have had at least entry experiences. They have observed others at work, and have either participated in, or have listened to, discussions by workers or experts on the subject of occupations. Most school and public libraries today keep up-to-date occupational information available in the form of books, pamphlets, and trade journals.

Many libraries utilize the Dictionary of Occupational Titles *coding system for the organization of their materials on occupations. Reference to the "D.O.T." itself will provide further information on the classification and description of occupations.*

Not all occupational information is of equal worth. The suggestions offered previously will aid in the evaluation of various occupational materials. Probably as much as anything, an attitude of objective skepticism will insure the reader against the dangers of overgeneralizations and glamorizing found in some occupational literature.

SUPPLEMENTARY SOURCES

A Guide to Colleges, Universities and Professional Schools in the United States. Washington: American Council on Education, 1945.

Baer, M. F., and E. C. Roeber, *Occupational Information; Its Nature and Use.* Chicago: Science Research Associates, Inc., 1951.

Bogue, J. P., *American Junior Colleges* (3rd ed.). Washington: American Council on Education, 1952.

Cohen, N. M., *Vocational Training Directory of the United States.* Washington: N. M. Cohen, 1953.

College Blue Book, Christian E. Burckel, Compiler and Publisher, Baltimore, Maryland: Universal Lithographers, Inc., 1956.

Counselors' Information Service. Washington: B'nai B'rith Vocational Service Bureau.

Dictionary of Occupational Titles, Part I, *Definitions of Titles,* Part II, *Titles and Codes,* Part IV, *Entry—Occupational Classification.* Washington: U.S. Department of Labor, U.S. Employment Service, U.S. Government Printing Office, 1949.

Erickson, Clifford E., ed., *A Basic Text for Guidance Workers.* Englewood Cliffs, N. J.: Prentice-Hall, Inc., 1947.

Forrester, Gertrude, *Occupational Literature; An Annotated Bibliography*. New York: H. W. Wilson Company, 1954.

Hansen, Harry, ed., *The World Almanac and Book of Facts*. New York: *New York World Telegram and The Sun*. Published annually.

Hoppock, Robert, *Occupational Information*. New York: McGraw-Hill Book Company, Inc., 1957.

Irwin, Mary, *American Universities and Colleges* (6th ed.). Washington: American Council on Education, 1952.

Junior Colleges and Specialized Schools and Colleges (2nd ed.). Boston: Porter Sargent, 1955.

Karl, S. D., *The College Handbook*, Princeton, N. J.: College Entrance Examination Board, 1955–6.

Lovejoy, C. E., *Lovejoy's College Guide*. New York: Simon & Schuster, 1954.

———, *Lovejoy's Vocational School Guide*. New York: Simon & Schuster, Inc., 1951–55.

Patterson's American Education, 51, Educational Directories, Inc., Compiler and Publisher. Wilmette, Illinois, 1954.

Shartle, Carroll L., *Occupational Information; Its Development and Application*. Englewood Cliffs, N. J.: Prentice-Hall, Inc., 1952.

U.S. Bureau of the Census, U.S. Census of Population: 1950, Vol. II, *Characteristics of the Population*, Part I, U.S. Summary, Chapter C. Washington: U.S. Government Printing Office, 1953.

U.S. Department of Labor, Bureau of Labor Statistics in cooperation with Veterans Administration, Office of the Assistant Administrator for Vocational Rehabilitation and Education, *Occupation Outlook Handbook*. Washington: U.S. Government Printing Office, 1951.

An *occupational* and educational research paper consists of the study of an occupation and the training and education required for entry into that occupation. The particular occupation chosen for research is a decision to be made by the student. It is intended that the research paper be an *individual research project*. The research essential to the completion of such a paper should yield, for each student, the following benefits: *(1)* A means of evaluating choice of an occupation; *(2)* a pattern for the evaluation of any subsequent

Chapter 16

OCCUPATIONAL
AND EDUCATIONAL
RESEARCH PAPER

changes in vocational choice; *(3)* contact with various sources of information about occupations; *(4)* a knowledge of the factors involved in making a vocational choice; *(5)* the opportunity to apply a research technique commonly used in an occupational study; *(6)* an extension of previous study in self-analysis and application of such study to individual needs.

As earlier stated, and as later reinforced in this chapter, it must be emphasized that it is not assumed that in completing a research paper on a particular occupation a student is making a definitive, non-revocable choice of a job or a vocation. The stress in this particular project is upon methodology and process. Occupational and educational data, self-knowledge, and the integration of both of these factors is necessary whenever occupational planning is considered. The research paper in this chapter is, in every sense of the word, *practice*. An occupational choice as reflected in this paper must be confirmed or denied by a conscious evaluation upon the conclusion of the project and in light of further education and investigation. Occupational and educational planning must be a continuous process for all students.

251

OCCUPATIONAL AND EDUCATIONAL RESEARCH

Students, prior to undertaking the task of a thorough occupational and educational research project, need to view the total problems involved in profitable research into vocations and training programs. An over-all view of the total project is in order before actual research procedures are begun.

Values

At one time it was believed that the sole key to successful occupational adjustment was reliable educational and occupational information. Many school programs exposed the students to an abundance of educational and occupational information with the hope that this would ensure appropriate vocational choices for all students. Today, many students are laboring through a program of studies leading toward an inappropriately chosen vocation. Many are doing so because they selected an occupation purely because of interest. Lacking any further insight into themselves, they have grasped this early choice as a guide to their higher education and possibly to their future vocations.

Underlying all that has been presented throughout this book is the thesis that sound educational and occupational information must be coupled with self-understanding in order to ensure wise vocational decisions and promise of successful occupational adjustment. Trained counselors and counseling are of course an integral part of the total process.

In undertaking a major research project such as is outlined in this chapter, the student has an invaluable opportunity to test his knowledge of self against the reality of the occupational world. Under no circumstances should the student, in making a decision as to the appropriateness of the occupation under investigation, mistake the decision to undertake the study of an occupation for the decision to prepare for and enter into a particular occupation. Self-understanding is an indispensable aspect of occupational decision-making. The outline offered in this chapter can promote such understanding provided it is undertaken as an opportunity to test one's knowledge of self against the requirements of an occupation. There is no right or wrong decision implicit within the project as outlined. Some students will reject their present choice, others will reaffirm their decisions. Others may suspend decisions pending investigation of another occupation. Whatever the decision, it will have been made on the basis of an abundance of information and critical analysis. Student planning will need to be based upon facts, interpretations, and applications. Many values are therefore involved in educational and occupational research.

Myth of a definitive choice

In an earlier chapter (14), the myth of success was discussed. Another myth important in the lives of young Americans is the persistent belief that everyone should make a definitive occupational choice during his high-school career or, at the very latest, during his freshman year in college. This myth of the definitive choice ignores the reality that individuals differ with regard to almost every measurable characteristic; proneness to make a vocational decision, although at present not measurable, is no exception to the principle of individual differences. As has been seen, many factors enter into the making of a vocational choice. The cumulative effect of the many physical and psychological influences from the environment varies from one person to another; the actual physiological and psychological growth of the individual also varies. With so many uncontrolled interacting variables it is indeed fallacious thinking to expect all young people to respond at the same chronological age with an appropriate occupational choice.

The outline for the study of an occupation is presented with the full understanding that the student now undertaking this study may well be at a strictly exploratory stage. For him this study will provide a valuable experience in critical thinking. Some students, in writing this paper, will have taken a valuable step toward the discovery of an appropriate vocational objective. Other students, upon completing the task, will have ruled out an occupational choice on the basis of an abundance of information about the job and the self. Each student will have profited.

SELECTING A TOPIC

The student ready to select a specific occupation for investigation should be fully aware of his potentialities, his strengths and weaknesses, and his dominant personality characteristics as well as his basic motivating values, needs, and emotions. Then he should turn his attention to the question of interest. Interest can be determined in a number of ways. In completing a self-analysis the student will have available considerable pertinent information on his basic interests. Favorite subjects in school, favorite hobbies, books, and leisure-time activities, as well as satisfying work experience, will all give clues to the student's basic pattern of interests. Various interest inventories are available that yield scores convertible into percentiles for comparison with interest patterns of workers in specific occupational areas. Other inventories enable the student to compare the relative strengths of his interests in several general areas.

The student should look first for broad interests that can be related to broad occupational fields. Later on it is possible to narrow one's choice to specific interests and vocations. At that time the student should begin to think in terms of occupational level as well as field, for, within each broad field of work there are various levels, each requiring different degrees of skill, aptitude, and ability. It may be that the student who is reasonably sure of his levels of skill, aptitude, and ability may choose to examine a number of fields on an appropriate level for himself, but this approach is not recommended unless the correct level has been determined through careful self-analysis.

People are not alike by nature, nor made alike by training, education, or inclination. Modern personnel studies show that it is not enough just to be able to do a job—one should also be temperamentally adapted to the job. The student must seek out fields of occupational endeavor that will match his capacities as a person with the demands of the occupation.

What are these fields of endeavor in which one may find a rewarding career? For most purposes the fields can be classified broadly as:

1. Proprietary — managerial
2. Professional — technical
3. Skilled
4. Semi-skilled
5. Office — sales
6. Domestic — personal
7. Unskilled

BOSTON UNIVERSITY PHOTO SERVICE

Achievement of the goal is sufficient reward

A brief examination of the *Dictionary of Occupational Titles* will demonstrate, within these broad fields, the myriad opportunities, demands, and varying degrees of specialization needed by the person seeking an entrance into a particular field.

Very few individuals can realistically enter into the process of self-analysis without the consideration of an occupation. Self-analysis and occupational analysis supplement each other. The question for most individuals is "What do I want?" Actually, this should involve a second question, "What can I get?" or perhaps, "For what can I qualify?" To the uninitiated, the occupational world can appear as a limitless expanse of confusion. Upon closer inspection this expanse is seen to be bounded by fields. Within any given field the opportunities are varied enough to suit one's preference.

The many opportunities within a single field allow the individual to take into consideration, in his final choice, many personal factors. The adventurous soul might choose to prepare for a career involving international travel. The stay-at-home may choose a career that would limit his travels to daily walks through a city park. The question of health must be considered. Some positions within a field will demand extreme changes of climate with attendant hazards. Other positions may require late hours and continuing high pressure from competitors. Varying degrees of socioeconomic status may be found within a particular field. Obviously, there are many other factors to be considered in deciding upon a particular vocation within a field. The research outline presented in this chapter will suggest some of the more important factors to be considered in making a choice.

In the final analysis only the individual concerned can determine the appropriateness of a vocational choice. Even after a careful study of a field of work and a consideration of the demands made on a worker the all-important but unpredictable factors that make for success still remain. Among these difficult-to-assess factors are motivation, energy, initiative, common sense, and emotional stability.

The student should utilize all of the occupational-information resources to be found in most libraries. Chapter 15 presented a discussion of the various sources that should not be overlooked, such as books, magazine articles, pamphlets, government reports, census reports, material from national associations and organizations, state employment services, state and national civil-service announcements, classified business directories, chambers of commerce, and community-service-organization bulletins.

STYLE AND PROCEDURE

At this stage in their careers, most students will have had some experience in writing various types of papers. The autobiography is usually one of the first assigned papers. Later, other types of writing are required, such as the writing of reports and descriptions. The college student is often confronted with a peculiar type of assignment called a "term paper." In it, he is required to present facts or opinions on a certain topic related to a given course and to demonstrate his familiarity with the subject. Another type of paper very often assigned to college students is the *research paper*.

The research type of paper differs from the usual term paper in that it calls for more objectivity on the part of the writer. It must be written in the third person and must present facts devoid of the author's personal opinion concerning them (unless interpretation of the facts is presented as a separate section of the paper). Furthermore, the facts presented in a research paper must be annotated—that is, footnotes must be used to show where the information was obtained. Usually the source will be from some other person who must be given credit for his ideas.

There are many styles of research writing. In all of them consistency is the keynote. Once a given style of headings, paragraphing and footnoting is adopted, the student must continue to use this style throughout the paper. The reader has perhaps noted that this text is written in a consistent pattern of headings, references, and sources. By referring to the table of contents it is possible to outline the basic ideas presented in the book. Chapter and paragraph headings actually summarize the content of any well written book.

The student should consult his English grammar book for supplementary information in the writing of a research paper. College bookstores usually have available style manuals for the writing of term papers and theses. Any such manual will serve as a guide to the proper techniques and style for research reporting. The paper is a report and should be as objective and as close to the facts as possible.

To the student beginning his first major research project, the mechanics of gathering information, analyzing data, and writing in a specified form with all sources of information annotated may seem hopelessly and needlessly cumbersome. Having once mastered the fundamentals of research writing, however, the student will have at his command a tool that should stand him in good stead throughout his college career and quite possibly in his career after graduation. Every student should make every effort to abide by the suggested procedures offered in whatever style manual is followed.

A RESEARCH OUTLINE

In analyzing an occupation it is necessary to take into account a number of considerations. To aid in developing a standard of judgment that will enable a person to study any occupation in which he might be interested, an outline should be presented on which to develop the paper.

When writing the paper students should use the part headings (Part I, II) as chapter divisions. Under the chapter headings the major subheadings should be used (for example, A. Name or title of occupation, B. Description of occupation); further outlining of material is not considered essential and is not encouraged. It is suggested that the outline details be developed in paragraph form, using the outline as a guide to the content.

It is important in a research paper to document all information secured from the work of others, including personal interviews. An English grammar book or a style manual needs to be followed for the correct form of footnotes and bibliography. The outline that follows, with detailed suggestions to students, is offered for both research and writing purposes. The outline is an outgrowth of many years of use with college students. It was originally adapted from a suggested outline for an occupational monograph by the National Vocational Guidance Association. (103)

PART I—THE OCCUPATION

A. Name or title of occupation.

B. Description of occupation: give as many of the following definitions as you can find:
   1. As determined by an official organization.
   2. *Dictionary of Occupational Titles.*
   3. As given in the law.
   4. Any other carefully formulated definition acceptable to those in the occupation.

C. A day's work in the occupation.

D. Employment outlook. (Give statistics that reveal the employment outlook in the occupation that you are considering and interpret their significance in terms of that outlook.)
   1. Number employed nationally and locally.
   2. Proportion of total labor force.
   3. Estimated future needs for workers.
   4. The effect of geography upon occupational opportunities.
   5. Chances of securing a position in the near future.
   6. Long-term trends in the occupation.

E. Relation to other jobs.
   1. Entry jobs that might lead to this occupation.
   2. Jobs to which workers may be promoted.
   3. Requirements for promotion.
   4. Jobs of similar nature for which this job would help to prepare workers.

F. Earnings, hours, working conditions.
   1. Beginners' average yearly earnings.
   2. Average annual wages received.
   3. Maximum wages that may be earned yearly.
   4. If there are any particular laws, union regulations, and the like, that may apply to this particular occupation, describe them and give their purpose.
   5. Surroundings in which the worker is employed.
   6. Average number of hours per day worked in the occupation, average days per week, average weeks per year.
   7. Health or accident hazards attached to this position.
   8. Security of worker in occupation—laws, company regulations, and so forth, that provide security.
   9. Provisions made for old age.

G. Advantages of workers in this occupation. (Consider such matters as the following: service opportunities, working conditions, opportunities for promotion, fellow workers, wages, security, and physical factors.)

H. Disadvantages of occupation. (Consider same points mentioned in G.)

PART II—THE WORKER

A. Personal qualifications necessary for success in the occupation. (Consider such points as the following: age qualifications, sex, race, nationality, physical qualifications, special abilities, and particular interests of the worker.)

B. Preparation for work in this occupation.
   1. Educational requirements for this job. (Be specific.)
   2. If there is any training on the job, describe the in-service training.
   3. Advanced or special training required to prepare for promotion to a higher position.
   4. Preliminary work experiences helpful in preparing for the job.
   5. Personality traits desired in occupation. (Consider such points as the following: courtesy, cheerfulness, common sense, good judgment, responsibility, promptness, initiative, and ability to get along with people.)
   6. Other requirements.

PART III—PLANNING YOUR CAREER IN THIS FIELD
(Utilize Chapter 13 in completing this section)

A. Personal factors and the occupation.
   1. Interests. (Compare your interests as ascertained in your counseling interviews with the interests involved in the occupation. Consider how your interests are similar to, and different from, the interests of those engaged in the occupation. What vocational interests should you seek to develop for this occupation? How may you develop these interests?)
   2. Aptitudes and abilities. (After conferences with your counselor, you should be able to arrive at a fairly objective appraisal of yourself.

The literature that you read should give you an estimate of the abilities needed for the occupation. Compare your aptitudes with the abilities required for success in the occupation. Consider how they are *similar* and how they are *different*. Discuss the abilities that you should seek to develop for success in the occupation. In your discussion indicate how you plan to strengthen the abilities in which you are weak.)

3. Occupational alternatives. (It is possible that conditions may be such that you will not be able to enter the occupation of your first choice. Describe other related occupations that (a) call for abilities similar to yours, and (b) vocational interests similar to yours. Show why you have selected various alternatives.)

B. Your preparation for the occupation.

1. Schools contemplated attended or courses planned that will be helpful.
2. Additional training you will need.
3. Schools and colleges where you plan to obtain this additional training.
4. Other schools offering similar training.
5. Schools offering training in related occupations.
6. Work experiences you have had that will be of assistance.
7. Work you may secure that would be helpful in preparing for your future occupation.
8. Total expense and time involved in securing your training. How do you plan to meet the necessary expenses?

C. Securing a job in your chosen occupational field.

1. Methods of securing a job in this field. (Consider such methods as the following: help from relatives; letters of application; contacts with former employers; want ads; assistance from acquaintances and friends; employment agencies, either school, public, or private; and personal interviews. Indicate the methods you propose to use and how you plan to use them.)
2. Employment opportunities. Name possible companies.
3. Holding and progressing in the job. (Consider in your discussion the qualities necessary for your success in the work and the lines of promotion possible.)

PART IV—SOURCES OF INFORMATION

This part of your study should list your sources of information. Use the form for a bibliography suggested by a style guide. *After each reference give a brief evaluation of that reference.*

Your bibliography should be divided into two parts:

1. Primary sources. (Direct, first-hand reporting of factual data.)
2. Secondary sources. (Additional references useful for background information.)

Below your reading references state the workers and employers whom you visited as follows:

1. Mr. Henry Adams, Salesman
   255 Commonwealth Avenue, Boston, Massachusetts.
2. Mr. John Smith, Electrical Appliances, Inc.
   1066 Boylston Street, Boston, Massachusetts.

The case of John James

In the following case, an attempt has been made to demonstrate an approach and methods that may be used in writing an occupational research paper. *This sample case, however, should not be accepted as a set pattern for all research papers, since initiative and originality are important characteristics in such a project.* Its main purpose is to show one method of attack that may be used as a point of departure.

John James, after concluding his self-analysis and determining his level of potential, decided that of his three fields of interest he knew the least about diplomacy, so this was the obvious choice for his occupational research paper. He had been told about the Occupational Library of the college and realized that this was the place to go to find the information he was seeking.

The Occupational Library comprises pamphlet files, books on various occupations, sources of statistics and trends, information about schools where required training may be obtained, and periodicals containing articles of interest on different occupations. The pamphlet files contain certain unbound information on different occupations. Each one has a separate folder.

John asked if the library had any information on diplomacy and he received a folder consisting of about ten pamphlets. He was informed that each folder contained a cross-reference sheet that listed any books in the library that dealt with diplomacy as a career, any related jobs or folders that might also contain information he desired, a list of periodicals that contained articles on the particular job he was looking up, and a list of related industries. In the case of diplomacy, John found no related industries on the cross-reference sheet, but did find a list of books of related occupations. The magazine articles had been clipped and placed in the folder, presenting all of the information for him in one place.

John read all the pamphlets in the folder and found that of the ten, five of the pamphlets contained the information he needed. He made a complete list of these, plus the two books he had decided to read, as follows:

1. *American Foreign Service*, Childs, J. Rives, Henry Holt and Co., New York, 1947.
2. *Diplomacy as a Career*, Wilson, Hugh, R., Riverside Press, Cambridge, 1941.
3. *The Foreign Service of the United States*, Department of State Publications 3612, Government Printing Office, Washington, 1949.
4. *Foreign Service*, Occupational Index, Inc., New York, 1947.
5. *Foreign Service Workers*, Science Research Associates Inc., Chicago, 1950.
6. *Preparing for a Career in the Foreign Service of the United States*, Department of State Publications 3668, Government Printing Office, Washington, 1950.

7. "Serving the United States Abroad," Cheever, Daniel S., *School and College Placement,* Vol. 10, No. 1, Oct. 1949.
8. *Handbook of Job Facts,* Frankel, Alice, Science Research Associates, Chicago, 1948.

It must be remembered that these pamphlets were chosen only after all of the information had been read. John read his outline thoroughly. He was told statistics could be found in the current census of the United States, but "diplomat" was not listed in the census. The same held true for the *Occupational Outlook Handbook,* another basic reference source. If he had been looking for information on "lawyer," he would have found it in both of these sources. Since two of the pamphlets he decided to use were government documents, however, he found employment statistics mentioned in them. He also found some in nongovernment documents.

Next, notes had to be taken from the pamphlets and books. John found that an easy method, one that would eliminate too many rough drafts, was to use small index cards, 3″ x 5″. Each section of the outline had a separate card on which he noted the source to be used for the corresponding information. John's card outline was as follows:

PART I—THE OCCUPATION

A. Introduction: Childs' book. By reading Childs' book, thorough background information such as history and practice of diplomacy may be obtained and used throughout the paper.
   Occupational Abstract, p. 2, 1st paragraph. A short history of diplomacy was given but it was not as good as Childs'.

B. Description: *Dictionary of Occupational Titles,* Pt. 1. Definition of duties of diplomat will be found here. Childs'—pp. 64-65 further defines diplomacy and functions of diplomats.
   Black's Law Dictionary—p. 580. Legal definition of diplomacy and diplomat.
   Preparing for a Career in the Foreign Service of the United States, p. 2: descriptions of positions in the foreign service.

C. Day's work: *The Foreign Service of the United States,* p. 5, 1st paragraph. Lists functions of foreign-service officers. There is no special day-by-day routine. Work is greatly varied. Information gathered from personal interview with someone already in the field may be used here. Information read in the books may be used throughout the paper wherever the facts fit.

D. Employment outlook: future prospects.
   Occupational Abstract—p. 2. Not too much information.
   Science Research Associates Occupational Brief No. 92—p. 2 for 1950 statistics, 1948 statistics on p. 4 of *Foreign Service of the United States* in 1949. No census data.

E. Relation to other jobs: For list of entry jobs in an occupation, Part IV of the *Dictionary of Occupational Titles* should be used. Diplomat was not listed so the information had to be found in other available sources and, namely, the pamphlets and books.

Occupational Abstract No. 105, p. 4—Information about testing given. Childs'—p. 247—Lists ranks in succession within the foreign service. *The Foreign Service of the United States*—p. 7, 4th paragraph. Definite information about tests—when and where they are given, also texts of tests.

F. Earnings, hours, working conditions:
Preparing for a Career in the Foreign Service of the United States, p. 2. Information about salaries, allowances, promotions, retirements.
Occupational Abstract No. 105—p. 5—Salaries, given according to class.
Childs', p. 157, *The Foreign Service of the United States.* Appendix for Foreign Service Act of 1946. *The Foreign Service of the United States* —p. 7. More information of salaries and vacations.

G. Advantages and disadvantages:

H. *Occupational Abstract* No. 105—p. 5.
Both Wilson and Childs have the information, although it is scattered throughout the material.

PART II—THE WORKER

A. Qualifications:
Serving the U. S. Abroad by Cheever—p. 19 and 20. Lists personal qualifications of foreign service officer.
Science Research Associates Occupational Brief No. 92—p. 2.
Slightly more detailed list than above source.
Handbook of Job Facts by Frankel—Gives per cent of women and Negroes in the field plus repetition of qualifications.

B. Preparation:
Preparing for a Career in the Foreign Service of the United States, p. 12-15. Gives educational requirements of foreign service officer. Perhaps best source for this information.
Occupational Abstract No. 105—Contains information already covered.
Serving the United States Abroad—p. 21. Information on the in-service training program scattered throughout.
Preparing for a Career in the Foreign Service of the United States, p. 7-8. Examination of information in detail.
Foreign Service of the United States—Contains usable information throughout.

PART III—PLANNING FOR A CAREER

A. All personal information was filled in here by John after he had reviewed his test data sheets, and had completed several interviews with his counselor.
Related occupations—Use Part IV of the *Dictionary of Occupational Titles,* if possible, or pamphlets. See Part I, Sec. E.

B. *Preparing for a Career in the Foreign Service of the United States,* p. 12-15. Best source for information on educational preparation. Excerpts from both *Diplomacy as a Career* and *American Foreign Service.*

C. *The Foreign Service of the United States*—pp. 6-7; Information about securing a job and different assignments possible. *Preparing for a Career in* the Foreign Service of the United States, p. 2, 7, 9, 10, 11. Contains information about progressing in the job. Regulations about examinations are fully discussed on pages 7, 8, 9, 10, 11. Sample questions found starting on page 21.

After all pertinent data were collected on the cards, John went back and took more complete notes on his reading. Having the cards in sequence according to the outline helped him with the continuity of his paper. He also reviewed his test data sheets. The test data sheets having already been completed by John, it was easy for him to make a comparison of his own aptitudes, abilities, and interests with those of successful diplomats. As it turned out, John found that his abilities, aptitudes, and interests corresponded very closely with those described as desirable for diplomats. Had they not done so, however, John would have then been in a position to make a decision about his future based on an abundance of realistic information about himself and diplomacy and would not in later years have entertained unrealistic notions concerning a possible career in diplomacy.

SUMMARY

The individual research project outlined in this chapter provides the basis for the application of critical thinking to the problem of vocational choice. The student has an opportunity to test his self-understanding against the requirements of an occupation. Whether the final result of this research is acceptance, rejection, or modification of plans, the student will have gained insight into the process of occupational and educational choice.

SUPPLEMENTARY SOURCES

Caplow, Theodore, *The Sociology of Work*. Minneapolis: University of Minnesota Press, 1954.

Gray, J. Stanley, *Psychology Applied to Human Affairs* (2nd ed.). New York: McGraw-Hill Book Company, Inc., 1954.

————, (ed.), *Psychology in Use* (2nd ed.). New York: American Book Company, 1951.

Hepner, Harry W., *Psychology Applied to Life and Work* (3rd ed.). Englewood Cliffs, N. J.: Prentice-Hall, Inc., 1957.

Hoppock, Robert, *Occupational Information*. New York: McGraw-Hill Book Company, Inc., 1957.

Roe, Anne, *The Psychology of Occupation*. New York: John Wiley & Sons, Inc., 1956.

Super, Donald E., *The Psychology of Careers*. New York: Harper & Brothers, 1957.

Roles are important in life as well as on the stage

APPENDICES

PSYCHOLOGICAL TEST PROFILES

THE PSYCHOLOGICAL TEST PROFILES included in this appendix may be used as actual blank profiles to be completed by students in connection with their course work. More frequently they will serve as models and as examples for class or group discussions on the psychological test program in the school or college.

The Psychological Test Data Sheet on page 268 is a general profile which might easily be reproduced by mimeograph or by similar duplicating processes. Local variations in style may be needed to include all of the results normally used in a particular program. The Differential Aptitude Test profiles may be secured from The Psychological Corporation in New York City. The Kuder Interest Inventory Profile may be obtained from Science Research Associates in Chicago, Illinois. Many programs provide for student scoring and profiling of Kuder Interest Inventory results. Similar measures of interest may be incorporated into varying counseling and testing programs.

No attempt has been made to include all published profiles or procedures for aiding students in understanding their own psychological test patterns. Considerable local variation in style of operation and counselor techniques are not only usually desirable but most often necessary if psychological test data are to be utilized successfully in a student-centered counseling and testing program.

PSYCHOLOGICAL TEST DATA SHEET

Name_____ Date _____

PSYCHOLOGICAL TEST	PERCENTILE RATING									
	10	20	30	40	50	60	70	80	90	99

I SCHOLASTIC APTITUDE

1. Name of Test_____
   Date Taken_____Form____
   Raw Scores   Percentiles

   _____ ____ _____

   _____ ____ _____

   _____ ____ _____

   _____ ____ _____

   Norm Group_____

2. Name of Test_____
   Date Taken_____Form____
   Raw Scores   Percentiles

   _____ ____ _____

   _____ ____ _____

   _____ ____ _____

   Norm Group _____

II READING ABILITY

1. Name of Test_____
   Date Taken_____Form____
   Raw Scores   Percentiles

   _____ ____ _____

   _____ ____ _____

   _____ ____ _____

   _____ ____ _____

   Norm Group_____

III INTELLIGENCE

1. Name of Test_____
   Date Taken_____Form____
   Raw Scores   Percentiles

   _____ ____ _____

   _____ ____ _____

   _____ ____ _____

   Norm Group_____

IV OTHER

1. Name of Test_____
   Date Taken_____Form____
   Raw Scores   Percentiles

   _____ ____ _____

   _____ ____ _____

   _____ ____ _____

   Norm Group_____

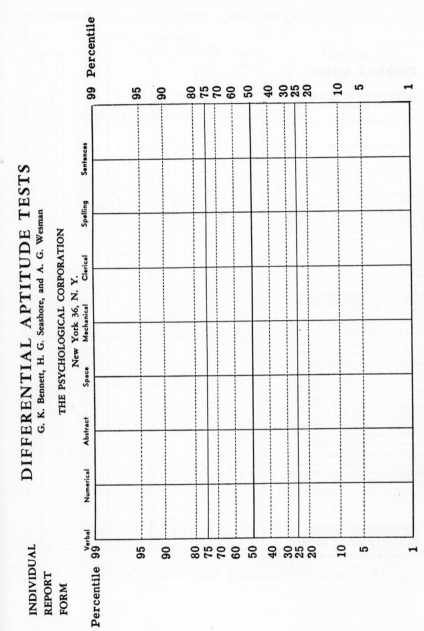

DIFFERENTIAL APTITUDE TESTS

G. K. Bennett, H. G. Seashore, and A. G. Wesman

THE PSYCHOLOGICAL CORPORATION

New York 36, N. Y.

INDIVIDUAL
REPORT
FORM

Reproduced with Permission of The Psychological Corporation

NAME _____ AGE _____ SEX _____ GROUP _____ DATE OF TEST _____
Print   Last   First   Initial   M or F

First Revision, February 1951
REPRODUCTION BY ANY MEANS STRICTLY PROHIBITED

SELF-INTERPRETING

PROFILE SHEET
for the
KUDER PREFERENCE RECORD
VOCATIONAL
Forms, CH, CM.

MEN and WOMEN

DIRECTIONS FOR PROFILING

1. Copy the V-Score from the back page of your answer pad in the box at the right.

   If your V-Score is 37 or less, there is some reason for doubting the value of your answers, and your other scores may not be very accurate. If your V-Score is 45 or more, you may not have understood the directions, since 44 is the highest possible score. If your score is not between 38 and 44, inclusive, you should see your adviser. He will probably recommend that you read the directions again, and then that you fill out the blank a second time, being careful to follow the directions exactly and to give sincere replies.

   If your V-Score is between 38 and 44, inclusive, go ahead with the following directions.

2. Copy the scores 0 through 9 in the spaces at the top of the profile chart. Under "OUTDOOR" find the number which is the same as the score at the top. Use the numbers under M if you are a man and the numbers under F if you are a woman. Draw a line through this number from one side to the other of the entire column under OUTDOOR. Do the same thing for the scores at the top of each of the other columns. If a score is larger than any number in the column, draw a line across the top of the column; if it is smaller, draw a line across the bottom.

3. With your pencil blacken the entire space between the lines you have drawn and the bottom of the chart. The result is your profile for the *Kuder Preference Record—Vocational.*

   An interpretation of the scores will be found on the other side.

The profile chart columns are numbered 0 through 9 with headings (each with M and F sub-columns): OUTDOOR, MECHANICAL, COMPUTATIONAL, SCIENTIFIC, PERSUASIVE, ARTISTIC, LITERARY, MUSICAL, SOCIAL SERVICE, CLERICAL. The left and right margins are labeled PERCENTILES, marked from 0 to 100.

Your INTEREST PROFILE

Your profile on the *Kuder Preference Record—Vocational* shows your interest in the ten important areas listed across the top of the chart. The profile will also help you learn how you compare with other people.

The lines you drew on the chart show whether your interest is high, average, or low. If your score is above the top dotted line in any column, it is a high score and shows that you like activities in that area. If your score is between the two dotted lines, your interest is about average. If your score is below the bottom dotted line, it is a low score and shows that you dislike activities of that type.

Like most people, you are probably high in some areas, low in some, and average in others. Look at your highest score first. This score shows the type of activities you probably like best. If you have more than one score above the top dotted line, you have a combination of high interests.

Look at your low scores, too. They should be considered in any plans you make because they indicate the kinds of activities you probably do not enjoy. Remember that high interests are not better or worse than low, nor are some interests better than others. It is your own *pattern* of interests that counts.

Here is what your scores on the *Preference Record* mean:

OUTDOOR interest means that you prefer work that keeps you outside most of the time and usually deals with animals and growing things. Forest rangers, naturalists, and farmers are among those high in outdoor interests.

MECHANICAL interest means you like to work with machines and tools. Jobs in this area include automobile repairmen, watchmakers, drill press operators, and engineers.

COMPUTATIONAL interest means you like to work with numbers. A high score in this area suggests that you might like such jobs as bookkeeper, accountant, or bank teller.

SCIENTIFIC interest means that you like to discover new facts and solve problems. Doctors, chemists, nurses, engineers, radio repairmen, aviators, and dieticians usually have high scientific interests.

PERSUASIVE interest means that you like to meet and deal with people and to promote projects or things to sell. Most actors, politicians, radio announcers, ministers, salesmen, and store clerks have high persuasive interests.

ARTISTIC interest means you like to do creative work with your hands. It is usually work that has "eye appeal" involving attractive design, color, and materials. Painters, sculptors, architects, dress designers, hairdressers, and interior decorators all do "artistic" work.

LITERARY interest shows that you like to read and write. Literary jobs include novelist, historian, teacher, actor, news reporter, editor, drama critic, and book reviewer.

MUSICAL interest shows you like going to concerts, playing instruments, singing, or reading about music and musicians.

SOCIAL SERVICE interest indicates a preference for helping people. Nurses, Boy or Girl Scout leaders, vocational counselors, tutors, ministers, personnel workers, social workers, and hospital attendants spend much of their time helping other people.

CLERICAL interest means you like office work that requires precision and accuracy. Jobs such as bookkeeper, accountant, file clerk, salesclerk, secretary, statistician, and traffic manager fall in this area.

The occupations listed for each area on this profile are only examples. Your counselor can help you think of many others that are suggested by your pattern of interests. He can also tell you about many books and pamphlets that will help you learn more about these occupations. You may find that many school courses and leisure-time activities fit into your high interest areas.

Another form of the *Preference Record*, the *Personal*, will help you find out more about the types of things you like to do. It will help you discover, for example, how much you like meeting new people, whether you prefer situations you are familiar with, if you would rather work with ideas or things, how much you prefer pleasant social situations, and if you like to direct others. Your scores in these areas, too, will help you plan your career.

What you can do well depends, of course, on many things in addition to interest. Your abilities are particularly important. Many abilities can be measured by tests. Here, again, your counselor is the person to see.

Try to get as much information as you can about your interests, abilities, and the jobs you want to consider. The more you know about yourself, the more opportunity you have to make wise plans for your future.

Reproduced with permission of Science Research Associates

STUDENT PSYCHOLOGICAL
TEST GLOSSARY

THE NUMBER OF TESTS in our culture is almost unbelievable to the casual lay observer. Buros, in his *Mental Measurements Yearbook* (22), which has had four editions through 1954, lists, describes, and evaluates thousands of tests. Each year many more appear. Various professional publications, such as those of Super (121), Anastasi (6), and Cronbach (39), and others for counselors, psychologists, and teachers have reviewed, analyzed, and compared these many tests. Needless to say, this student psychological test glossary is not intended to be a competing source with any of these professional publications. This glossary is intended to be a functional, student-centered description of the major psychological test instruments used in college guidance and personnel programs.

Almost every school and college in America administers psychological tests and uses the results. It has been traditional, however, to treat these test results as confidential information; the school utilizes the material, the student does not. In many cases this is necessary; in many cases this is not necessary. When trained counselors are available, and students are prepared, the use of such material can be a valuable part of the individual student's education.

This book can help the trained guidance counselor and the responsible student to make the use of test results become a learning experience. The entire book attempts to provide a basis for critical thinking and decision-making. The use of test results requires the effective understanding of both the principles of psychological measurement and the test instruments themselves.

TEST ANALYSIS PATTERN

This appendix presents tests in an order paralleling that of the chapters in Part III, the "self-analysis" section of the book. Reference back to the corresponding topic chapters, and to Chapter 8, "Individual Differences," for an over-all view, will give more meaning to the discussions of tests in the pages that follow.

The glossary will deal separately with several groups of tests—interest, aptitude, intelligence, and personality—discussing each in terms of these three questions:

1. Its purpose—what does it intend to do? What is it designed to measure? Was the test developed and defined for nationwide usage? The answers to these questions will aid students in understanding the particular use for each test and how it differs from other, perhaps similar, tests.

272

2. Its description—how does it operate? How does this particular psychological instrument achieve its purpose? What areas are measured and how are they measured? How many "subtests" are there and what are the time limits? Is the test timed or untimed? The answers to these questions will help each student to understand the structure of the test.

3. Its uses—what do the results mean? Are its results consistent with its purpose? How precise and applicable are the results?

VOCATIONAL INTERESTS (Chapter 9)

Vocational interest has been an area in which much psychological history has been written. Many inventories have been developed and standardized that measure vocational interest. Research has been voluminous and productive. The vocational interest inventory offers a wealth of source material for all students.

Vocational interest inventories (since actually the word "test" is inappropriate) operate upon more than one premise. Certain inventories measure interest directly: "Do you or don't you like to do——?" Others measure attitudes toward various activities and then compare students' attitudes with the attitudes of successful workers in selected occupations.

The vocational interest inventories listed in this glossary are:

1. The Kuder Preference Record—Vocational (74)
2. The Occupational Interest Inventory (Lee and Thorpe) (102)
3. The Strong Vocational Interest Blank for Men (and Women) (120)

Kuder Preference Record—Vocational (74)

PURPOSE

The Kuder Preference Record attempts to show the relative strengths of interests in ten general areas of activity. These areas are not directly related to a specific occupation or vocation, but rather to families of occupations or vocations. Many occupations require high interest in two, three, or more areas.

DESCRIPTION

This inventory attempts to measure relative areas of interests by a "forced choice" method that requires each person to choose the activity (among three listed) "most liked" or "least liked." Relative interests and relative interest patterns can thus be obtained. Percentile scores are available on general-population (male or female) norms. The ten areas included in the Kuder Inventory can be described as follows:

Interest area:	*An interest and liking for:*	*Persons with high interest in this area are usually found in occupations such as:*
0. Outdoor	Activities performed out of doors involving nature and things found out of doors.	Tree surgeon, forest ranger, telephone lineman, etc.
1. Mechanical	Mechanical or machine type activities—working with, around, and upon machines.	Mechanical engineer, machinist, tool and die maker, etc.
2. Computational	Working with numbers, statistical reports, figures, accounts.	Accountant, auditor, statistician, bookkeeper, etc.
3. Scientific	Experimental and laboratory work, precise methodological approaches.	Physician, medical technologist, research chemist, etc.
4. Persuasiveness	Verbal persuasion, interpersonal relationships.	Lawyer, salesman, receptionist, etc.
5. Artistic	Use of good line, color, and proportion in creative activities.	Interior decorator, set designer, window dresser, etc.
6. Literary	Working with books, written materials, writing criticisms.	Librarian, book seller, book reviewer, author, etc.
7. Music	Instrumental or vocal performance, listening to, and reading about, music.	Musician, composer, record sales clerk, disc jockey, etc.
8. Social service	Working with and for other people, serving, helping, aiding.	Social worker, train information clerk, teacher, etc.
9. Clerical	Filing, categorizing, office work, typing and general office detail.	Office clerk, bookkeeper, file clerk, typist, etc.

The inventory is untimed, but is usually completed in about 45 minutes.

USES

The Kuder Preference Record—Vocational has wide use as a general screening device in helping the student locate broad areas of activities that appeal to him. These results indicate a relative degree of liking for activities, and may have no relation to amount of ability or aptitude the person may have in these areas. Thus, after the areas of interests have been located, areas of ability and aptitude must be located and compared to the areas of interests. The Kuder Preference Record indicates relative like or dislike; this interest tells nothing about ability or aptitude.

A second valuable use of this inventory is in helping the student to understand the curve of normal distribution, how norms are derived, and some differences in male versus female interest norms, due to social expectation. These points are illustrated on the profile sheet that each student can make for himself. Reference back to the chapter entitled "Individual Differences" (Chapter 8) will explain this point further.

Strong Vocational Interest Blank (120)

PURPOSE

This blank attempts to measure the degree of similarity of interests between persons in various occupations and the student filling out the blank. The likes and dislikes of the student are compared to those of successful persons in various occupations. In this way, the student can learn the degree to which his pattern of interests corresponds to that held by persons already successful in a field he may wish to enter.

DESCRIPTION

Four hundred kinds of school subjects, amusements, occupations, and peculiarities of people are listed. The student indicates "like," "indifferent," or "dislike" according to his own preference for the items listed by encircling the letters L, I, or D. Since tangible differences in patterns of like, indifference, and dislike exist among persons in separate occupations, forty-five separate scoring keys are provided for the men's form and twenty-five scoring keys can be used on the women's form.

USES

The results of the Strong Vocational Interest Blank can indicate occupations for which the student's pattern of interest closely approximates that of persons already successful in the work. Thus, this instrument yields results that are narrower, or in a sense, more precise, than the broader fields of interest indicated by results of the Kuder Preference Record. For example, if one student were to have taken both of these interest inventories, one high area on the Kuder might be social service. On scoring his Strong, the specific occupation of teacher might be highly rated. These two inventories are alike, however, in locating only interests.

Occupational Interest Inventory (102)

PURPOSE

This interest inventory has three purposes:

1. To measure preference for activities and tasks that are used in six vocational areas,

2. To measure preference for three types of activity, and,
3. To indicate the level in the occupation at which the student is most interested in working.

DESCRIPTION

The student selects his preferences of tasks and activities that are drawn from these six vocational areas:

Personal–social	Business
Natural	Arts
Mechanical	Sciences

Scoring keys are arranged such that the student's interests can also be classified as *verbal, manipulative,* and *computational.* An additional score is designed to indicate the "occupational level" in which the student is currently interested, varying from unskilled to skilled and professional grades.

USES

Specific information regarding the development and standardization of this test has not been published. (22) For this reason, it is used most often in conjunction with other interest inventories. Its unique features include types of activity scores and level of interest scores that make it useful in obtaining leads that other inventories do not provide. It is generally used as a supplemental counseling tool.

APTITUDES (Chapter 10)

Aptitudes have been defined as learning potentials. Persons with superior aptitude in one field would be expected to reach a higher level of performance than those persons having less aptitude, after both groups had had equal chances to learn.

Specific aptitude tests have been developed in many fields, including mechanical, spatial relations, clerical, musical, and art. The likelihood of a person's success in an academic program can also be predicted by the results of scholastic aptitude tests. The content of scholastic aptitude tests may include an emphasis on verbal, mathematical, and abstract reasoning components, depending on the use for which the test is designed. Along with scholastic aptitude, reading ability is an important predictor of academic success. For this reason, one reading ability test is included in the aptitude section of the glossary.

A series of separate tests can be organized into a battery. This grouping is to meet needs that are better served by a unified approach than a piecemeal approach. Two general aptitude test batteries are presented.

As defined above, the following aptitude tests are included in the glossary:

1. Test of Mechanical Comprehension (Bennett) (126)
2. Minnesota Paper Form Board (Revised) (94)
3. Seashore Measures of Musical Talents (112)
4. Meier Art Tests: Art Judgment (90)

5. Ohio State University Psychological Examination (104)
6. Co-operative English Test: Reading Comprehension (36)
7. Differential Aptitude Tests (44)
8. General Aptitude Test Battery (55)
9. Co-operative School and College Ability Tests (37)

Test of Mechanical Comprehension (Bennett) (126)

PURPOSE

Bennett's Test of Mechanical Comprehension attempts to measure the ability to recognize and understand mechanical principles and relationships as expressed in practical situations. This is a test of mental processes rather than manual skills. Superior understanding is assumed to be an index of superior aptitude.

DESCRIPTION

Sixty diagrams are presented in the test booklet. Each illustrates some mechanical principle. The testee must understand the principle to answer the item correctly. Principles are illustrated in simple form, using applications found in everyday life—scissors, ice, or roads. Particular acquaintance with machinery is not necessary. No time limit is prescribed, but most students are finished within thirty minutes.

USES

The test is designed to help predict success in educational programs or occupations in which an understanding of mechanical principles is necessary. It has had widespread use, and thus norms have been established for many occupations and educational programs. Many advisement and screening batteries use this test, with other evidence, to predict success in engineering, drafting, and mechanical work. This test is often used with the Minnesota Paper Form Board, which is next described. The two tests are different, but overlap in their results and applications.

Minnesota Paper Form Board (Revised) (94)

PURPOSE

Many training programs and occupations require the understanding of objects in three dimensions, or spatial-relations ability. This test is a more convenient means of measuring this ability to think in three dimensions—length, width, and depth—than were the older form boards and apparatus tests that are its ancestors.

DESCRIPTION

A form board is a flat piece of wood into which a series of pieces (or forms) must be inserted or assembled. This is the "apparatus" referred to above. The Minnesota Paper Form Board is a paper-and-pencil test developed to measure the same factors as did the more cumbersome types of wooden form boards. It includes sixty-four questions. Each item consists of a group of from two to five disarranged pieces of a geometric figure. From the five possible answers given, the student must select that group which is the correct assembly of the original pieces. In some items, assembly can be accomplished by mentally bringing together pieces from existing positions; in others, components must first be turned around or turned over. Twenty minutes is the time limit.

USES

The Minnesota Paper Form Board (MPFB) can be used with school groups ranging from eleventh grade through the freshman year of college. The presence of comparatively large amounts of spatial-relations aptitude can be partially predictive of success in engineering, dentistry, art, and many trade fields. If this factor is absent, the student may be advised to consider alternate objectives. This test is used for screening and selection purposes in all of the above-named fields.

Seashore Measures of Musical Talents (112)

PURPOSE

High achievement in music—singing, playing, composing—is closely related to the refined discriminations that the performer's ears are capable of making. Without the presence of these precise physical attributes, training and practice may be mere empty form. This series of records measures the ability to make such precise auditory discriminations.

DESCRIPTION

Three 78 rpm phonograph records are used to present the six subtests:
1. Pitch: among 50 pairs of tones, the student tells whether the second is higher or lower than the first.
2. Loudness: similar to the pitch test, but the second tone is judged on being stronger or weaker than the first.
3. Rhythm: 30 pairs of rhythmic patterns are given. The student judges whether the second is the same as the first or different.
4. Time: from 50 pairs of tones, the student judges the second as being longer or shorter than the first.
5. Timbre: in judging harmonic structure, the student chooses whether the second in each of 50 pairs of tones is of the same or different tonal quality from the first.

6. Tonal memory: 30 pairs of sequences of tones are presented. The student judges whether the second is the same as the first, or different.

Answers are recorded on standardized answer sheets. The test must be given under good audio and acoustic conditions.

USES

With students of college age, the results of this test can be helpful in advising students the extent to which they may be able to enter the music field professionally. It is usually given to students who already display both training and accomplishment in music, and are considering further study in the field of music.

Meier Art Tests: Art Judgment (90)

PURPOSE

Art judgment is the discerning of relationships of proportion, balance, and rhythm that exist in all good art. In this test, students must apply this esthetic judgment by telling good art from bad. Students whose opinions match those of experts are judged to have this ability. The test can be used, with other evidence, for both advisement and screening.

DESCRIPTION

One hundred pairs of pictures are presented. One in each pair of pictures is an original, previously judged as good art, and illustrating some essential art principle. In the other of the pair, that principle has been altered to some extent, but the two pictures are nearly duplicates. The student judges which picture in the pair represents the better art.

USES

College students who already possess art training and skill often wonder about their chances for success in art as a vocation. The results of this test, along with samples of work, and other factors, can be used in advising these students. Success in art fields, however, requires much more than just the ability to judge good art.

Ohio State University Psychological Examination (104)

PURPOSE

The Ohio State University Psychological Examination is considered one of the better instruments for the measurement of scholastic aptitude in the field of psychological testing today. It is designed to measure this single aspect of general intelligence. When administered as an untimed, power-type test it has been demonstrated that performance on the "OSU" is highly predictive of academic achievement in college.

DESCRIPTION

The test is made up of three parts and yields, in addition to the total score, the following subtest scores:

1. Same versus opposites: a vocabulary test involving recognition of synonyms and antonyms.
2. Analogies: a test of word relationships related to the ability to carry on abstract thinking.
3. Reading comprehension: a measure of ability to read and understand paragraphs.

The Ohio State Psychological Examination is among the most accurate predictors now available for an over-all academic aptitude instrument at the college level. Essentially an untimed power-type test, the OSU does not penalize the slower, more deliberate worker.

USES

The "OSU" is widely used as part of college admissions batteries. It has been used at Boston University as a screening device for admission to most undergraduate schools and colleges. Both national and local norms are available for high-school, junior-college, and senior-college groups. The student is thus able to compare his performance with that of students in other academic situations. Inasmuch as the total score is reliable as a measure of scholastic aptitude it is a valuable measure for use in future educational and vocational planning.

At the Boston University Junior College, research has demonstrated that improvement in reading skills fostered by the communications program results in marked over-all improvement on the OSU. This improvement is apparent mainly when the original test scores were depressed by low reading ability due to reading-skill deficiencies, but generalized improvement in the other two verbal measures is also possible.

Co-operative School and College Ability Test (SCAT) (37)

PURPOSE

The Cooperative School and College Ability Test, or SCAT, is designed to aid teachers, counselors, and "students themselves," in the words of the manual, in understanding student capacity or ability for *future* academic or scholastic training. The test is concerned with the measurement of present "developed ability" in order to predict the degree of academic success that may be expected in the future. The test is therefore a scholastic aptitude test.

DESCRIPTION

The test includes four subtests: Part I is a series of "sentence-completion" tasks; Part II is a series of "number-computation" tasks; Part III is a measure of vocabulary; Part IV is a series of "numerical problem-solving" tasks. The test takes 70 minutes to administer and is usable in grades 10, 11, and 12, and for college freshmen and sophomores. There are two levels (I and II) of difficulty in order to obtain proper results in a wide variety of school populations.

USES

The SCAT is one of the latest in a series of attempts to measure accurately scholastic aptitude. This test differs from many previous measures of this particular aptitude in that users are cautioned *not* to use any of the subscores. A total score is the only predictor recommended by the publishers.

The norm groups for this test are representative of widely dispersed student groups and attempt to offer a representative sampling of ability levels. Students planning to enter college may use this test in high school. College students and administrators also can use this test to measure academic potential.

Cooperative English Test: Reading Comprehension, Form C2 (36)

PURPOSE

The Cooperative English Test: Reading Comprehension, Form C2 (higher level) attempts to measure not only skill in the mechanics of reading, but to measure reading ability as a thinking process. Skill in manipulating verbal concepts is measured not by the speed of reading (the number of words covered in a given time) but the speed at which reading can be comprehended, and the depth to which it can be understood. Although the test is not primarily a diagnostic tool, a great deal of information may be derived by the careful study of an individual's performance on the test.

DESCRIPTION

The test is divided in two parts: the first part is a recognition vocabulary test of sixty items in which the student is asked to choose synonyms from a choice of five words per item in an allotted time of fifteen minutes; the second part of the test, for which twenty-five minutes are allowed, contains paragraphs to read. There are ninety items of five choices each in which the student answers questions based on the textual material of the paragraphs. These items are grouped so that two scores, speed of comprehension and level of comprehension, may be obtained. The total score is a compilation of the other three scores.

Uses

An unusually good feature of this test is that it measures the ability of the student to understand word meaning in context and to consider the mood and purpose of the author. Reading ability is measured as a thinking process rather than as a mechanical process of looking at words.

The most obvious application is the use of the Cooperative English Test: Reading Comprehension to discern those students who need remedial work in reading skills. It is helpful when it is used in conjunction with other tests as a counseling tool. In addition, the test has about the same relation to school achievement as do general intelligence tests. It can be concluded that the test has considerable predictive value for academic achievement. It may be given in successive administrations of different forms of the test to provide a measure of improvement in reading skills. It is generally considered one of the better conceived and better executed tests within the limits of its objectives.

Differential Aptitude Test (44)

Purpose

Aptitude tests for particular fields have been in use for some time. It has been possible to determine how a student performed on a mechanical aptitude test and on another of spatial perception, but until recently all of these were compiled with separate norms, making comparisons difficult, if not impossible.

The Differential Aptitude Test (DAT) is an integrated battery, with common norms. With this condition, it is possible to draw profiles from the results of the battery, and to see clearly the student's relative performance in each test within the battery.

Description

Eight different tests are included in seven booklets. The entire battery can be administered in just over three hours of testing time, usually divided into two or more sessions. The following tests are included in the battery:

1. Verbal Reasoning: with double word analogy items, testing complex verbal relationships.
2. Numerical Ability: arithmetic problems serving as a measure of facility in handling number concepts and understanding numerical relationships.
3. Abstract Reasoning: testing for logical thinking ability without language through recognition of the principle on which a series of diagrams changes.
4. Space Relations: visualizing concrete materials by judging either what form a pattern will make after construction, or imagining how an object will look if rotated.
5. Mechanical Reasoning: this is essentially a new form of the Bennett Test of Mechanical Comprehension. The student answers simple questions about pictures of mechanical situations. The test measures understanding of physical and mechanical principles.
6. Clerical Speed and Accuracy: is measured by having the student compare two sets of numbers or letters, one in the test booklet, the other on the answer sheet.

7. Language Usage:
   A. Spelling: distinguishing between correct and incorrect spelling of common words.
   B. Sentences: choosing good over bad punctuation, grammar, and word usage.

USES

Profiles plotted from the results of the DAT will indicate relative areas of aptitude strengths and weaknesses. These profiles, with supporting information, can be used as evidence that may answer some educational and vocational questions. The results can be applied toward specific occupational questions (laboratory technician, journalist, pharmacist), but may have even more use on questions of area (in which tests did I do best?), and on questions of level, (how high were the highs?). As with all test results, other evidence must be added to substantiate conclusions drawn from the tests.

General Aptitude Test Battery (GATB) (55)

PURPOSE

The General Aptitude Test Battery or the "GATB" was developed by the United States Employment Service for use in employment procedures. Applicants seeking aid in placement may be scheduled to take this battery of aptitude tests in order effectively to utilize their aptitudes on a job.

Many high-school and occasionally college students (junior-college terminal students) may also be tested on this battery in order to aid them in their placement problems. In public school testing, the United States Employment office officials administer, score, and interpret the test results. Results are also available to the co-operating institutions.

DESCRIPTION

The GATB includes individual tests in twelve areas:

1. Name comparison	7. Form matching
2. Computation	8. Mark matching
3. Spatial relations	9. Placing
4. Vocabulary	10. Turning
5. Tool matching	11. Assembling
6. Arithmetic reasoning	12. Disassembling

These twelve subtests are designed to measure nine traits or aptitudes:

G. Intelligence	Q. Clerical
V. Verbal	K. Motor co-ordination
N. Numerical	F. Finger dexterity
S. Spatial	M. Manual dexterity
P. Form perception	

The GATB includes the manipulation of apparatus, and in these measures there is a stress on manual or physical aptitude.

USES

The GATB is primarily a test to be used in the vocational guidance process or, more precisely, placement. The norms have been established by testing workers on the job. Prospective job holders can thus compare their performance with actual employees working on a particular job. The inclusion of clerical and manual measures aids in placing prospective employees accurately. The "battery" approach of this test combines various ability, aptitude, and skill areas in one instrument.

INTELLIGENCE (Chapter 11)

Intelligence was one of the first factors to be measured by psychologists. The first and most effective method of measuring intelligence is through an individually administered clinical test. Such test instruments are beyond the scope of this book although they are occasionally used. Personal consultation with a professionally trained counselor is necessary to understand these individual instruments.

A second method of measuring intelligence is through group paper-and-pencil tests. Such are the tests described in this section of the glossary. The purposes, designs, and uses are given for each of the following tests:

1. The Army General Classification Test. (7)
2. The California Test of Mental Maturity. (26)
3. The Otis Quick-Scoring Test of Mental Ability. (105)

Army General Classification Test: First Civilian Edition (7)

PURPOSE

The Army General Classification Test (AGCT) serves as a measure of general learning ability. It was originally designed to screen candidates for officer-training school during World Wars I and II, and to classify military personnel in general, according to their potential to learn their duties as soldiers. The civilian edition of the AGCT is used primarily as a test of general intelligence, and is a form similar to the World War II test.

DESCRIPTION

Although this test renders but a single score, it does attempt to measure three specific areas of intelligence—namely, verbal comprehension, quantitative reasoning, and spatial thinking. Three types of test problems are employed: vocabulary to measure reasoning factors, arithmetic problems testing quantitative reasoning, and block counting to measure the space factor. The vocabulary and arithmetic problems are presented in written fashion, and the space problems pictorially.

USES

A similar form of this test was administered to more than twelve million inductees. It was thus possible to compute a variety of useful and highly reliable occupational norms. Thus, if a student aspires to a specific occupational area, such as accountant, medical student, toolmaker, plumber, or barber he can compare his AGCT score with the median score obtained by a particular occupational group. In addition to occupational norms the AGCT also is useful in giving a general level of intelligence when compared to the male population at large.

With its emphasis on quantitative reasoning and spatial thinking, the AGCT test appears to be especially useful for screening engineering or other technology-school applicants. For this very reason, males tend to score higher on this test than females. This is not because females are less intelligent than males in these areas, but probably it is a reflection of cultural differences. It is of only fair reliability when a predictive instrument is warranted for evaluation of women students or for students contemplating a predominantly verbal program, such as the humanities or fine-arts curricula.

California Test of Mental Maturity: Advanced Form 1950-S (26)

PURPOSE

The California Test of Mental Maturity is a test of general intelligence. This test yields three scores, a language score, a nonlanguage score, and a total score. The language part of the test deals with vocabulary, reading, and reasoning problems, and appears to be rather closely related to scholastic aptitude and success in verbal programs. The nonlanguage section deals with items involving numbers, spatial relations, and motor co-ordination, and although the nonlanguage score appears to be of little value for purposes of predicting scholastic success, it does appear to have some diagnostic value. A student who presents a reading or language problem may do well on this part of the test and poorly on the language section. If this is found to be the case, he *may* be a good prospect for remedial reading since his problem may be a verbal handicap rather than a real lack of ability.

DESCRIPTION

A variety of subtest scores is available. The California Test of Mental Maturity purports to measure memory, spatial relationships, logical reasoning, numerical reasoning, and vocabulary. The brevity of these subtests, however, tends to lower the accuracy of the part-score measures.

The language score includes subtests entitled "Inference," "Numerical Quantity," and "Verbal Concepts" (vocabulary). Four subtests are in the nonlanguage section: sensing right and left, manipulation of areas (both being activities related to spatial-relations ability), similarities, and numerical-series items.

Uses

The California Test of Mental Maturity serves as a reliable measure of general intelligence. As a diagnostic instrument, it serves to assist the student in an analysis of his particular assets and weaknesses. As a predictive device, the language and total scores are valuable instruments for selecting potential college freshmen. Students who fare well on this test also tend to do well academically, although, as mentioned in an early chapter, the relationship is far from a perfect one.

The nonlanguage score has not appeared to be significantly related to college success but may be important for nonverbal environments.

Otis Quick-Scoring Mental Ability Test (105)

Purpose

The Otis mental ability test intends to measure mental ability, or how well the student can think. This is done indirectly by measuring the extent to which the student's mental ability has helped him to acquire certain mental skills and information. It gives a single score in a short time and is easy to administer.

Description

The test is complete on one sheet of paper that folds into a three-leafed booklet. The test attempts to measure mental ability as it exists in verbal, arithmetical, and spatial areas. Its 80 questions are arranged in "spiral-omnibus" order, meaning in order of ascending difficulty, and rotating from vocabulary items, to arithmetic questions, to spatial problems, and back to vocabulary. Students choose from multiple-choice answers and have thirty minutes in which to complete the test.

Uses

Results are given in a single, global score. This can be used to give a general idea of how the student may be expected to do in an academic program. When local norms are used, this index of comparative mental ability can serve as a check on potential versus performance. As with any guidance test, its results must be used with other substantiating information.

PERSONALITY (Chapters 6 and 7)

The most intangible aspect of the self is personality. Personality is therefore the most difficult area to test. Hundreds of tests of personality have been developed, used, and discarded. The field of personality testing is still the most *inexact* of all areas of psychological testing.

Selected clinical personality tests of an individual nature are more reliable and valid than group tests, but must be administered, scored, and interpreted on an individual basis. Most personality tests can only tell if there are *problems* or *areas of concern* within the personality. Direct, positive statements are very difficult to derive from existing personality-test instruments. Therefore, the test within the scope of this book is a screening or identifying device.

Personality-test interpretation should be discussed only with a trained counselor.

The personality inventories described in the glossary are:

      1. California Test of Personality (27)
      2. Bell Adjustment Inventory (Student) (10)

California Test of Personality—
Secondary, Form A (27)

PURPOSE

The California Test of Personality purports to give "a profile of personal and social adjustment." The test yields twelve subscores in areas of personal and social adjustment.

DESCRIPTION

The test is not timed, but can generally be administered in a one-hour period. There are twelve subtests of fifteen questions each, all to be answered "yes" or "no." Adding the raw scores of the first six tests gives a total score for the principal unit, self-adjustment, and the total of the second six is a score for the second unit, social adjustment.

The total of 180 questions are arranged so that they measure areas listed as follows:

1. Self-adjustment
   a. Self-reliance
   b. Sense of personal worth
   c. Sense of personal freedom
   d. Sense of belonging
   e. Freedom from withdrawing tendencies
   f. Freedom from nervous symptoms

2. Social adjustment
   a. Social standards
   b. Social skills
   c. Freedom from antisocial tendencies
   d. Family relations
   e. School relations
   f. Community relations

USES

Since personality is the least tangible aspect of the self, it is the most difficult to test. This is especially true in this particular test, since it allows the student to react with only "yes" or "no." For these and other reasons the necessity for checking results of this one measure with other supporting evidence is even more true with this test than with others.

A trained counselor may use the test results in the counseling situation as a springboard to subjective evaluation on the part of the counselee *if* the counselor keeps in mind that to accept the profile is to accept an instrument of low objective value, and *if* the counselor can be successful in convincing the counselee of the validity of his profile as a general indication only of personality patterns.

The test has some value when used with care with large groups to screen out those with markedly deviant scores whose profiles suggest the need for further clinical testing in accordance with accepted clinical practice.

Bell Adjustment Inventory (Student Form) (10)

PURPOSE

The Bell Adjustment Inventory attempts to assess adjustment problems in four major areas of personality. These areas of personality are important to students in college. This inventory aids sincere students to uncover problem areas that may then be discussed in counseling interviews.

DESCRIPTION

The Bell Adjustment Inventory is designed to measure adjustment in the areas of:

1. Home
2. Health
3. Society
4. Emotion

The inventory is completed by answering "yes," "no," or "?" to 140 questions. These questions cover usual and unusual problems in the four areas listed above.

USES

The Bell Adjustment Inventory is most often usable in schools and colleges as a screening device. It is administered in group situations in order to isolate students with problems that may be helped by counseling and guidance programs.

SUPPLEMENTARY SOURCES

Anastasi, Anne, *Psychological Testing.* New York: The Macmillan Company, 1954.

Buros, Oscar, editor, *The Fourth Mental Measurements Yearbook.* Highland Park, N. J.: The Gryphon Press, 1953.

Cronbach, Lee J., *Essentials of Psychological Testing.* New York: Harper & Brothers, 1949.

Super, Donald E., *Appraising Vocational Fitness.* New York: Harper & Brothers, 1949.

————, *The Psychology of Careers.* New York: Harper & Brothers, 1957.

Army General Classification Test, First Civilian Edition, Science Research Associates, Chicago, Illinois.

Bell Adjustment Inventory, Stanford University Press, Stanford, California, 1938.

California Test of Mental Maturity, Advanced level, Short-form 50-S, California Test Bureau, Los Angeles 28, California.

California Test of Personality, Secondary, Form A, Ernest W. Tiegs, Willis W. Clark, and Louis P. Thorpe, California Test Bureau, Los Angeles 28, California.

Cooperative English Test, Reading Comprehension, Form C2 (S, T, Y.), Frederick Davis, Harold V. King, Mary Willis, Clarence Derrick, Harry R. Neville, Jeanne M. Bradford and Geraldine Spaulding, Co-operative Test Division, Educational Testing Service, Princeton, N. J.

Cooperative School and College Ability Test, 1955, Cooperative Test Division: Educational Testing Service, Princeton, N. J.

Differential Aptitude Tests, George K. Bennett, Harold G. Seashore, Alexander G. Wesman, The Psychological Corporation, New York, New York.

General Aptitude Test Battery, 1956, U.S. Dept. of Labor, Bureau of Employment Security, U.S.E.S., Washington, D. C.

Kuder Preference Record—Vocational, Form CH, G. Frederic Kuder, Science Research Associates, Chicago, Illinois.

Meier Art Tests: I. Art Judgement, Norman Charles Meier, Bureau of Educational Research and Service, State University of Iowa, Iowa City, Iowa.

Minnesota Paper Form Board (Revised) Form AA, Donald G. Paterson, Richard M. Elliott, L. Dewey Anderson, Herbert A. Toops, and Edna Heidbreder. Revised edition by Rensis Likert and William H. Quasha. The Psychological Corporation, New York, New York.

Occupational Interest Inventory, Form A, Edwin A. Lee, and Louis P. Thorpe, California Test Bureau, Los Angeles, California.

Ohio State University Psychological Examination, Form A and 23, Herbert A. Toops, Ohio College Association, Ohio State University, Columbus, Ohio.

Otis Quick-Scoring Mental Ability Tests, Arthur S. Otis, World Book Company, Yonkers-on-Hudson, New York.

Seashore Measures of Musical Talents, 1939 Revision, Carl E. Seashore, Don Lewis, Joseph Saetveit, The Psychological Corporation, New York, New York.

Strong Vocational Interest Blank, 1938, Stanford University Press, Stanford, California.

Test of Mechanical Comprehension, Form AA, and BB, George K. Bennett, The Psychological Corporation, New York, New York.

SELF-ANALYSIS STUDENT WORKBOOK

INDIVIDUAL DIFFERENCES *

1. Ways in which I think I am different from others:

    A. Physically: ....

    ....

    B. Mentally: ....

    ....

    C. Socially: ....

    ....

    D. Other: ....

    ....

2. Ways in which others have told me I am different from others are:

    ....

    ....

    ....

MOTIVATION AND COLLEGE

1. The person(s) who decided that I should attend college was: ....

    ....

* This workbook is included in Wilcox, Glenn W., *Basic Study Skills,* Boston: Allyn and Bacon, Inc., 1958, which is designed as a companion volume to *An Introduction to Personal Adjustment.*

2. The person(s) paying for my education is: ....

....

3. I came to college because:

A. ....

B. ....

4. I study .... hours a week.

5. My attitude toward study is: ....

....

6. My attitudes (values) toward high school were: ....

7. My attendance so far has been: ....

8. My primary occupational goals (values) are:

A. ....

B. ....

C. ....

D. ....

9. I hope that college will benefit me by: ....

....

10. My basic goals in life are: ....

....

VOCATIONAL INTERESTS

1. My strongest vocational areas are (see Psychological Test Data Sheet, Appendix A):

....

....

....

2. My hobbies have been and/or are: ....

....

....

3. My work experience has been in: ....

....

....

4. Subjects I liked best in high school were:

   A. ....

   B. ....

   C. ....

   D. ....

5. Subjects I most disliked in high school were:

   A. ....

   B. ....

   C. ....

   D. ....

THE CONCEPT OF APTITUDES

1. My work experience (full and part-time service) has demonstrated the following skills:

   ....

   ....

2. My high-school and community activities have been:

   ....

   ....

3. My high-school grades were highest in these areas:

....

4. My current skills are (other than above):

....

....

5. Specific aptitudes that I may have in above-average degree are:

....

....

6. Specific aptitudes that I may have in average degree are:

....

....

7. Specific aptitudes that I may have in below-average degree are:

....

....

8. My evidence for these judgments of specific aptitudes is:
   A. Test scores, which are:

.... (test) .... (indication)

.... (test) .... (indication)

   B. Other evidence, which is (include data in Sections 1-4):

....

....

9. Vocational aptitudes that I may have are:

....

....

10. My evidence for these judgments of vocational aptitudes is:

....

....

11. My interests, skills, and aptitudes seem to overlap in the following areas:

....

....

12. My evidence for these judgments on the overlapping of my interests, abilities and aptitudes is:

....

....

....

13. Occupations that I have considered entering are:

....

....

14. These aptitudes are necessary in the occupations I am currently considering:

       APTITUDE   OCCUPATION

....

....

15. There seems to be HIGH AVERAGE LOW (circle one) correspondence between the requirements of my current occupational goals and my aptitudes.

Explain: ....

....

....

....

INTELLIGENCE AND SCHOLASTIC APTITUDE

1. My intelligence level is, when compared with most college freshmen: (*check one*)

   Low.... Below average.... Average.... Above average.... High....

2. My scholastic aptitude when compared with college freshmen is:

   Low.... Below average.... Average.... Above average.... High....

3. My reading ability, when compared with college freshmen is:

   Low.... Below average.... Average.... Above average.... High....

4. An analysis of intellectual abilities according to the multiple factor approach suggests that my potential strengths and weaknesses are located as follows:

Strengths	*Weaknesses*
....	....
....	....
....	....
....	....

5. Some of the nonintellectual factors operative in my situation are:

   ....

   ....

   ....

6. A summary of my intellectual and perceptual factors that serve to encourage the continuation of my educational and vocational plans are:

   ....

   ....

   ....

7. A summary of my intellectual and perceptual factors that serve to discourage the continuation of my educational and vocational plans are:

   ....

   ....

   ....

THE OTHER FACTORS

1. My time schedule involves the following apportionment of hours (on the average) in the listed areas:

   A....travel   F....college events

   B....classes (all types)   G....sleep

   C....homework   H....work

   D....meals   I....other

   E....recreation (coffee also) J....total

2. The person(s) paying for my education is: ....

3. My four-year investment of funds will total approximately $...........

4. My health is: ....

   A. Handicaps are: ....

   B. Poor habits are: ....

   ....

5. My study skills are: ....

   ....

6. My family's attitudes toward my attending college are:

   ....

   ....

   toward my vocational plans: ....

   ....

7. My attitude toward dating is: ....

   ....

8. My plans for the armed forces are: ....

   ....

PERSONALITY APPLIED

1. Significant family influences that have been factors in shaping my personality have been: ....

....

....

2. Significant attitudes I have toward my future role as a parent are: ....

....

....

3. My schooling has affected my personality by:

....

....

....

4. Cultural forces that have been important in my life are:

....

....

....

5. My attitudes (values) toward or about work are:

....

....

....

6. I probably will be the sort of employee who will:

....

....

....

7. All in all I would say my personality is:

....

....

A SUGGESTED OUTLINE

    I. My strengths and weaknesses as a student and person
   II. My goals in life
  III. My motivation for college
  IV. My vocational interest pattern
   V. My aptitudes
  VI. My intelligence and scholastic aptitude
 VII. Other significant factors
VIII. My personality
  IX. A look ahead
   X. Summary and conclusions

CASE STUDIES

MIKE

Mike Russell was facing the problem of which curriculum to elect for his last two years. He had just completed two years of a general-studies course in the state university and now he would be forced to elect a liberal-arts, business, or technical-training program. Mike had been an above-average student for most of the two years he had spent at the state university, but he felt that somewhere along the line he must have "missed connections" because he was not at all certain of which way to turn with regard to the selection of courses for his junior and senior years.

When Mike had first entered the state university after his Korean service he had been very sure that he wanted business administration. He wondered why and how he had changed from being so certain of what he wanted to do to his present position, which left him unsure of which way to turn.

. . .

Mike had enrolled with one of the first groups of Korean veterans, and had worked hard to secure his admission to the state university, since he had been discharged during the first week in September. Mike was very concerned that he should be able to attend college. He had worked for two years following his graduation from high school before going into the service, since his family did not have the financial means to support him in college. During the two years that Mike had worked before going into the service, he was not sure whether or not he wanted to attend college. After working as milling-machine operator for two years, however, he had become more and more certain that college ought to be a part of his future plans.

"This Korean Bill of Rights is a real deal," Mike said, as he was very enthusiastic about college that first September. He did not mind telling anyone that he wanted to go to college in order to "get ahead."

"I worked for two years and I saw plenty of guys with a lot less stuff than I have passing me by in promotions simply because they had been to college— they weren't half as good as I was on the job, but they had been to college and I hadn't been."

. . .

Mike's first few days at the state university were not too happy, for he had counted on being pledged to the outstanding fraternity on the campus. As it turned out during the first week of registration, during rush week, Mike had been passed over by his hoped-for fraternity and several others as well. Mike became involved in a serious argument with several of the upper-class students who were members of the interfraternity council of the university, and the result was that Mike had ended up as a confirmed "independent."

. . .

Mike's father was a minister. Mike had never gotten along well with his father, and he did not mind telling others about the sort of person that his father was: "Dad is a real nice guy—but he's always wrapped up in his books and philosophy—he's always dressed so darned shabbily—poor mother, she's always had it rather hard."

Mike's father had graduated from a small denominational college in the Midwest, and had lived as a lower-middle-class minister in Mike's home town. He and Mike's mother were respected members of their community and served as a pastor and wife at one of the small churches on the edge of town. When Mike had decided to attend the state university his father had been very pleased, and had talked a great deal with Mike about making a success of his college career. He had always been interested in having Mike further his own education, and was very much concerned that he succeed academically. As Mike said, "Whenever we talk about college his eyes light up and he's always just about ready to give me a sermon." He also had talked with his father about his choice of curriculum, but his father had told him that he would have to work it out himself, which caused Mike to say, "That's the old man—he's always a big help in a practical problem!"

. . .

Mike had worked part time in a clothing store for his first two years at college, and during the first summer he had worked as a turret-lathe operator, and during the second summer as a milling-machine operator. He described it in the following terms:

"It was a real fine job for the first summer. They wanted a turret-lathe operator, and although I had never actually worked one of these, I had watched the operators many times, and felt sure that if they gave me a chance I could do it. I got the job and was able to hold down the position. I wouldn't have been able to get into the factory if I had told them that I was a college student on vacation, so I just had to keep my mouth shut. I finally got to be supervisor before the summer was over, and was able to make a good piece of change. They were somewhat upset and a little mad when I left, but why should they care. I worked hard for them during the summer. I wasn't able to get the job back this last summer, but I did get a good one as a milling machine operator."

Mike thought about his experience working in the "shops" during the past few summers as well as the two years he had spent in them before he went into the service. He did not want to work in that sort of atmosphere the rest of his life, whether he was a supervisor or an engineer. Mike felt that the "shops" were no place for a person of ability. He was therefore able to rule out the technical-training curriculum, but that still left him with a choice of whether to take one of the social sciences and liberal-arts majors or whether to go into the many business-administration areas.

. . .

Mike's grades were average to above average for his four semesters. He had just missed the Dean's List in his last semester. Mike always said that he did not care a "damn" about grades. All he wanted to make sure of was that he was getting everything he ought to from his courses. He felt that he had really been given a "short deal" during the last semester, though—his grades were very close to Dean's List quality, and if it hadn't been for the instructor in the sociology class disliking him Mike felt sure that he would have been able to be on the Dean's List.

During his freshman year his best grades were in the social sciences, and his poorest were in the science area. The math and the formulas in science had given him difficulty, but he had liked the courses in which there were a lot of discussions. He had always been able to talk easily and he found that the social-science courses were much more to his liking. During the second semester there did not appear to be any pattern to his grades.

. . .

Student activities were an area in which Mike had achieved mixed success. He was known in college as a "crackerjack" master of ceremonies. He was always able to draw laughs with his parodies of various faculty members. He got into trouble once because one of the older, more eccentric faculty members objected to Mike's caricature of him. Mike patched things up, but was reported to have said afterward: "He's a real old goat. I'll make more money in my first two years after college than he's making right now!"

Mike was elected to the student council for the second semester of his freshman year as a representative of the independents on campus. He participated very actively during the first few months of his term as a student-council representative, but during the last part of the semester his attendance dropped off and he appeared to have lost interest. He was not re-elected during his sophomore year and during his sophomore year he maintained that he had always felt that the student council was nothing but "a bunch of kids trying to play as if they were the faculty in the university."

Mike's closest friend, Jim, had not been of much help although they had always been close to one another during the freshman year. Many times they had discussed what they would do, what courses they would take, and what sort of success they hoped for in later life.

The last time that Mike and Jim had sat down to have a talk about what courses they were going to take it had ended in a big argument. Mike had been telling Jim what he wanted to get out of life and how he was simply confused as to which road would be the most effective path for him to achieve his goals. Mike did not understand Jim's last comment as they had broken off in an argument, which was, "Why don't you major in banking so that you can practice foreclosing mortgages on old ladies' homes and churches!"

Mike sat at the registration table for juniors and just stared at the registration blank. . . .

PEGGY

Peggy found the aptitudes chapter easy enough to read. Farmer Brock seemed to have a good thing. But she was not so sure about that case that was written into the chapter. It was that one about he fellow who wanted to be an engineer, and the tests that said he would make a better history teacher. How could tests tell that? And besides, there were a lot of loose ends in that case about Al Morris. Peggy did not think that the counselor had helped Al very much because in the end Al's choice was still up in the air. She thought that the counselor had not told Al what would be best for him, and had left a lot of parts of the case dangling.

The reading was not too hard. Now that she had finished the chapter, she could start—but what was this? What are all those blanks for? Work experience, high-school grades—that sounded like the way Al Morris began. Now that she thought of it, her counselor had told the group about the purpose of that part of the chapter—something about an orderly way of organizing one's abilities, aptitudes, and interests. Peggy remembered that he seemed to emphasize the evidence or the facts the student had for claiming this ability or that interest.

The assignment was not as easy as it looked. Peggy invested a long time and some hard thought in the process.

1. My work experience (full and part-time service) has demonstrated the following skills:

   Typist   *Receptionist*
   Office work   *Crafts instructor*
                                                    Camp counselor

2. My high-school and community activities have been:

   Italian Club   *All sports*
   Girls' Athletic Club

3. My high-school grades were highest in these areas:

   Italian, art
   All others (except stenography and transcription, which I hated) were B's

4. My current skills are (other than above):

   Piano   *Craft hobbies—leatherwork*
   PBX switchboard

5. Specific aptitudes that I may have in above-average degree are:

   Clerical   *Verbal*
   Numerical   *Abstract*

6. Specific aptitudes that I may have in average degree are:

   Writing—composition   *Music—piano*
   Reading ability   *Art*

7. Specific aptitudes that I may have in below-average degree are:

   Space   *Mechanical*

8. My evidence for these judgments of specific aptitudes is:

   A. Test scores indicating:

      DAT   *High in verbal, numerical, abstract, clerical*
      C2T   *Reading ability average for freshmen*

   B. Other evidence, which is (include data in Sections 1-4):

      Clerical experience   *Music lessons came hard*
      High-school grades in Italian language class

9. Vocational aptitudes that I may have are:

   Scholastic—see both OSU and DAT: verbal, numerical, and abstract
   Clerical—business

10. My evidence for these judgments of vocational aptitude is:

    Putting together parts of the DAT, with the Ohio State, and my work experience.

11. My interests, skills, and aptitudes seem to overlap in the following areas:

    Being a successful student, first, then maybe a service position in business

12. My evidence for these judgments on the overlapping of my interests, abilities, and aptitudes is:

    Adding the Kuder results (and my own likes and dislikes) to 10 above. Kuder highs in computational, artistic, social service

13. Occupations that I have considered entering are:

    Public relations   *Advertising*

14. These aptitudes are necessary in the occupations that I am currently considering:

APTITUDES	OCCUPATIONS
I think these would be the same for both—scholastic, numerical, clerical, desire to serve, business ability	*Public relations* *Advertising*

15. There seems to be HIGH AVERAGE LOW (circle one) correspondence between the requirements of my current occupational goals and my aptitudes. Explain:

. . . .

. . . .

. . . .

    Peggy got as far as question 15. She wondered if she had really gotten anywhere with the project, or had she just started it?

    Peggy looked further at her test scores. Her notes were as follows:

Differential Aptitude Test	*12th grade norms*
Verbal	80th %ile
Numerical	92nd %ile
Abstract	75th %ile
Space	30th %ile
Mechanical	15th %ile
Clerical	75th %ile
Spelling	75th %ile
Sentences	70th %ile

O.S.U.	(total)	50th %ile college freshman norms
C2T	(total)	50th %ile college freshman norms
Otis	(total)	65th %ile college freshman norms
Kuder		Highs: computational, artistic, social service Lows: outdoor, mechanical, scientific

BILL

Excerpts from Bill's autobiography

I learned to walk at an early age. My mother has always bragged about this. I don't remember my father, because I was only four years old when he passed away.

My older sister married when she was quite young and is now living in another state. My sister Belle never got along with mother and always had a number of arguments. Belle used to say, "I am going to lead my own life my own way."

I guess I've always been considered a mother's boy. She always treated me wonderfully and we've always gotten along together almost too well. She's had to work hard all her life and is now one of the head nurses in a large metropolitan hospital.

We hardly ever argue because I always make sure I do the right thing. This way there is never anything to argue about, although I sometimes "bang the furniture around" when I don't like to study nights.

She has high hopes for me I guess, but so far I've been a big disappointment. She always talks about my being a doctor and the possibility of my ending up in the same hospital ward as she, but I don't know.

I did very poorly in high school, except in math and science, which were both "C." I don't know why I did poorly, I always studied exactly four hours every night. If I put in less time, my mother worries.

Sometimes I think I want to be a doctor more than anything else, and other times I want no part of it. I feel I could do it if I really wanted to in spite of my poor academic record. Something seems to be holding me back. Perhaps I'll find myself at college.

Bill's guidance test results		*Percentile*	*Norm*
Otis Test of Mental Ability	Total score	95	General population
Ohio State Psychological Exam	Total score	98	Entering college Freshman national
Bennett Mechanical Aptitude	Total score	98	Freshman students Engineering school
Minnesota Paper Form Board	Spatial relations	98	1st year students
Kuder Preference Record	Interest inventory		General population

High in scientific, social service, mechanical, computational

Low in musical, literary, clerical

Counselor's summary of initial interview

Bill was anxious to talk, and wanted to co-operate in every possible way. He spoke easily, appeared entirely at ease, and presented a neat appearance. He is doing average work in all his subjects. We discussed study habits to some extent. Bill emphasized the fact that he studies exactly four hours every night.

THE "WONDERER"

"Write a self-analysis paper." That's what the man said, "looking at one's self, describing what you see there, and giving evidence to back up your statements."

Looking into myself. "Introspection," the man called it. I'm always doing that. I keep describing myself, but the picture I see keeps changing. Do I keep changing? Am I ever the same person? Or is it this "evidence" he talks about? Do the yardsticks keep changing? Or are both changing, both myself and the evidence about myself?

An example: My high school principal told my father that he had written on my college application, "This student has ability, but has never achieved high enough grades to warrant recommendation to college." But look at my grades for the first semester:

Humanities	B+
Science	B+
Psychology	B
Social relations	B+
Communications	B—

Maybe the old boy was looking backward when he wrote those words. I did get expelled from school as a behavior problem in fourth grade. Then I became an educational vagrant—three schools in four years; they didn't suit my folks. But the next one was really good for me. When Kennedy School was started in the early 30's, it was real gone—"progressive," "developmental," "unleashing unchallenged potential," and all that, but I really went for it. They thought kids learned by doing, learned by using their hands as well as their heads. It sure agreed with me. I worked in the dairy barns with the milking machines and really loved it. The rural environment showed me a side of life that I want to go back to. Pretty soon the classes seemed more worthwhile than I remembered from other schools. I still remember reading *Walden* there. Before leaving for high school, I changed my work assignment to the kitchen. I helped prepare the noon meal and had charge of the food orders.

I guess the high school never did figure me out. They said they wanted me to go out for sports because they needed all the big men and they couldn't understand it when I said I was interested in other things about school. These kids all seemed to be interested in nothing but the "good time," the "jalop," and a job with the biggest pay check. At Kennedy I learned to stick up for what I believed in, but in high school no one even wanted to discuss my opinions. Since my ideas were so different, I began to doubt myself some. I graduated as 59th in a class of 87, with no future educational plans.

The Navy is what did it. Boot camp was rough, but storekeeper's school was a breeze. I eventually was transferred to a storeship of the Sixth Fleet in the Mediterranean. I think it was while we were working hardest—during a three-day replenishing period—that I started to feel important again. By then I had gotten a storekeeper-second-class rate, but that isn't what I mean by "feeling important." It was that in the terrific amount of work we did on board our ship, I began to see that I was doing my part—more than my part lots of times. There was 100 per cent teamwork in all of our operations. Our contribution to the success of mission and to the health of the whole Sixth Fleet showed in our ship spirit and the morale of the crew.

Some of this became mine. I knew I was a part of this spirit, and it made me feel better. It built up my confidence considerably. I learned to roll with some of the punches of life and accept those things I couldn't change. I think I grew up partly from this working experience, partly from my travels in Europe, and partly from the bull sessions we had off duty. There were all kinds of men on board, and plenty of chances to sound off on all ideas.

So when I got out I worked as a shipper for eight months while waiting to enter here. And now, so help me, I'm shot with the program. I can talk when I want to, or brood if I feel like it (which is seldom). I can always find some other crackpot to talk over my ideas with. I just wish the school was out in the country.

So, going back to what I said in the beginning, I'm always looking within myself. What I saw in high school is a lot different from what is there now. How do I know? Well, for one thing, I can just feel the difference—like drinking three bottles of Serutan. For a while I was wondering about teaching, maybe in a school like Kennedy. But now I'm thinking more about hotel management. I've had school and Navy experience in the food-service line, and I like to meet people.

I guess above all I want to be able to manage my own affairs, and more especially, those of my future family and children. I want to know why people "do what they do" and to know how I can help them. I would like to be able to support myself and my family well enough to give them what they really need—a healthy home environment, proper direction, and good solid companions. Also, enough responsibilities to keep their minds busy in constructive activities.

So there you are. I think I'm a much different person now. The high-school principal wouldn't know me. But now how do I put all this together? I've just been pondering here and haven't organized the paper.

What in the world can I do with my notes on the test scores?

O.S.U.	65th %ile	College freshman norms
C2T	40th %ile	College freshman norms
Otis	60th %ile	College freshman norms

DAT		12th grade norms
Verbal		90th %ile
Numerical		60th %ile
Abstract		80th %ile
Space		65th %ile
Mechanical		80th %ile
Clerical		40th %ile
Spelling		60th %ile
Sentences		65th %ile

Kuder	General population male
Outdoor	40th %ile
Mechanical	30th %ile
Computational	10th %ile
Scientific	30th %ile
Persuasive	85th %ile
Artistic	50th %ile
Literary	5th %ile
Musical	70th %ile
Social service	98th %ile
Clerical	10th %ile

TOM AND SALLY

Tom and Sally were thinking of getting married. They had been going with one another for almost a year and a half. They were fairly sure of the responsibilities of marriage, and they felt that they could be reasonably sure of being happy together.

Tom met Sally in high school last year. They had been in the same class but somehow had never gotten to know each other until the beginning of their senior year. Tom had been in the college curriculum, whereas Sally had been in the commercial course, training to be a secretary. Perhaps this had been one of the reasons that they had never gotten to know one another, as they never had any classes together. Tom and Sally had had a wonderful time while they were in their last year in high school. They had both been active in many of the school affairs and both had attended most of the dances and other social affairs that had taken place in their last year at high school. Tom had an old jalopy of a car that he used while in school, and he was also able to borrow his father's car when there was a special occasion, such as the prom.

In the summer following their graduation from high school both Tom and Sally had obtained jobs. Sally's job was more or less permanent since she had wanted to do secretarial work and was fortunate to find a good position as a secretary and receptionist. Tom had taken a job with one of the construction gangs in the city, for he wanted to earn as much money as he could in order to help him through college, which he was going to enter that fall. Tom and Sally went out together a good deal during the summer months. They went to the beach, had picnic suppers, took drives in the country, went to the movies, and all in all, had a wonderful time. Sally enjoyed her work and although Tom was not relishing the construction-gang work, he at least had the satisfaction of earning a good pay check each week, and he managed to save a good portion of it in spite of the fact that he and Sally spent a good deal of it while going out. In fact, this was one of the gripes that his Dad had kept harping on, saying, "If you are going to go to college, and you don't expect me to pay all the expenses, what are you going to use for money if you spend it all this summer with Sally?" Tom agreed with his father, but they still spent a lot each weekend whenever they went out.

One particular occurrence in the late summer had bothered Tom a bit, and he was doing a lot of thinking about it. He and Sally had gone to a wonderful dance at the town hall in a neighboring town with two other couples, and they had all had a good time. After the dance they had all gone to one of the night spots on the outskirts of the two towns, and had a few drinks and something to eat. Maybe it was the drinks that they had had, he was not sure—but one thing was sure, he was bothered and confused after that night. He had dropped the other two couples at their homes since he was driving his father's car, and then he took Sally home. They stopped to park for a while before they went on home, as they often had done in the past, but somehow this time things had been different. They had always necked and petted a good deal after many of their dates, but neither one of them had any intention of doing anything more serious than this. This night, however, before either of them had realized it, they had gone much farther than they had ever done before. No, they had not done anything to regret, but as Tom thought about it, it was not something that he liked to remember when he thought of getting married to Sally. They had always talked seriously about sex and marriage and had agreed that they would never do anything that "they would be sorry for" later on. Perhaps it was because of this night that things had seemed strained between the two of them for a little while. After a couple of weeks of this strained relationship, however, it seemed to pass and they were the same old couple again.

After the summer was over, Tom had entered Wiley Tech and was able to see Sally only on weekends as the school was about fifty miles away from their home town where Sally worked as a receptionist and secretary. Tom had, in the beginning, come down more often, but now he found that coming down weekends was less expensive in terms of money and in his grades. Tom liked the work at Wiley Tech and he liked the courses that he had, but if he had not been able to see Sally on weekends, he did not think he would ever have been able to stay at college. The weekends were really all that Tom existed for. He could keep his mind on his work pretty well during the week, but when the weekend rolled around, even though sometimes he tried to do some work, he always found himself going back home to see Sally.

The first semester at college was almost over, and Tom and Sally had been talking about their getting married. Maybe it was because of the Christmas vacation that was just over. They had had a wonderful time. They had gone out almost every night. Tom had given Sally a beautiful watch for a gift, and she had given him an onyx birthday ring. It was on the first time that they had seen each other after vacation that they had talked about getting married. Neither one had seemed to bring up the subject, but suddenly they both had been talking about it. They had discussed some of the problems that would be involved, but they had seemed to see their way through most of them. Sally could take a job at Rockdale where the school was, and she could continue working while Tom studied. Tom was not sure yet what his parents would say about his getting married, since it would be difficult for him to go to school unless his father continued to pay for his tuition and the other expenses. Although he felt that if Sally worked and he also got a job they could probably swing the deal alone if his Dad took that attitude, he did not think his Dad really would, so it was not too much of a serious problem.

Tom was back at college after the talk he and Sally had had. Tom was thinking about Sally:

"She certainly is a wonderful girl. . . . We have had a wonderful time for the last year and a half, and it sure would be wonderful if we could get married. We could live together while I went to school. . . . This business of coming home every weekend is expensive and a lot of bother anyway. . . . I am Jewish and Sally is Protestant, but that won't make any difference anyway. . . . Sally's Mom was a little upset when we first started to go together, but I think she really likes me now, and religion doesn't mean too much to either of us anyway. . . . Dad and Mom might object a little bit but they seem resigned to it anyway at this point. . . . She's a really wonderful girl. . . . All the fellows sure like her, and I bet they would be surprised if we came back here married, and she was living with me while I went to college. . . . Jim's married and he gets good grades, and I bet mine would go up after we got married, and I could stop this running back to see her every weekend. . . . I bet we could find a nice place to live in Rockdale. . . . I've seen a lot of nice little houses that might be for rent, and even if we couldn't find a house, we could find a nice little apartment. . . ."

Sally was also doing a little dreaming while she was not too busy at work: "Tom certainly is a wonderful guy. . . . We have had such good times together. . . . This past summer was out of this world, and this fall, even though it's just weekends, we still have a good time and get to go out a lot together even though Tom is in school. . . . Tom really should stay in school. . . . He is a smart guy and he does so want to be an engineer. . . . I could work while Tom went to school and we could make ends meet that way. . . . Tom would be studying nights, but we still could have a good time on weekends. . . . Dad and Mom really haven't objected to Tom. They did in the beginning but they both like him now. . . . Mom was the most upset, but now I think she likes Tom. . . . Gee, it would really be nice if I could chuck this job and get one up in Rockdale while Tom went to school and we could really have a wonderful time if we were married and could be living in Rockdale together."

SELF-ANALYSIS ESSAYS

(Examples of student writing)

MR. "X"

I believe the most important aspect of anyone's life today is to know what you want and how to get it. I would like to be a good husband and parent. Eventually I hope to own my home, and retain social respect within my society as well as being an understanding and helpful person. Last, and very important, I would like to do creative work in a field that fits my qualifications. I believe that these goals may be obtained if I can devote my efforts toward acquiring an education.

Part of any educational training is to become critical and evaluate the accumulation of facts which support a theory or belief.

As a person and student, I feel my strengths have been formulated through age and experience. These two factors have helped me realize the necessity of an education. I have a good foundation of scientific knowledge concerning the human body. I also have the power to employ common sense in reasoning and forming opinions. From this has been derived the will to learn and the persistence to overcome my weaknesses. My weak points as a student seem to focus upon the fundamentals of communication. These fundamentals have been stimulated in the adjustment period of the last few months. A true conclusion cannot be formed until all of the factors have been combined. The retesting of my reading ability and the second-semester grades will help me to draw a final conclusion which should coincide with my vocational interests.

Vocational interests form different patterns for each individual. A vocational pattern will naturally fall into an area where there has been some previous enjoyment or experience. My Kuder profile on the test data sheet reveals that my strongest areas of interest lie in social service, scientific and persuasive. These are areas that I have found most enjoyable in the past because of their affiliation with people. It was within my ability to help these people, and in return I received a great deal of self-satisfaction. My part-time hobbies have consisted of donating my time to older people at the Boston Dispensary and working with children at the West Newton Community Center. From these experiences and my service time, I have concluded that I must work with people, preferably with those who have physical and psychological problems. A physical therapist must contend with problems similar to these, and must be motivated in every way to help correct them.

My present motivation is the result of many factors. I have recognized a great waste of time and energy in the past five years. Possibly, the insecure feeling of knowing my abilities has been the stimulus to go to school and improve. My parents and my wife must have made me realize, in their own ways, that school and doing work that is satisfying to myself is important in classifying possible success. Regardless, I am motivated and my future depends a great deal on this year's studying. This first year will also allow me to assimilate my scholastic aptitude with my special aptitudes to give me a better over-all picture of my abilities.

The psychological test profile has indicated that I am in the lower portion of my class in scholastic aptitude and intelligence. Basically, I believe this is the result of a poor high-school record and poor reading skills. I have devoted a great deal of time in trying to improve my reading speed and comprehension, and, as a result, I do feel as though I have improved. The degree of improvement will be seen in the reading re-testing. The marks I received the first semester do show some capabilities. The total marks averaged 2.9, with my lowest grade in communications, which I hope to bring up this semester.

My specialized aptitudes seem to depart slightly from my scholastic aptitudes, probably because of the time element invested in them. Much of my time in the past has been spent on doing work with my hands. Through my high-school years, I worked in a gas station doing mechanical work. In massage, the co-ordination of my hands was important. In the Navy I worked as a cook, then on the assembly line at General Motors as a civilian again. Except for one, these jobs could be classified as labor. There has been a great tendency on my part to be attracted to the proper functioning of the human body. I believe I would like to spend the rest of my life co-ordinating hands and mind for the benefit of someone who is ill. This type of work is done best by a person with a special type of personality.

My strongest personality traits have probably been derived from my parents. Our home was well balanced, with love, sadness, sincerity, and a belief in people. This has created a cheerful and happy life, yet flexible enough to see a serious side. I appear to be the strong, reliable type character, mainly because I think for myself and speak my mind. I like to be understanding and try to help others by listening to their problems. I have probably adopted as many roles as there are, but I enjoy most the roles of a happy husband and a serious student. My weakest personality traits seem to come under the titles "stubbornness" or "meticulosity." These unfavorable aspects of my personality can easily be concealed when necessary, and many times be altered to fit any situation that may arise. Many of these situations will arise in the field of physical therapy.

A therapist is liable to find that he will demand a great deal from his personality. Probably the most important traits are to be emotionally stable, friendly, and self-confident. You must have the desire to help people, and the ability to inspire confidence and faith in physical therapy procedures. A person in this field must have a sense of humor, and have sympathetic understanding. He must be patient, tolerant, and tactful. Neatness and courtesy are also necessities for a therapist. Adaptability to different patients and changing circumstances also seem to be an important aspect of the physical therapist's personality. These traits, in some manner, hold a position in my self-concept. I enjoy the happiness that accompanies the natural phenomenon of living in good health and would like to help restore some of this happiness to others.

The only other factors that appear to have any weight in my situation are my wife and money. Granted, they could be heavy burdens, but they seem to represent no problem at the present time. Because of my wife's wonderful attitude and financial contributions to our household, this process of education is possible. My parents have always been happy people. They believe that doing work that offers self-satisfaction in return for your efforts is the key to happiness, and I am inclined to agree with them. The future is hard to predict, but being happy and having a happy family will be of prime importance.

In order to take a look ahead, a person must be a little optimistic. I seriously believe that my objectives will be satisfactorily fulfilled in the future. I am also a true believer in the saying "every goal in life has its price." There is a lot of work in store for my wife and myself before we can settle down to a normal married life, but we do know why and for what we are working.

Although there are many opportunities in physical therapy, I believe that I would like most to be an instructor. I could have my own practice on the side or work as a trainer with college athletic teams.

In summary of the past few paragraphs I would like to say the following:

My goals in life are clear.

My vocational interest pattern coincides with my aptitudes.

My strengths as a person and student are stronger than my weaknesses.

My intelligence and scholastic aptitude scores should rise as I improve my reading speed and comprehension.

My personality is, in general, similar to the required traits of a physical therapist.

There seems to be no other factors that will hinder a successful look ahead. My conclusions have been drawn from facts, assumptions, and hopes. The field of physical therapy is where I should be, but if something unforeseen should appear, I am sure I can adapt myself accordingly.

MISS "Y"

As I attempt to analyze myself in view of my strengths and weaknesses, I must consider the surrounding elements that influence me. I feel that my ability to mingle and get along with people of all ages may be attributed to the organizational work I have done. This type of work has served as a basis for a few other personality traits as well. In order to be able to associate successfully with people, one must be sincere, thoughtful, and respectful. My religious background has also furnished me with basic strengths—a power to reason out situations, to assume an unbiased attitude toward all races and religions, and to accept people first and then question them. The most essential contributor to these strengths has been my closely-knit family.

My personality weaknesses as a person and a student are due to a varied number of factors. A very difficult task arises when I explain why I lack a certain amount of self-confidence. I must admit I don't know the basic reason for this; however, since my work with a certain counselor at the Reading Laboratory, I feel I have improved in this respect. Because I have a great deal of confidence in this individual, I, in turn, have acquired more confidence in myself. Another habit which I still have from my childhood is that of stubbornness. I think this weakness first started when the usual arguments between a brother and sister occurred. I get along very well with my brother, but this habit of arguing has extended out of the family relationships. Perhaps it is self-pride. One of my weaker study habits is that of not settling down to work and continuing to concentrate. I am easily distracted. When I have to take an exam, I become extremely nervous, although this weakness has also been greatly improved through my work at the Reading Laboratory.

My motivation for achieving scholastically at college results largely from my desire to attain a substantial education for my future life, whatever path it might follow. I feel an education is vital for making a well-rounded, stable individual, for acquiring a job or position, or just for carrying on an intelligent conversation. My parents also urge me to study not only verbally, but they are paying for my education. Competition between students for grades serves as a motivating factor. My motivation to obtain a religious background lies within my family, as I am accustomed to living a religious life. Since I have been brought up in this manner, I now feel I should like to follow this way through.

My goals in life almost coincide with a look into the future. I should like to raise a family in the same warm, closely-knit, sensible, and religious manner in which I was fortunate to be brought up. I want people to respect me for myself, my morals, and my beliefs. I want to achieve a well-rounded education not only in a general sense, but also in one particular aspect: whatever vocation I decide to select.

Because I have been attending Hebrew School for some twelve-odd years, I have acquired an aptitude to read, write, and speak Hebrew rather fluently. Camp ———, which is affiliated with the Jewish Theological Seminary of America, has also helped me considerably in developing this aptitude. Camp activities, along with those of organizational work, have aided me in developing aptitudes in singing and dancing. Since an extremely young age, my family has taught me several sports so that now I possess quite a few aptitudes in sports, also. For the past eleven years I have taken piano lessons so that now I feel proficient in this area. Because of my summer jobs as a counselor and instructor, and my occasional winter position in leadership experiences, I feel I am able to lead certain types of groups in specific activities.

My intelligence and scholastic aptitude are above average in comparison to that of the general population and above average in comparison to that of college freshmen. My reading ability compared with other college freshmen was below average when I entered this college. However, since I have attended the Reading Laboratory, I have not only built up my reading speed to a score above that of the average college freshman, but I have also increased my power of comprehension.

For a great number of years I always felt I wanted to be a piano teacher, however, my vocational interest pattern has been extended. I know I enjoy working with children immensely, but I decided that I wanted to teach Hebrew, too. Now, Hebrew educators are very much in demand, aside from the fact that I would like to utilize some of the religious knowledge and background I have received. Thus, if I can acquire a position as a Hebrew teacher, along with a position as an instructor of Hebrew singing and dancing, I think my work would be ideal. My experiences in working with people (more so than the average individual at my age) began as I associated with my parents' friends, who assume positions in various organizations. I have held several officers' positions in organizations; recently, my work experience consists of that of a counselor of a "bunk" and of sports at camp, and that of a substitute Hebrew teacher. As I review my Kuder Preference Record, I find similar indications of interests in social service and music, in which I received high scores.

When I examine a possible vocation, I must consider several other factors besides those previously mentioned. I must consider monetary values, health, family conditions, time, and even the possibility of a boy friend's interfering. A couple of these problems I can account for before my training, but others I have to cope with during my education.

If one were not afforded the opportunity to write this type of analysis, he may not appreciate what he himself is, wants to become, and possibly will become. The essential step for selecting a way of life for the future is to discover one's self; for only through knowing who we are, can we hope to learn what we may become.

MR. "Z"

Like most students, I have many strong points, and as many, if not more, weak ones. All my life I have always been very independent in my ideas. In fact, until recently, I never realized how much more I could have benefited from my high-school education but I had not been so obdurate in listening to the advice of persons more qualified to know what was best for me. However, I have always been a hard worker and have never minded doing work which I enjoy, regardless of how long and tedious it might be. I think that this ability to work hard, which I have as a person, will be a great asset to my life as a college student. In college, since I will be more willing to work than I was in high school, where all my courses were relatively mandatory.

Since I haven't definitely decided to strive for any one particular field, my goals in life, at this point, are not ultimate ones, but rather just general ideas. At the present time the primary thing which I am seeking, is a liberal education, later to be supplemented by further education in some specific field at graduate school. I am also looking for a way to find financial and self-satisfaction by doing work which will help others as well as myself. Fields I have seriously been contemplating are personnel, real estate, and education. They all seem to "sit well" with the ideas and interests I have at the present time.

Before I began college, my motivation in high school was more or less an attitude of indifference. However, now that I have an idea of what a college education really is, I realize more than ever exactly what it will mean to me in later life. This realization of educational value has, I believe, greatly strengthened and increased my motivation toward studying. A greater interest in my subjects has also been a contributing factor.

I do not know whether it is a good sign or a bad one, but during the last few years my interests have seen a great deal of change. There are several factors which have helped me to form a vocational interest pattern. In high school I was interested very much in scientific and mechanical ideas. My hobbies of photography and woodworking were also very close to these interests. However, since last summer I have been more interested in working with other people, and studying their social relations in conjunction with business. The Kuder Preference Record showed that my three highest areas of interest are computational, persuasive, and literary.

Unfortunately, I have not had as many vocational aptitude tests as I should like to have had up to this point. I have never done any work in the areas in which I am interested, mainly because I could always make more money doing other summer jobs. Likewise, I have never taken any written aptitude tests, with the exception of tests in scholastic aptitude. Perhaps the only good measure of aptitude I have is my success with different courses in school. So far this year I have done well in Social Relations and Science, but not as well in Humanities. My marks in Social Relations could be an indication of aptitude in this area.

During this last year I have taken several tests indicating measures of intelligence and scholastic aptitude. The California Test of Mental Maturity showed that I have a high intelligence compared with general population norms, and average intelligence in comparison with entering college freshmen. I did not have the opportunity to take the Ohio State University Psychological Examination or the Co-operative Reading Comprehension Test. However, I did take the Scholastic Aptitude Test given by the College Entrance Examination Board, and this showed that my scholastic aptitude was just above the median for entering college freshmen. My high school marks, another indication of scholastic aptitude, were also average. In the twenty courses I studied, I had ten certifying grades.

I have always been interested in social activities of all sorts, and especially in meeting other people. I find it very interesting to note common characteristics and differences in individuals, and likewise, to compare the opinions of different persons regarding one particular individual. I also enjoy discussing different matters, but oftentimes I am too outspoken when voicing my opinion to others in a group. I have found that it is very helpful for me also, to open myself to the criticism of others in matters concerning my personality, and I fully realize the value of their opinions.

My self-concept seems to fit in fairly well with my plans for the future, in that I enjoy associating with people, and sharing different pleasures and problems with them. However, my self-concept might differ greatly from the opinions of others.

In order to continue with, and to fulfill all my plans for the future, it will be necessary for me to maintain a high level of motivation. Since my parents cannot pay too much toward my education, I must work hard and save as much money as I can each summer. My motivation should help me a great deal in continuing through graduate school with my education.

As soon as possible I would like to take some aptitude tests in order to fill in my background and help me in choosing a career for which to strive. These should also be helpful for me in determining my educational plans for the future.

If I work hard, my tests and background seem to indicate that I should be able to do well in college, and in later life. However, all my success will still be decided by the amount of work which I contribute.

MISS "J"

My strengths as a person seem to center around the fact that I am extroverted. I am broadminded. I like to learn new things which will not only increase my knowledge, but help me to understand myself and others around me. I am told that I am understanding and in my own crowd I am singled out to listen to problems. I like to help people, not give them advice, but to try to make them understand their own problems so that they can help themselves. I am more ambitious for others than I am for myself. I seem to be able to give them strength that they oftentimes need. I oftentimes place others before myself. I get pleasure out of giving assistance to others. I am very frank, which at times is good, but I have found that when dealing with people, honesty, especially about themselves, is not always the best policy. I am thrifty. I not only like to save my own money, but I get a great deal of pleasure out of saving others' money.

My weakest personality traits seem to center around my insecurity. This insecurity often results in little self-confidence. Sometimes I am afraid to make decisions even in the smallest of matters for fear of making a mistake; or if I am doing something for another person I am afraid he won't like it. I strive to be an individual. Being an only child and a girl, my parents watch me constantly. They treat me like a baby to the extent that I will be sitting down at the dinner table and I will get my bread buttered for me. This may seem trivial, but to me it is a sign of dependence and I am striving for independence. I do not like to be told what to do in matters that are governed by common sense, such as being able to get in out of the rain. This brings on negativism and stubbornness in me. I have not yet learned to accept this "help." I have a bad temper and malicious tongue. These often appear as a defense when I get hurt. I am much too sensitive. I tend to procrastinate. I have the ability to set up mental blocks which enable me to use the device called selective forgetting. That is to say, I forget until the activity I am trying to forget is a few days off.

My main goal in life is happiness. To me that means a home, husband, children, and the education which will enable me to understand my family, and, if necessary, to secure a job. Now more than ever I wish to read, but I don't have the time. I want to be able to read "deep" books, which, with an education, I can more easily understand.

I am motivated by many different forces. My father was the person who decided I should go to college. I didn't get good marks in high school, however, I was given an opportunity to attend college by enrolling at the Boston University Junior College. I want to prove to myself, my parents and my team that I can succeed in college; I want to go to school four years and get my bachelor's degree; I want to make my parents proud of me; I want to be able to get a good job; I want to be able to keep up with my future husband.

From the Kuder Vocational Preference Test my greatest interests lie in computational (99th %ile), social service (85th %ile), and clerical (75th %ile). I always liked mathematics and received very good grades in algebra. As I have said I like helping, working with and for other people. Last summer I did clerical work in the Jordan Marsh Company and enjoyed it very much.

I believe I have a computational aptitude and I also have a liking for working with figures. I think I may have an aptitude and an interest for people, especially "what makes them tick."

As far as scholastic aptitude and intelligence, as shown in the Ohio State University Psychological Examination, the Co-operative Reading Comprehension Test and the California Mental Maturity Test, there is definite evidence to prove that I do have a reading speed and comprehension difficulty. I believe that as soon as this deficiency is rectified, my scholastic aptitude scores will rise.

My personality has been greatly influenced by my parents. I am strong willed and if I put my mind to something I can usually do it (if I try and my goal is within my limits). In many roles I have been trusted and respected, but I lack self-confidence, which stems from my insecurity. I like to laugh and have fun—this has helped me use selective forgetting. I am, however, using this device (laughing) less and less. I want responsibility but on some occasions I fear it. At home, as independent (negative) as I try to be, I am still dependent. I must get over the fear of responsibility if I am to grow up. Since school started I have, as told to me by one of my team of instructors, grown up "a lot" in the last four months. I hope I will be able to continue to grow up as time goes on.

Last summer was the first time I had had a job for five days a week. I enjoyed working and assuming responsibility. Liking people as much as I do I got along fine in the office. At that time, being more immature than now, I did not take my job as seriously as I would now. College has helped me a great deal and I know it will continue to do so.

The most important other factors in my life are my parents. My mother, who is more introverted than I, and I don't get along. I am often pampered, which makes me negativistic. My father and I have always gotten along since he tries to understand me and he can remember when he was my age. He has much more influence over me than does my mother.

Next year I should like to go to the College of Business Administration and take up accounting and secretarial work. I feel that I can do it if I am transferred. I believe that the Junior College has helped me a great deal to understand myself. I still have much to learn. I want to be able to learn it. My marks last term averaged a B+, and I am trying even harder this term. I hope I can be and get all the things I want, but most important I would like to continue to grow wiser.

TEST DATA ON MISS "J"

Ohio State University Psychological Examination

	June %ile	April %ile	
Same–opposites	66	34	
Verbal analogies	73	84	College freshman
Reading comprehension	16	21	norms
Total	51	58	

Co-operative Reading Comprehension Test

	June %ile	April %ile	
Vocabulary	27	42	
Speed of comprehension	34	34	College freshman
Level of comprehension	42	34	norms
Total	34	34	

California Test of Mental Maturity (September)

	%ile	
Verbal	66	General
Non-verbal	66	population norms
Total	66	

MR. "ROCK HUDSON"

This is an endeavor to analyze myself. If, at times, this essay seems similar to "Will Success Spoil Rock Hudson?" remember that it is your duty as the reader to bear with me until the sketch is completed. In accordance with my conscience, I will not paint myself as I have often seen myself in moments of glory, but rather will sketch how I see myself in not-so-frequent moments of modesty. In all fairness to myself, concerning the first issue, "strengths and weaknesses as a person and student," I will start off with my weaknesses and conclude with a grand finale of attributes and better qualities.

I am sometimes labeled by those of authority (i.e. headmasters, parents, etc.) as one who is a bit immature in that I am not as serious as they would have me. This seems quite appropriate to me for I see that my lack of seriousness reflects to an extent upon my life in and out of the classroom. I am, actually, a "joker," and consequently I take things rather lightly. This has a tremendous effect upon me as a student and a person.

As a person, I sometimes seem quite egotistical. This is caused by a false sense of superiority, which is caused by a natural sense of inferiority. Another personal fault is that I expect too much in life to be given me. I have no idea of what causes this, but feel it is not caused by being spoiled because I have always been fairly well disciplined. Because of a combination of these two faults, I have a tendency to ask for more than I can possibly get.

As a student, my faults lie in the fact that I have poor study habits, practically no will power, even less power of concentration, and no ability to study those subjects in which I am not interested.

As personal strengths, I have chosen the fact that I practically always get along well, and am always at ease, with people and groups of people. I am free and easy, not prejudiced toward any one group, and am always willing to go out of my way for almost anyone without being a "patsy."

My strengths as a student are as follows: I have the will to learn, I realize the necessity of a college education, and I try to stimulate or cultivate interest in all of my courses.

My "goals in life" are really not too much to ask for, but can only be reached, I realize, by my working hard. I wish to fulfill that which is expected of me by my parents, friends, and self. For instance, I want to make college a success. I also want to be successful in a vocation which I enjoy and am successfully suited for. These are the only concrete examples of goals I have at the moment which I feel are worth including in a self-analysis.

Without first looking at my Kuder results, I can tell you that I am interested most strongly in a vocation involving both business and people. Something in the line of a public-relations man for a firm or corporation would be to my preference. After examining the Kuder results, I find I have a high score in clerical, persuasive, and literary. To me this indicates that I am best suited (as far as interest is concerned) in a vocation where both business and people are involved and combined. Unfortunately, I have no interest in social-service work; the Kuder and I agree unanimously. This is, no doubt, caused by my being principally concerned with myself. Although I am somewhat concerned about people's welfare, I am not in the least way interested in that sort of thing as a vocation.

Concerning my intelligence and scholastic aptitudes, I only have two bits of information to submit. This is simply because the results of my tests taken during and prior to orientation week were somehow lost in the shuffle. I feel compelled to say that this is not a swing at the administration; it is not intended as such.

The two bits of information mentioned are the results of the California Mental Maturity and Snader General Math examination. The results are as follows:

C.M.M.:

	R. S.	C. F. %ile	G. P. %ile
N. L.	36	10	40
L.	36	40	70
Total	72	30	60

Snader General Math:

R. S.	12th grade %ile
112	85

In my own opinion, without any flattery, my intelligence and scholastic aptitude are about average. The problem lies, if anywhere, in the application of these two.

I feel that my personality, in regards to character, will be very influential in my final choice of a vocation and my success in that vocation. I am very amiable and persuasive to an extent, and feel this would help me to be successful in a vocation such as public relations. I am good-natured, can get along well with all kinds of people, and can influence people to a certain extent; I feel this would help in such a vocation as public relations.

Information concerning the "other factors" (i.e. my home, school background, friends, etc.) can be found in my autobiography. I say this because I feel this information is too lengthy to supply in this particular essay when it has already been stated in a previous essay.

In summarizing, I would like to say that the self-analysis has benefited me in that it has shown me how I am, in my own opinion, best suited for, in ability and interest, a vocation in the line of public relations. If this be true, I would like to go on to a second year of general education at the Junior College, and then go to the School of Public Relations and Communications.

AUTOBIOGRAPHICAL ASSIGNMENT SHEET

Written assignment . . . . Autobiography
Length . . . . 1,000 words minimum
Reader . . . . Your teacher-counselor
Grades . . . . Papers will be rated as "S" (satisfactory) or "U" (unsatisfactory). Those rated as unsatisfactory will be returned for revision.

This assignment is designed to serve two purposes:

1. To permit you to analyze your own life history up to this point.
2. To demonstrate your ability to write an interesting composition in effective English.

The contents of your autobiography will be kept confidential. Except by permission, no person other than your guidance counselor will read your paper.

All of us are concerned from time to time with re-examining our lives. We frequently go back over our careers to see where we succeeded and where we failed; we often endeavor to find from a study, casual or systematic, of our past, lessons that will guide our present and future action. There is no time in life when this can be done to greater advantage than in youth. Then the past has been short and the future lies all before us. Careful reflection now, which results in a wise plan for the rest of life, will be of much more value than revisions made later under the pressure of frustrating experiences.

The following topics may help you in recalling pertinent incidents for the paper. You may possibly get a better effect by beginning with the present and retracing your steps. You may possibly combine two or three areas of thought. The method is up to you, but each paper should have only one central idea to which other ideas should be subordinated.

My strengths and weaknesses as a student and person
Early home influences
Family relationships
How your educational pattern has affected your present-day thinking.
Personal values in work experience or travel
Reactions to military experience
Personal, racial, religious, and social problems that have proved significant to you
Advantages and disadvantages of your present and past home environment
Factors that have influenced your choice of educational objectives
An analysis of development of special talent, hobbies, interests
Future vocational and educational plans

OCCUPATIONAL AND EDUCATIONAL RESEARCH PAPER CHECK SHEET

Title _Accountant_   Name _John J. Jones_

Counselor _Glanz_   Grade _B +_

I. The Occupation

    ( ) 0. No adequate information or irrelevant information.
    ( ) 1. Poorly treated on the whole.
    ( ) 2. Below average treatment of topic.
    ( ) 3. Average treatment of topic, or some parts well done, some poorly.
    ( ) 4. Above average treatment of topic.
    (✓) 5. Superior selection and treatment of relevant information.

II. The Worker

    ( ) 0. Omitted or no adequate information.
    ( ) 1. Very poor understanding of requirements.
    ( ) 2. Below average treatment of this part of paper.
    ( ) 3. Average treatment, or some parts well done and some poorly.
    (✓) 4. Substantial information and good understanding.
    ( ) 5. Superior grasp of educational and occupational requirements.

III. Planning your career in this field

    A. U.   Relating personal analysis of:
        (S.)   interests, aptitudes, abilities, specific skills and personality, to the field.

    B. Plans for job preparation and securing employment.

    ( ) 0. Omitted or no evidence of realistic planning.
    ( ) 1. Poor treatment, little attempt to think ahead.
    ( ) 2. Limited understanding of the ways and means available.
    ( ) 3. Average treatment, or some parts well done and some poorly.
    (✓) 4. Above average evidence of realistic planning.
    ( ) 5. Excellent; thoughtful and realistic planning.

IV. Sources of Information (including interview)

    ( ) 0. Choice does not meet minimum demands, or omitted.
    ( ) 1. Choice meets minimum demands of assignment only.
    ( ) 2. Poorly selected and well selected materials; unbalanced.
    ( ) 3. Average treatment; well balanced selection.
    (✓) 4. Above average; considerable attention given to selection.
    ( ) 5. Excellent; special effort to secure and use materials.

Counselor's Comments.

GLOSSARY

This glossary defines technical terms largely as they have been used in the chapters of this book. In some instances, the definition has been limited in its meaning to specific applications suitable to the beginning student in psychology. For more comprehensive definitions, reference may be made to H. C. Warren, *Dictionary of Psychology*, Houghton Mifflin Company, Boston, 1934. Chapters in which a primary consideration is given to these concepts are listed in parentheses after the definition.

Ability: The power to perform responsive acts both physical and mental. (9, 10)

Abnormal: Actions, mentality, physical characteristics, modes of behavior, etc., that deviate significantly from the accepted norm or average. (6, 12)

Adjustment process: The accommodation to circumstances both environmental and internal that is necessary for solving man's problems or fulfilling his needs. (4, 7)

Adolescence: The period in the individual's life in which the reproductive functions mature. The ages between childhood and adulthood. (6)

Age score: Point of average performance of persons of a particular age. (8, 11)

Aptitude: A learning potential or capacity that can be developed by training. (9, 10)

Association: The process of establishing relationships. (5)

Autocratic society: A society in which the ruler makes or can make all decisions and is responsible only unto himself. (3)

Basic interest pattern: The broad areas of interest that remain relatively stable. (9)

Canalization: A learning process involving the formation, in the central nervous system through the repeated passage of nerve impulses, of pathways of permanently lowered resistance. A process of selecting and utilizing need satisfiers. (5)

Capacity: The full potential of an individual for any function limited only by his native constitution and developed under optimal conditions. (9, 10, 11)

Case history: A systematic record of all pertinent items of information concerning an individual. (6)

Central tendency: The general tendency of judgments, test scores or other measures regarding a quality or trait to group toward the middle of a distribution. (8)

Chronological age: The actual age of an individual in years, months, and days. (8, 11)

323

Compensation: A defense mechanism by which an individual unconsciously covers up or disguises an undesirable trait by developing what is commonly accepted as a more desirable trait. (6)

Conditioning: A process of learning in which a new stimulus may be substituted in a previously acquired stimulus-response bond. (5)

Correlation: A term showing the tendency of certain paired measures to vary so that knowledge of one gives information as to the mean value of measures paired with it. (8)

Counseling: A verbal process involving direct personal contacts with an individual to assist him in changing his attitudes and behavior and in the solution of personal and social problems. (2, 3)

Critical score: The score on some instrument representing the dividing line between acceptability and nonacceptability for some particular purpose. (3, 8)

Critical thinking: A careful and unbiased examination of data to form a considered judgment. (1, 13)

Defense mechanism: The unconscious mental device or mechanism by which an individual seeks adjustment to his environment. (6)

Democratic society: A society that allows for individual differences and decisions. (3)

Derived score: A score that has been placed in a statistical frame of reference for purposes of interpretation. (8)

Deviation: The amount by which a test score differs from some reference point. (8)

Distribution: A graphic presentation of the variability of a set of test scores. (8)

D.O.T. (Dictionary of Occupational Titles): A dictionary composed of three volumes and a supplement developed by the United States Employment Service. It lists (over 39,000 job titles), classifies, describes (over 25,000 jobs) and relates occupations. (14, 15, 16)

Drive: An organic, physiologically based stimulator to action. (4)

Ego: The portion of the "id" in contact with reality. A controlling force in personality (Freud). (4)

Emotion: An internal feeling, state, condition, or response involving either pleasantness or unpleasantness usually accompanying, preceding or following an experience. (2, 4, 9)

Entry job: An occupation that does not require previous experience and that leads to a goal set by the individual. (14, 16)

Environment: A term covering all conditions and factors (internal or external) that act upon an individual. (4, 6)

Experiment: A controlled observation or series of observations used to test a hypothesis or theory. (1, 11)

Expressed interests: The individual's verbal statement of preferences or likes. (9)

Figure and ground: A characteristic of perception in which part of the situation is seen as the foreground or primary aspect. (4, 5, 6)

Frequency: The number of times a particular score appears in a distribution of such scores. (8)

Frequency distribution: A presentation of the manner in which the scores on a particular test are distributed. (8)

"G" factor: According to Spearman's two-factor theory of intelligence, the general intelligence fundamental to all correlated abilities as distinguished from the specific "S" or variable factor. (11)

Gestalt psychology: The belief that mental processes and behavior cannot be analyzed as separate units but must be regarded as parts of one whole. (5)

Grade score: Point of average performance anticipated at a particular grade level in school. (8)

Group: A social collection of individuals that may be treated as a unitary whole. (3)

Group dynamics: The interactions among individuals leading to identification of the individual in relation to the group. (3)

Group structure: A number of individuals functioning as a unit under a totality of principles or ideas unique to the unit. (3)

Growth curve: A graphic representation of the changes that take place in a given mental or physical characteristic or function with increasing maturity. (11)

Heredity: The transmission of mental and physical characteristics to offspring biologically through the genes. (4, 6, 11)

Human relations: A composite expression pertaining to the study of interactions among individuals and groups in a society. (3)

Identification: An adjustive device in which the individual unconsciously relates his behavior to that of another individual. (6)

Illusions: Distortion or falsification in the interpretation of experiences through addition, omission or substitution. (6)

Individual differences: The variations or deviations in mental and physical characteristics occurring in the individual members of a group. (8)

Insight: Mental discernment; the process of seeing all relevant factors in a total perspective. (5)

Integration: The process by which materials (ideas, theories, principles) are brought into a complex whole at a higher level. (1, 10, 3)

Intelligence: The ability of the individual to solve problems and to adjust to his environment. (11)

Interaction: A relationship between two individuals or systems in which the activity of one influences or alters the activity of the other. (3)

Interest: A feeling of appeal and liking that accompanies special attention to an object or activity. (9)

Interest inventory: An evaluation device for determining the basic interest pattern of an individual. (9)

Interest pattern: A pattern of interests having significance for a particular field of work or activity. (9)

Interest profile: A graphic representation of an individual's basic interest pattern. (9, Appendix A)

Inter-individual differences: See individual differences. (8)

Intra-individual differences: The usually slight variability of individual performances at various times. (8)

I.Q.: Intelligence quotient of $\dfrac{\text{mental age}}{\text{chronological age}} \times 100.$ (8, 9)

Job analysis: A systematic and detailed study of all the facts about a specific occupation. (14-16)

Laissez faire: Literally, to allow to act—i.e., to interfere as little as possible. (3)

Language test: A type of mental test that involves the use of verbal symbols. (11)

Learning: The modification of a response; the development of a behavior pattern through experience. (3, 4, 5, 6)

Learning curve: A graphic representation of certain aspects of progress in ability during successive periods of practice in terms of equal time or of equal accomplishment units. Also, a graphic representation of learning ability according to age levels. (8, 11)

Maturation: The development or growth that occurs in most members of a species and is independent of learning. (4, 5, 6, 7)

Mean: An arithmetical average—i.e., the sum of all scores divided by the number of scores. (8)

Measured interests: Interests as measured by inventories. (9)

Median: The middlemost score in a distribution of scores. (8)

Mental age: The age for which a given score is the average (a method of expressing a test score). (8, 11)

Mode: The score in a distribution that appears the greatest number of times. (8)

Motivation: A force or combination of forces that provides a basis for action. (2, 4, 7)

Motive: The incentive or reason underlying human behavior. (4, 6)

Multiple-factor theory: The theory that intelligence is a pattern of an indefinite number of specific capacities. (11)

Need: A fundamental human condition marked by a feeling of deprivation or want or requiring some action. (3, 4, 5)

Nonentry job: An occupation that requires experience before one may enter it. (14-16)

Norm: The usual or standard performance for a given group in a particular characteristic. (7, 8)

Normal curve: A bell-shaped frequency distribution obtained mathematically from the operation of chance. An approximation of the normal curve is often found in a distribution of measures of a particular biological or psychological trait. (8)

Norm group: A standard against which a given person's score may be appropriately compared. Such a standard is obtained through the testing of a large number of persons who are comparable in some respect. (7, 8)

Occupational and educational research paper: The study of an occupation and of the training and education required for entry into the occupation. (16)

Organism: A complex being capable of maintaining itself as a living unit. (4, 6, 7)

Overachiever: An individual who, through unusual effort, is performing at a level above that which is predictable for his ability. (11)

Percentile: Indicates by hundredths the percentage of individuals in a given group who have scores equal to or lower than the given one. (8)

Perception: The mental process by which the nature of an object is recognized. (4, 5)

Performance test: A type of mental test in which the role of language is greatly diminished, and consisting of the manipulation of objects. (11)

Personality: The integrated characteristics and reaction to environment that make each individual unique. (6, 7)

Phenomenal field: The universe, including the individual, as it is experienced by the individual at the instant of action. (3, 6, 7, 14)

Population: A group of individuals selected on some particular basis. (8)

Prediction: A description of probable results or events that is based upon the evaluation and projection of data or information presently available. (7, 8)

Prestige: Recognition by general members of a social group. The attainment of a temporary or permanent reputation that distinguishes the individual from the group. (3, 6, 7)

Primary mental abilities: The theory that intelligence is composed of basic mental abilities relatively independent of each other. (11)

Primary source: The original reference material; eyewitness or original report. (15, 16)

Projection: A defense mechanism in which the individual sees in another his own characteristic motives or behavior. (6)

Range: The interval between the highest and lowest scores in a group of scores. (8)

Rationalization: A conscious or unconscious attempt to make behavior that is inferior or unapproved appear to be socially acceptable. (6)

Raw score: The total number of correct items in a given test. (8)

Reality: The objective world as it exists rather than as it is perceived by an individual. (2, 3, 6)

Response: Any activity of an organism that results from internal or external stimulation. (4)

Role: A particular pattern of behavior or method of behaving or acting, usually developed in terms of what is expected of one. (3, 6, 7)

Sample: A selection of a number of cases taken at random from a group or population. (8)

Scholastic aptitude: The learning potential of an individual; involves ability to deal successfully with abstract ideas expressed in words and quantitative symbols. (11)

Secondary source: A reference prepared by someone not actively engaged in the area under discussion. (16)

Self-analysis: An attempt by the individual to determine his own personal strengths and weaknesses. (Part III)

Self-appraisal: An attempt by the individual to evaluate his own characteristics in comparison with the characteristics of others (Part III)

Self-concept: The self as seen by the self. (1, 3, 6, 13)

Self-understanding: The process of assimilating and appreciating the concept of self resulting from self-analysis and self-appraisal. (1, 3, 6, 13)

Sensory stimuli: Forces acting on the sense organs (receptor cells) with sufficient intensity to cause the individual to respond. (4)

Set: A mental attitude or predisposition that tends to predetermine the outcome of an experience. (3, 5, 6, 9)

"S" factor: The specific "S" or variable factor according to Spearman's two-factor theory of intelligence; the specific factor of intelligence which, in contradistinction to the "G" factor, varies with different abilities. (11)

Social drive: The force of other individuals and general environment operating on man. (4)

Social intelligence: The ability to deal effectively with situations involving mutual relations with members of a group. (11)

Socialization: The process by which individuals acquire socially acceptable habits and become members of a social group. (4, 6, 7)

Spatial visualization: The ability of an individual to perceive the relationships of objects in space. (10, 11)

Standardization group: A group for which norms of performance, on a particular test, are available. (8)

Status: A position in reference to an environmental situation or among individuals in a social structure. (7, 8)

Stimulus: An external or internal energy change that effectively activates or excites a receptor. (4)

Sublimation: The development of a substitute activity to satisfy a frustrated motive. (6)

Student-centered learning: A process of acquiring knowledge by emphasizing the role of the learner as well as the material to be learned. (3)

Tension: A state of imbalance within the individual that leads to behavior tending to restore balance. (4, 6, 7)

Test profile: A graphic representation of an individual's test scores for purposes of reporting, comparison and interpretation. (Appendix A)

Traditional learning: Knowledge acquired through systematic study in any field with emphasis upon the material to be learned rather than upon the learner. (3)

Trial-and-error learning: Learning through chance or blundering. (5)

Two-factor theory: The theory that intelligence is composed of a common factor of general intelligence and many special abilities. (11)

Underachiever: An individual who is performing at a level lower than would be predicted for a person of his ability. (11)

Validity: The agreement between a test score and what it purports to measure. (8)

Value judgment: The subjective estimate or appreciation of the importance of a given factor in relation to other factors in the same class. (4, 6, 7)

Values: The primary learned and personal beliefs of an individual. (4, 6, 7)

Vocational interest: A liking for and enjoyment of a particular kind of work activity. (11)

BIBLIOGRAPHY

1. *A Guide to Colleges, Universities, and Professional Schools in the United States.* Washington: American Council on Education, 1945.

2. Alexander, Franz, "Emotional Maturity," *Mental Health Bulletin,* Illinois Society for Mental Hygiene, 26 (1948), pp. 1-4.

3. Alexander, Franz, *Fundamentals of Psychoanalysis.* New York: W. W. Norton and Company, Inc., 1948.

4. Allport, Gordon W., Philip E. Vernon, and Gardner Lindzey, *The Study of Values, a Scale for Measuring the Dominant Interests in Personality* (rev. ed.). Boston: Houghton Mifflin Company, 1951.

5. Anastasi, Anne, *Differential Psychology, Individual and Group Differences In Behavior.* New York: The Macmillan Company, 1949.

6. Anastasi, Anne, *Psychological Testing.* New York: The Macmillan Company, 1954.

7. *Army General Classification Test,* First Civilian Edition. Chicago: Science Research Associates, Inc., 1947.

8. Baer, M. F., and E. C. Roeber, *Occupational Information; Its Nature and Use.* Chicago: Science Research Associates, Inc., 1951.

9. Bayley, Nancy, "On the Growth of Intelligence," *The American Psychologist,* 10 (1955), pp. 805-818.

10. *Bell Adjustment Inventory.* Stanford, California: Stanford University Press, 1938.

11. Benjamin, James, "Changes in Performance in Relation to Influence upon Self-Conceptualization," *Journal of Abnormal and Social Psychology,* 45 (1950), pp. 473-480.

12. Benne, D. and N. Muntyan, *Human Relations in Curriculum Change.* New York: Dryden Press, 1951.

13. Bennett, M. E., *College and Life* (4th ed.). New York: McGraw-Hill Book Company, Inc., 1952.

14. Bernard, Harold W., *Toward Better Personal Adjustment* (2nd ed.). New York: McGraw-Hill Book Company, Inc., 1952.

15. Bingham, Walter Van Dyke, *Aptitudes and Aptitude Testing.* New York: Harper & Brothers, 1937.

16. Bischof, L. J., *Intelligence, Statistical Concepts of Its Nature.* New York: Doubleday & Company, Inc., 1954.

329

17. Blau, P. M., J. W. Gustad, R. Jessor, H. S. Parnes, and R. C. Wilcock, "Occupational Choice: A Conceptual Framework," *Industrial Labor Relations Review,* 9 (1956), pp. 531-543.

18. Bogue, J. P., *American Junior Colleges* (3rd ed.). Washington: American Council on Education, 1952.

19. Boring, E. G., *A History of Experimental Psychology* (2nd ed.). New York: Appleton-Century-Crofts, Inc., 1950.

20. Bulgelski, B. R., *The Psychology of Learning.* New York: Henry Holt and Company, Inc., 1956.

21. Burgess, Ernest W., and Leonard S. Cottrell, Jr., *Predicting Success or Failure in Marriage.* Englewood Cliffs, N.J.: Prentice-Hall, Inc., 1939.

22. Buros, Oscar, ed., *The Fourth Mental Measurements Yearbook.* Highland Park, N.J.: The Gryphon Press, 1953.

23. Burtt, Harold E., *Applied Psychology* (2nd ed.). Englewood Cliffs, N.J.: Prentice-Hall, Inc., 1957.

24. Calia, Vincent, "No Vocational Choice—A Function of Self-Concept," unpublished article.

25. Calia, Vincent, "The Counselor and the Teacher-Phone Program," *Junior College Journal,* 25 (1954), pp. 224-228.

26. *California Test of Mental Maturity,* Advanced level, Short-form 50-S. Los Angeles: California Test Bureau.

27. *California Test of Personality,* Secondary, Form A. Los Angeles: California Test Bureau.

28. Caplow, Theodore, *The Sociology of Work,* Minneapolis: University of Minnesota Press, 1954.

29. Carmichael, Leonard, "The Onset and Early Development of Behavior," *Manual of Child Psychology* (L. Carmichael, ed.). New York: John Wiley & Sons, Inc., 1946.

30. Cartwright, D., and A. F. Zander, *Group Dynamics: Research and Theory.* New York: Rowe, Peterson & Company, 1953.

31. Cattell, P. "Constant Change in Stanford-Binet I.Q.," *Journal of Educational Psychology,* 22 (1921), pp. 544-550.

32. Cohen, N. M., *Vocational Training Directory of the United States.* Washington: N. M. Cohen, 1953.

33. Cole, Luella, *Psychology of Adolescence* (4th ed.). New York: Rinehart and Company, Inc., 1954.

34. *College Blue Book,* Christian E. Burckel, Compiler and Publisher, Baltimore, Maryland: Universal Lithographers Inc., 1956.

35. Combs, Arthur W., "Intelligence from a Perceptual Point of View," *Journal of Abnormal and Social Psychology,* 45 (1952), pp. 662-673.

36. *Cooperative English Test,* Reading Comprehension, Form C2 (S,T,Y.). Princeton, N.J.: Cooperative Test Division, Educational Testing Service.

37. *Cooperative School and College Ability Test.* Princeton, N.J.: Cooperative Test Division, Educational Testing Service, 1955.

38. Crawford, Albert B., and Paul S. Burnham, *Forecasting College Achievement: A Survey of Aptitude Tests for Higher Education,* Part I: General considerations in the measurement of academic promise. New Haven: Yale University Press, 1946.

39. Cronbach, Lee J., *Essentials of Psychological Testing.* New York: Harper & Brothers, 1949.

40. Dashiell, John F., *Fundamentals of General Psychology.* Boston: Houghton Mifflin Company, 1949.

41. Davis, Frederick B., *Utilizing Human Talent.* Washington: American Council on Education, 1947.

42. Deese, James, *The Psychology of Learning.* New York: McGraw-Hill Book Company, Inc., 1952.

43. *Dictionary of Occupational Titles,* Part I, *Definitions of Titles,* Part II, *Titles and Codes,* Part IV, *Entry—Occupational Classification.* Washington: U. S. Department of Labor, U. S. Employment Service, U. S. Government Printing Office, 1949.

44. *Differential Aptitude Tests* (2nd ed.). New York: The Psychological Corporation, 1952.

45. Doll, Edgar A., *Vineland Social Maturity Scale, Manual of Directions.* Minneapolis: Educational Test Bureau, 1947, pp. 1-2.

46. Dollard, J., and N. E. Miller, *Personality and Psychotherapy, An Analysis in Terms of Learning, Thinking and Culture.* New York: McGraw-Hill Book Company, Inc., 1950.

47. Drazin, Nathan, "History of Jewish Education from 515 B.C. to 220 C.E." *The Johns Hopkins University Studies in Education,* No. 29. Baltimore: Johns Hopkins Press, 1950.

48. Dysinger, D. W., and W. S. Gregory, "A Preliminary Study of Some Factors Related to Student Achievement and Grades in the Beginning Course in Psychology," *Journal of General Psychology,* 24 (1941), pp. 195-209.

49. Erickson, Clifford E., ed., *A Basic Text for Guidance Workers.* Englewood Cliffs, N.J.: Prentice-Hall Inc., 1947.

50. *Flanagan Aptitude Classification Tests,* John C. Flanagan. Chicago: Science Research Associates, Inc., 1953.

51. Forrester, Gertrude, *Occupational Literature; An Annotated Bibliography.* New York: H. W. Wilson Company, 1954.

52. Freud, Sigmund, *An Outline of Psychoanalysis* (trans. James Strachey). New York: W. W. Norton and Company, 1949.

53. Gamble, Alice H., "Teaching by Telephone on the College Level," *College and University Business,* June, 1955, pp. 35-36.

54. Garrett, H. E., "The Relation of Tests of Memory and Learning to Each Other and to General Intelligence in a Highly Selected Adult Group," *Journal of Educational Psychology,* 19 (1928), pp. 601-613.

55. *General Aptitude Test Battery*. Washington: U.S. Department of Labor, Bureau of Employment Security, U.S.E.S., 1956.

56. Gesell, Arnold, Frances L. Ilg, *et al.*, *Child Development*. New York: Harper & Brothers, 1949.

57. Ginzberg, Eli, and associates, *Occupational Choice*. New York: Columbia University Press, 1951.

58. Gray, J. Stanley, *Psychology Applied to Human Affairs* (2nd ed.). New York: McGraw-Hill Book Company, Inc., 1954.

59. Gray, J. Stanley, ed., *Psychology in Use* (2nd ed.). New York: American Book Company, 1951.

60. Grunes, W. F., "On Perception of Occupations," *The Personnel and Guidance Journal*, 34, No. 5 (January 1956).

61. Guthrie, E. R., *The Psychology of Learning*. New York: Harper & Brothers, 1935.

62. Haiman, Franklyn S., *Group Leadership in Democratic Action*. Boston: Houghton Mifflin Company, 1951.

63. Hepner, H. W., *Psychology Applied to Life and Work* (3rd ed.). Englewood Cliffs, N.J.: Prentice-Hall, Inc., 1957.

64. Hoppock, Robert, *Occupational Information*. New York: McGraw-Hill Book Company, Inc., 1957.

65. Irwin, Mary, *American Universities and Colleges* (6th ed.). Washington: American Council on Education, 1952.

66. Jersild, Arthur T., *Child Psychology* (4th ed.). Englewood Cliffs, N.J.: Prentice-Hall, Inc., 1955.

67. Jersild, Arthur T., *In Search of Self*. New York: Bureau of Publications, Teachers College, Columbia University, 1955.

68. Jersild, Arthur T., *The Psychology of Adolescence*. New York: The Macmillan Company, 1957, pp. 193-201.

69. Jervis, Fred, *Self Description Inventory*, Test Manual, Unpublished, Durham, New Hampshire, 1955.

70. Jones, Ernest, *What is Psychoanalysis?* New York: International Universities Press, 1948.

71. *Junior Colleges and Specialized Schools and Colleges* (2nd ed.). Boston: Porter Sargent, 1955.

72. Kingsley, Howard L. (rev. by Ralph Garry), *Nature and Conditions of Learning* (2nd ed.). Englewood Cliffs, N.J.: Prentice-Hall, Inc., 1956.

73. Koffka, K., *The Growth of the Mind*, New York: Harcourt Brace & Company, Inc., 1924.

74. *Kuder Preference Record—Vocational*, Form CH, G. Frederic Kuder. Chicago: Science Research Associates, Inc.

75. Landis, Paul H., *Adolescence and Youth*. New York: McGraw-Hill Book Company, Inc., 1947.

76. Lecky, P., *Self-Consistency*. New York: Island Press, 1945.

77. Lehner, George F. J. and Ella Kube, *The Dynamics of Personal Adjustment*. Englewood Cliffs, N.J.: Prentice-Hall, Inc., 1955.

78. Levy, John and Ruth Munroe, *The Happy Family*. New York: Alfred A. Knopf, Inc., 1938.

79. Lewin, Kurt, Ronald Lippitt, and Ralph K. White, "Patterns of Aggressive Behavior in Experimentally Created Social Climates," *The Journal of Social Psychology*, 10 (May 1939), pp. 271-299.

80. Lindgren, Henry Clay, *Psychology of Personal and Social Adjustment*. New York: American Book Company, 1953.

81. Lovejoy, Clarence E., *Lovejoy's College Guide*. New York: Simon and Schuster, Inc., 1954.

82. Lovejoy, Clarence E., *Lovejoy's Vocational School Guide*. New York: Simon and Schuster, Inc., 1955.

83. Marshall, M. V., and E. W. Simpson, "Vocational Choice and College Grades," *Journal of Educational Research*, 27 (1943), pp. 303-305.

84. Maslow, A. H., "The Influence of Familiarization on Preference," *Journal of Experimental Psychology*, 21 (1937), pp. 162-180.

85. Maslow, A. H., and Bela Mittlemann, *Principles of Abnormal Psychology*. New York: Harper & Brothers, 1951.

86. McDougall, William, *An Introduction to Social Psychology* (2nd ed.). Boston: John Luce and Company, 1926.

87. McKinney, Fred, *Psychology of Personal Adjustment* (2nd ed.). New York: John Wiley and Sons, Inc., 1949.

88. Mead, Margaret, *Male and Female*. New York: William Morrow & Company, 1949.

89. Mead, Margaret, *And Keep Your Powder Dry*. New York: William Morrow & Company, 1942.

90. *Meier Art Tests:* I. Art Judgement, Norman Charles Meier. Iowa City, Iowa: Bureau of Educational Research and Service, State University of Iowa.

91. Melby, Ernest, "Leadership is Release of Creativity," *School Executive*, 68 (November, 1948).

92. Miles, W. R., and C. C. Miles, "The Correlation of Intelligence Scores and Chronological Age from Early to Late Maturity," *American Journal of Psychology*, 44 (1932), pp. 44-78.

93. Miner, John B., *Intelligence in the United States, A Survey of Manpower Utilization*. New York: Springer Publishing Company, 1957.

94. *Minnesota Paper Form Board* (rev. ed.), Form AA. New York: The Psychological Corporation.

95. Morgan, Clifford T., *Introduction to Psychology*. New York: McGraw-Hill Book Company, Inc., 1956.

96. *Multiple Aptitude Test*. Los Angeles: California Test Bureau, 1955.

97. Munn, Norman L., *Psychology* (3rd ed.). Boston: Houghton Mifflin Company, 1956.

98. Murphy, Gardner, *Personality, A Biosocial Approach to Origins and Structure*. New York: Harper & Brothers, 1947.

99. Murray, H. A., *Explorations in Personality*. Oxford: Oxford University Press, 1938.

100. Mursell, James L., *Psychological Testing*. New York: Longmans, Green & Company, 1947.

101. Nelson, A. Gordon, "Vocational Maturity and Client Satisfaction," *Journal of Counseling Psychology*, 3 (1956), pp. 254-255.

102. *Occupational Interest Inventory*, Form A. Los Angeles: California Test Bureau.

103. Occupations Research Section, National Vocational Guidance Association, "Contents of a Good Occupational Monograph—The Basic Outline," *Occupations*, 19 (October, 1940) pp. 20-23.

104. *Ohio State University Psychological Examination*, Form A and 23. Columbus, Ohio: Ohio College Association, Ohio State University.

105. *Otis Quick-Scoring Mental Ability Test*. Yonkers-on-Hudson, N.Y.: World Book Company, 1937.

106. *Patterson's American Education*, 51. Educational Directories, Inc., Compiler and Publisher, Wilmette, Illinois, 1954.

107 Patty, William L., and Louise S. Johnson, *Personality and Adjustment*. New York: McGraw-Hill Book Company, Inc., 1953.

108. Plato, *The Dialogues of Plato* (tran. B. Jowett), 2 vols. New York: Random House, 1937, p. 632.

109. Pressey, Sidney L., and Raymond G. Kuhlen, *Psychological Development Through the Life Span*. New York: Harper & Brothers, 1957.

110. Prothro, E. Terry, and P. T. Teska, *Psychology: A Biosocial Study of Behavior*. Boston: Ginn and Company, 1950.

111. Roe, Anne, *The Psychology of Occupations*. New York: John Wiley Sons, Inc., 1956.

112. *Seashore Measures of Musical Talents* (1939 revision). New York: The Psychological Corporation.

113. Shaffer, Laurance F., and Edward J. Shoben, *The Psychology of Adjustment*. Boston: Houghton Mifflin Company, 1956.

114. Shartle, Carroll L., *Occupational Information; Its Development and Application*. Englewood Cliffs, N.J.: Prentice-Hall, Inc., 1952.

115. Smith, J. R., "The Frequency Growth of the Human Alpha Rhythms During Normal Infancy and Childhood," *Journal of Psychology*, 11 (1941), pp. 177-198.

116. Snygg, Donald, and Arthur W. Combs, *Individual Behavior*. New York: Harper & Brothers, 1949.

117. Spearman, C., *Abilities of Man*. New York: The Macmillan Company, 1927.

118. Spranger, E., *Types of Men*. New York: Hafner Publishing Company, Inc., 1928.

119. Strong, Edward K., Jr., *Vocational Interests of Men and Women*. Stanford, California: Stanford University Press, 1943.

120. *Strong Vocational Interest Blank*. Stanford, California: Stanford University Press, 1938.

121. Super, Donald E., *Appraising Vocational Fitness*. New York: Harper & Brothers, 1949.

122. Super, Donald E., *The Dynamics of Vocational Adjustment*. New York: Harper & Brothers, 1942.

123. Super, Donald E., *The Psychology of Careers*. New York: Harper & Brothers, 1957.

124. Super, Donald E., "Vocational Development: The Process of Compromise or Synthesis," *Journal of Counseling Psychology*, 3 (Winter, 1956), p. 251.

125. Terman, Lewis M., *Psychological Factors in Marital Happiness*. New York: McGraw-Hill Book Company, Inc., 1938.

126. *Test of Mechanical Comprehension*, Form AA, and BB. New York: The Psychological Corporation.

127. Thelen, H., *Dynamics of Groups at Work*. Chicago: University of Chicago Press, 1954.

128. Thorndike, E. L., *The Measurement of Intelligence*. New York: Bureau of Publications, Teachers College, Columbia University, 1927.

129. Thorndike, E. L., E. O. Bregman, J. W. Tilton, and E. Woodward, *Adult Learning*. New York: The Macmillan Company, 1928.

130. Threlkeld, H., "Educational and Vocational Plans of College Seniors in Relation to the Curricula and Guidance Programs in Forty-five Pennsylvania Colleges," *Teachers College Record*, 37 (1936), pp. 331, 332.

131. Thurstone, L. L., and T. G. Thurstone, *Factorial Studies of Intelligence*. Chicago: University of Chicago Press, 1941.

132. Topps, Robert F., "You Cannot Always Do It If You Try!" *Elementary School Journal* (December, 1953), pp. 230-234.

133. U. S. Department of Labor, Bureau of Labor Statistics in cooperation with Veterans Administration, Office of the Assistant Administrator for Vocational Rehabilitation and Education, *Occupational Outlook Handbook*. Washington: U. S. Government Printing Office, 1951.

134. *Vineland Social Maturity Scale, Manual of Directions*. Minneapolis: Educational Test Bureau, 1947.

135. Watson, R. I., *Readings on the Clinical Method in Psychology*. New York: Harper & Brothers, 1949.

136. Weitz, H., M. Clarke, O. Jones, "The Relationships between Choice of a Major Field of Study and Academic Preparation and Performance," *Educational and Psychological Measurement*, 15 (1955), pp. 28-38.

137. Woodrow, H., "The Ability to Learn," *Psychological Review,* 33 (1946), pp. 147-158.

138. Woodworth, Robert S., *Contemporary Schools of Psychology* (rev. ed.). New York: Ronald Press, 1948.

139. Woodworth, Robert S., *Psychology* (4th ed.). New York: Henry Holt and Company, 1940.

140. Young, Kimball, *Personality and Problems of Adjustment.* New York: Appleton-Century-Crofts, Inc., 1952.

INDEX